Semantic Relations Between Nominals

Second Edition

Synthesis Lectures on Human Language Technologies

Editor
Graeme Hirst, *University of Toronto*

Synthesis Lectures on Human Language Technologies is edited by Graeme Hirst of the University of Toronto. The series consists of 50- to 150-page monographs on topics relating to natural language processing, computational linguistics, information retrieval, and spoken language understanding. Emphasis is on important new techniques, on new applications, and on topics that combine two or more HLT subfields.

Semantic Relations Between Nominals, Second Edition
Vivi Nastase, Stan Szpakowicz, Preslav Nakov, and Diarmuid Ó Séagdha
2021

Embeddings in Natural Language Processing: Theory and Advances in Vector Representations of Meaning
Mohammad Taher Pilehvar and Jose Camacho-Collados
2020

Conversational AI: Dialogue Systems, Conversational Agents, and Chatbots
Michael McTear
2020

Natural Language Processing for Social Media, Third Edition
Anna Atefeh Farzindar and Diana Inkpen
2020

Statistical Significance Testing for Natural Language Processing
Rotem Dror, Lotem Peled, Segev Shlomov, and Roi Reichart
2020

Deep Learning Approaches to Text Production
Shashi Narayan and Claire Gardent
2020

Semantic Relations Between Nominals, Second Edition

Vivi Nastase, Stan Szpakowicz, Preslav Nakov, and Diarmuid Ó Séagdha

ISBN: 978-3-031-01050-7   paperback
ISBN: 978-3-031-02178-7   ebook
ISBN: 978-3-031-00189-5   hardcover

DOI 10.1007/978-3-031-02178-7

A Publication in the Springer series
SYNTHESIS LECTURES ON ADVANCES IN AUTOMOTIVE TECHNOLOGY

Lecture #49
Series Editor: Graeme Hirst, University of Toronto
Series ISSN
Print 1947-4040   Electronic 1947-4059

Semantic Relations Between Nominals

Second Edition

Vivi Nastase
Institute for Natural Language Processing, University of Stuttgart

Stan Szpakowicz
School of Electrical Engineering and Computer Science, University of Ottawa

Preslav Nakov
Qatar Computing Research Institute, Hamad Bin Khalifa University

Diarmuid Ó Séagdha
Computer Laboratory, University of Cambridge

SYNTHESIS LECTURES ON HUMAN LANGUAGE TECHNOLOGIES #49

ABSTRACT

`Opportunity and Curiosity find similar rocks on Mars.` One can generally understand this statement if one knows that OPPORTUNITY and CURIOSITY *are instances of the class of* MARS ROVERS, and recognizes that, as signalled by the word on, ROCKS *are located on* MARS. Two mental operations contribute to understanding: recognize how entities/concepts mentioned in a text interact and recall already known facts (which often themselves consist of relations between entities/concepts). Concept interactions one identifies in the text can be added to the repository of known facts, and aid the processing of future texts. The amassed knowledge can assist many advanced language-processing tasks, including summarization, question answering and machine translation.

   Semantic relations are the connections we perceive between things which interact. The book explores two, now intertwined, threads in semantic relations: how they are expressed in texts and what role they play in knowledge repositories. A historical perspective takes us back more than 2000 years to their beginnings, and then to developments much closer to our time: various attempts at producing lists of semantic relations, necessary and sufficient to express the interaction between entities/concepts. A look at relations outside context, then in general texts, and then in texts in specialized domains, has gradually brought new insights, and led to essential adjustments in how the relations are seen. At the same time, datasets which encompass these phenomena have become available. They started small, then grew somewhat, then became truly large. The large resources are inevitably noisy because they are constructed automatically. The available corpora—to be analyzed, or used to gather relational evidence—have also grown, and some systems now operate at the Web scale. The learning of semantic relations has proceeded in parallel, in adherence to supervised, unsupervised or distantly supervised paradigms. Detailed analyses of annotated datasets in supervised learning have granted insights useful in developing unsupervised and distantly supervised methods. These in turn have contributed to the understanding of what relations are and how to find them, and that has led to methods scalable to Web-sized textual data. The size and redundancy of information in very large corpora, which at first seemed problematic, have been harnessed to improve the process of relation extraction/learning. The newest technology, deep learning, supplies innovative and surprising solutions to a variety of problems in relation learning. This book aims to paint a big picture and to offer interesting details.

KEYWORDS

natural language processing, computational linguistics, lexical semantics, semantic relations, nominals, noun compounds, information extraction, machine learning, deep learning

Contents

Preface to the Second Edition

RELATIONS AND TEXTS

Every non-trivial text describes interactions and relations: between people, between other entities or concepts, between events. What we know about the world comprises, in large part, similar relations between concepts representing people, other entities, events, and so on. Such knowledge contributes to the understanding of relations which occur in texts. Newly found relations can in turn become part of the knowledge people store.

If an automatic system is to grasp a text's semantic content, it must be able to recognize, and reason about, relations in texts, possibly by applying and updating previously acquired knowledge. We focus here in particular on semantic relations which describe the interactions among nouns and compact noun phrases, and we present such relations from both a theoretical and a practical perspective. The theoretical exploration shows the historical path which has brought us to the current interpretation and view of semantic relations, and the wide range of proposals of relation inventories; such inventories vary according to domain, granularity and suitability for downstream applications.

On the practical side, we investigate the recognition and acquisition of relations from texts. We look at supervised learning methods. We present the available datasets. We discuss the variety of features which can describe relation instances, and learning algorithms successfully applied thus far. The overview of weakly supervised and unsupervised learning looks in detail at problems and solutions related to the acquisition of relations from large corpora with little or no previously annotated data. We show how enduring the bootstrapping algorithms based on seed examples or patterns have proved to be, and how they have been adapted to tackle Web-scale text collections. We also present a few machine learning techniques which can take advantage of data redundancy and variability for fast and reliable relation extraction.

Semantic relations play a fundamental role in ontology-based learning and information extraction from documents. They can also provide valuable information for higher-level language-processing tasks, including summarization, question answering and machine translation.

THE AUDIENCE

We expect that this book will appeal to graduate students, researchers and practitioners interested in computational semantics, information extraction and, more generally, modern natural language processing technology. We have tried to make the presentation broadly accessible to anyone with a little background in artificial intelligence. Even so, it helps to have some familiarity with computational linguistics and a modicum of tolerance for mathematical formulae. A basic understanding of machine learning is useful but not strictly necessary.

A NOTE ON THE SECOND EDITION

Two meaty chapters, 3 and 4, were the heart of the first edition. Most of the new material in this edition appears in an even more substantial Chapter 5. We have reorganized and edited all other parts of the book—Chapters 3 and 4 most thoroughly—to bring the facts, statistics and links seven years forward, and to correct previous omissions. The enlarged and restructured Chapter 1 delineates the topic of the book better, and explains what we will not discuss and why. There is also a brand new conclusion, now in Chapter 6. Chapters 3 and 4 aged well, although inevitably not all material we discussed seven years ago has survived intact on the Web. On the other hand, time flies in natural language processing. In the years since the book first appeared, deep learning has taken our discipline by storm. This edition brings the semantic relation research up to date with the new developments.

The substance of this edition owes its existence to Vivi, and the form to Stan. In particular, the new Chapter 5 is Vivi's brainchild; Stan helped whip it into shape. We are both grateful to Deniz Yuret for his constructive comments on much of Chapter 5, and to Preslav Nakov for a few incisive observations on its draft. Two anonymous reviewers made a number of most useful suggestions on the book: thank you.

Vivi Nastase and Stan Szpakowicz
January 2021

CHAPTER 1

Introduction

1.1 MOTIVATION

The connection is indispensable to the expression of thought. Without the connection, we would not be able to express any continuous thought, and we could only list a succession of images and ideas isolated from each other and without any link between them [Tesnière, 1959].

The connection is indispensable. Any non-trivial text describes a group of entities and the ways in which they interact or interrelate. To identify these entities and the relations between them is a fundamental step in understanding the text. It is a step which human language users perform rapidly and reliably, assisted by their language skills and their world knowledge about entities and relations. If natural language processing[1] systems are to reach the goal of producing meaningful representations of text, they too must attain the ability to detect entities and extract the relations which hold between them. If a language understanding system is to adapt to new information just as people do, it must also use and then update existing repositories of knowledge about entities and about the way they interact.

Entity recognition (identify tokens which correspond to entity mentions) and entity resolution (identify the real-world entities or entity classes mentioned) are well-studied problems in NLP, with a voluminous associated literature. In this book, we will generally make the simplifying assumption that these steps have already been completed before the relation-processing stage—our main concern here—begins.

When a human reader interprets the relational content of a text, she draws on a spectrum of knowledge acquired from past experience, and on explicit and implicit signals in the text itself. Consider an example:

NASA flew its final three space shuttle missions—one per orbiter remaining in the fleet—earlier this year.

Discovery, one of the space shuttles in NASA's fleet, bound next year for the Smithsonian's Steven F. Udvar-Hazy Center in northern Virginia, was retired first in March. Endeavour landed June 1 and is now being prepared for display at the California Science Center in Los Angeles.

---

[1]The term *natural language processing* will henceforth be abbreviated to NLP.

> Atlantis flew the 135th and final shuttle mission, STS-135, last month. It will be exhibited near where it and all the other shuttles launched and most landed, at the Kennedy Space Center Visitor Complex in Florida.[2]

The first entity which this text mentions, NASA, must be recognized as referring to the U.S. space agency, not the National Auto Sports Association or the Nasa people of Colombia. As noted, we assume that this can be done before attempting to extract relational content. The recognition may trigger associations with a number of entities, such as SPACE, SPACE SHUTTLE, ORBITER, KENNEDY SPACE CENTER, DISCOVERY and ATLANTIS, some of which may appear in the text. Such associations—and the specific relations between the trigger concept and the triggered one—may help interpret the text.

The second entity mention refers to the *final three space shuttle missions*. *Space shuttle mission* is a compound of three nouns. It can only be fully interpreted by unpacking the semantic relations which hold between the concepts referred to as *space*, *shuttle* and *mission*—we already need relational processing! Roughly stated, *space shuttle mission* denotes a MISSION fulfilled (performed? aided?) by a SPACE SHUTTLE.[3] Even if the term *space shuttle mission* is unfamiliar, its meaning can be understood if we know enough about what *space shuttles* and *missions* are, and how they usually interact. Next question: what is a *space shuttle*? This term may be familiar, or can be looked up in a dictionary. While it is a relatively opaque compound, the reader can make an informed guess that such a thing moves around in space, if only she knows other uses of the word *shuttle* and sees the context. The parenthetical comment *one per orbiter remaining in the fleet* can be interpreted as implying that a SPACE SHUTTLE is a kind of ORBITER.

The second sentence in the example explicitly states that the entity referred to as *Discovery* is an instance of SPACE SHUTTLE. It does so by means of the construction "X, one of Y". This information is very useful if we do not already know what DISCOVERY is. And so on; a full explanation of the relational content of a text tends to be much longer than the text itself.

Like a human reader, an NLP system must avail itself of both new information present in the text and pre-acquired knowledge about the world. The latter is often construed as a *knowledge base*, and its content may be either fixed or dynamically updated as more texts are read. So, there is a clear interaction between the tasks of knowledge acquisition and text understanding. The interest in the organization of knowledge and the principles behind the understanding of utterances can be traced back to classical antiquity. In modern times, the two tasks have been the object of computational research throughout the history of artificial intelligence (AI), even though they have often been treated as separate problems. Their tight interaction came into clear focus rather recently. It was noted when people began to develop text understanding systems— the task requires lexical, world and common-sense knowledge. At the same time, such automated text-understanding systems could produce formal representations of the knowledge in texts, and those representations could be used to build, or to add to, knowledge bases. This book surveys

---

[2]www.space.com/12804-nasa-space-shuttle-program-officially-ends.html
[3]This is not the only interpretation. The compound may also denote a *shuttle mission* performed in *space*.

the research landscape and the state of the art in these often intertwined tasks. Many questions arise when one deals with relations between entities. Here are some questions worth considering.

- Can one design a parsimonious and general representation of the semantic relations which appear in text?
- What linguistic signals in text can help identify semantic relations?
- Can background knowledge enhance the understanding of relations in text?
- Can the understanding of relations help acquire new world knowledge and distinguish relational information of lasting value (DISCOVERY is a SPACE SHUTTLE) from contingent information with a one-off benefit (ENDEAVOUR is now prepared for DISPLAY)?

1.2   APPLICATIONS

There is much promise in the ability to identify semantic relations in texts and to locate relations in structured knowledge repositories. Swanson [1987] demonstrated the potential of using relations from text for knowledge discovery. He combined relations extracted from articles in different scientific domains, and discovered previously unknown but ultimately important connections between, e.g., fish oil and blood circulation or magnesium and migraines. The biomedical literature has been growing at a double-exponential pace [Hunter and Cohen, 2006], so researchers find it impossible to keep track of everything that is being published. Yet, billions of dollars can be saved by finding out what costly experiments have already been done, and what their outcomes were, and by discovering likely new interactions between known concepts. There are simply no practical alternatives to the automatic relation extraction from text in biomedicine.

Many of the techniques we discuss in this book, already quite mature, have worked in some of these NLP applications. For example, Nakov's [2008b] work helps improve *Statistical Machine Translation*. Suitable paraphrases make explicit the hidden relations between the nouns in a noun compound. This makes it easier to translate English noun compounds into languages in which phrases are not as compact, and enables the recognition of different variants of the same phrase. Suppose that the phrase *oil price hikes* is interpreted as *hikes in oil prices* and *hikes in the prices of oil*. A system may find it easier to translate the more syntactically parallel *hikes in the prices of oil*—rather than the very compact *oil price hikes*—into Spanish as *alzas en los precios del petróleo*.

Another case in point: information retrieval and question answering. Suppose that one wants to ask a search engine what causes cancer. Many causes are possible, so one might want to pose this query: "list all x such that x causes cancer". This can be seen as a special kind of search, called *relational search* [Cafarella et al., 2006]. It asks for a list of things in a given relation with a given entity. Relational search can find components of objects (every x which is part of an AUTOMOBILE ENGINE), materials with specific properties (every x which is material for making a SUBMARINE'S HULL), or types of entities (every x which is a type of TRANSPORTATION). Naturally, these examples are just the tip of the iceberg.

1.3 WHAT THIS BOOK IS ABOUT

1.3.1 RELATIONS BETWEEN NOMINALS

The book talks about relations between entities mentioned in the same sentence, and expressed linguistically as nominals. Relations are the connections we perceive among concepts or entities. A connection may come from general knowledge about the world (CHOCOLATE *is-a-kind-of* FOOD), or from a text fragment (`Chocolate is a psychoactive food`).[4] When one talks casually about a relation, one refers either to its type, such as *part-of* or *is-a*, or to its instance in which arguments accompany the relation name, such as `chocolate contains caffeine`. Throughout the book, we write simply "relation" if the context makes it clear which of the two usages is intended; otherwise we write "relation type" or "relation instance".[5]

The term *nominal* usually refers to a phrase which behaves syntactically like a noun or a noun phrase [Quirk et al., 1985, p. 335]. For our book, we have adopted a narrower definition. A *nominal* can be a *common noun* (`chocolate, food`), a *proper noun* (`Godiva, Belgium`), a *multi-word proper name* (`United Nations`), a *deverbal noun* (`cultivation, roasting`), a *deadjectival noun* (`[the] rich`), a *base noun phrase* built of a head noun with optional premodifiers (`processed food, delicious milk chocolate`), and recursively a sequence of nominals (`cacao tree, cacao tree growing conditions`).

The relation itself can be signalled by a phrase which links the entity mentions in a sentence (`Chocolate` *is a* raw or processed food `produced from the seed of the tropical Theobroma cacao tree.`), or it can be only implied, e.g., when the entity mentions are compressed into a noun compound (consider `cacao tree` and `cacao tree growing conditions` again).

Superficially, it seems easier to learn or detect relations when some linguistic clues exist than when the relation is only implied by the adjoining of terms. We will see, however, that, in order to rely on the linguistic expression of relations in texts, one must deal with *ambiguity*. For example, the word `in` may indicate a temporal relation (`chocolate` *in* `the 20th century`) or a spatial relation (`chocolate` *in* `Belgium`). Another difficulty is *over-specification*. Consider, for example, the ornate relation between chocolate and cultures in `Chocolate` *was prized as a health food and a divine gift by* `the Mayan and Aztec cultures`. When there are no surface indicators, the clues about the type of relation will come from knowledge about the entities (`milk chocolate`: CHOCOLATE, which is a kind of FOOD made with lots of MILK, which is an INGREDIENT of many FOODSTUFFS).

A special situation arises when an entity is actually an occurrence—event, activity or state—expressed by a deverbal noun such as `cultivation`. Relations between a deverbal noun and its modifiers mirror the relations between the underlying verb and its arguments. For example, in the clause `the ancient Mayans cultivated chocolate`, chocolate is the *theme*. So, one

---

[4]www.cacao-chocolate.com
[5]Chapters 1–4 will observe the following font conventions: *relation*, ENTITY/CONCEPT, text/example/pattern.

can also discern a *theme* in `chocolate cultivation`. We do not single out such relations for separate discussion, because the methods do not differ significantly from what is required to deal with any other relations and any other types of nominals.[6]

1.3.2   RELATIONS IN KNOWLEDGE REPOSITORIES

This book is also about relations between entities, stored for use outside a specific textual context. The relations describe the same connections as those found in a textual context, which explain how these entities interact. The difference is the absence of context. Depending on the knowledge repository, one would associate a universal or an existential quantifier with a particular relation instance. For example, the universal quantifier applies to a WordNet-style lexical semantic relation such as APPLE *is-a* FRUIT; this is always true (unless our knowledge of botany becomes revised). On the other hand, an existential quantifier should be associated with each relation instance in ConceptNet, where there are such relations as CHARACTER *located_in* NOVEL or CHARACTER *located_in* A PLAY IN A THEATRE. In repositories like Freebase or Cyc,[7] there are relations which are, or have been, true for a specific time interval, e.g., BARACK OBAMA *president_of* UNITED STATES OF AMERICA. While some systems give additional attributes to relation instances (including time span), our book will not focus on that.

By *knowledge repository*, we mean a variety of resources which store semantic relations. They have somewhat different properties and applications. When it is relevant, we will refer to a particular type.

A **taxonomy** categorizes things or concepts. Taxonomies are often based on the *is-a* relation, or on hyponymy/hypernymy when organizing linguistic information. The relation brings about the hierarchical structure of the taxonomy.

An **ontology** captures general knowledge. It covers a variety of relations one needs to express such knowledge. Ontologies often include taxonomies: *is-a* and *part_of* relations usually belong to the inventory. An ontology is built for a specific domain, where the pre-specified types of relevant concepts and relations—the ontology schema—are the scaffolding for the resource.

A **knowledge base (KB)** is a collection of facts which express knowledge, either general or in a narrower domain. Like ontologies, KBs contain a variety of relation types and concepts. Unlike ontologies, they are not structured around pre-specified schemata; new facts—maybe with new nodes or new types of edges—may be added *ad hoc*.

A **knowledge graph (KG)** is any of the knowledge repositories noted above if it is perceived as an interconnected network of entities—as opposed to separate relation instances. The graph is a powerful and expressive mathematical construct. This view of knowledge repositories makes possible a variety of solutions to issues in relation extraction and classification, as the book will show. In the context of KGs, the task of relation classification becomes *link prediction*: build a

---

[6]Even so, nominalization has been treated differently in some linguistic theories [Levi, 1978] and in some computational linguistic work [Lapata, 2002].

[7]The book will revisit both of them repeatedly.

model based on existing information in the graph, and use it to predict additional links (i.e., relations) between nodes in the graph.

1.4   WHAT THIS BOOK IS NOT ABOUT

1.4.1   ARGUMENT IDENTIFICATION – ENTITY RECOGNITION – WORD SENSE DISAMBIGUATION

We will not deal separately with *argument* identification, although it will be discussed in the context of the task of simultaneous argument identification and relation classification. A simplifying assumption is often made: argument identification (including possibly entity identification/disambiguation) is a task separate from relation extraction. That is why one can employ a pipeline system which first identifies, and possibly disambiguates, the entities of interest, and only then moves on to identifying semantic relations. In evaluation settings such as the ACE or SemEval relation classification tasks,[8] gold-standard entity annotations are usually part of the dataset. In some cases, such annotations may also be linked to WordNet or to another semantic network, and so mimic the output of a sense-disambiguation step.

1.4.2   DISCOURSE RELATIONS

Apart from relations in a noun compound and between entities in a sentence, there are other relations between nominals in a text, notably discourse relations. Coreference relations in particular are not included in this survey. They usually cross sentence boundaries, their arguments may be complex noun phrases (the girl next door) or pronouns, or they may not be explicitly expressed if ellipsis is at work. In the text below, for example, Angela Merkel and German chancellor are co-referents; the elided noun meeting is marked with square brackets.

> Angela Merkel's spokesman has insisted that the German chancellor's first meeting with François Hollande, France's president-elect, will be a "getting to know you" exercise, and not [a] "decision making" [meeting].

1.4.3   TEMPORAL RELATIONS

Temporal relations between nominals, such as *morning exercise* or *afternoon snack*, are quite frequent. While they belong to the inventory of semantic relations we review in Chapters 2 and 3, they most commonly hold between two events, or between an event and a time indicator. When temporal relations are studied separately, not as part of a more general analysis of semantic relations between nominals, the emphasis is on events, which are often expressed by verbs. That is why we will single out neither the datasets for work with temporal relations,[9] nor the methods designed to detect such relations.

---

[8]We will return to both in Chapter 3.

[9]Consider the TempEval task (paperswithcode.com/sota/temporal-information-extraction-on-tempeval-3) or the clinical TempEval task (competitions.codalab.org/competitions/15621).

1.4.4   ONTOLOGY BUILDING / KNOWLEDGE BASE POPULATION

The book concentrates on relations between nominals in texts and in knowledge repositories: what they are and how one can identify or recognize them. We will discuss relations in existing ontologies, KBs and other repositories only insofar as they are relevant to semantic relations between nominals. While building such resources may also require interesting methods or techniques, that is not our focus. They are, however, of particular interest as sources of seed examples or training data for learning or for developing other techniques of extracting relation instances. Also, the purpose of relation extraction often is the enrichment of knowledge repositories; this *will* be discussed in the book.

There is a similar task: knowledge base population (KBP), run annually since 2009 as part of the Text Analysis Conferences (TAC);[10] Ji and Grishman [2011] describe the task, and discuss the systems which participated in the 2010 edition. KBP does not, strictly speaking, perform relation extraction or classification but the actual tasks—entity linking and slot filling—are relevant to relation extraction. *Entity linking* detects mentions of entities of predefined types, and links them to the entities in a knowledge repository provided. *Slot filling* takes an entity and relation types (e.g., BARACK OBAMA, *birthPlace*, *birthDate* and *marriedTo*), and fills in the missing arguments. The book will not look at the particular data and systems for KBP but it will review some of its methods which touch on relation classification or extraction.

1.4.5   DATABASES AND SOCIAL NETWORKS

Databases and social networks do capture relations between entities but this book will not discuss them.

It is not always obvious where the boundary between KBs and databases lies. According to Brodie and Mylopoulos [1986], "an important difference between KBs and databases is that the former require a semantic theory for the interpretation of their contents, while the latter require a computational theory for their efficient implementation on physical machines". Our guiding principle is this: the knowledge repositories we consider here (taxonomies, ontologies, KBs and KGs) contain concepts and relations between them relevant to a wide range of applications. As positive examples, consider WordNet's lexical-semantic knowledge and Freebase's world knowledge focused on relations which connect such varying entities as people, places, artifacts, and so on. Negative examples include a network of interconnected publications, authors and citations, and a database of movie reviews: movies, users and ratings. The latter has been popular in statistical relational learning, and was among the first to undergo collective matrix factorization. (Matrix factorization is a successful technique of link prediction in KGs; Section 5.3.2 will discuss these matters at length.)

A social network is by its nature a graph, and one can interpret some databases as graphs. Knowledge repositories are often processed as graphs. The structure thus perceived benefits sev-

---

[10]tac.nist.gov/tracks/

eral typical operations on a repository, which rely on the interconnectedness of relation instances: derive entity and relation representations, find links, weigh entities and relations, and so on.

Because of the commonalities between databases and KBs, and between social networks and KBs, there is an overlap in the methods which can be applied to these structures to create new information or new models. Some techniques—e.g., link prediction by matrix factorization or statistical relational learning, or link prediction in social networks—have been first applied to such data. We acknowledge the proponents of such new methods but our focus is the discussion of research which explicitly applies such methods to semantic relations in texts and KBs. On the other hand, some of the techniques developed for databases and social networks are suitable to knowledge repositories but have not been applied yet. We leave it to the reader to discover such innovative applications of established methods, and to bring them into the field of semantic relations.

1.4.6   RESULTS AND COMPARISONS

The focus of this book is the interplay between linguistic information and clues on one hand, and formal organization of such information and learning methods on the other. A reader who needs a method for a concrete purpose and a concrete dataset may desire a ranking of the suitable methods by their appropriateness to the task. The variety of datasets and performance measures precludes a neat summary in a few tables, which would rank by their results the methods surveyed here. The level of performance is affected by a number of factors which interact in intricate ways: the annotation procedure for the training data, the amount of training data available, the number and nature of relations to be classified, the distribution of those relations in data, the source of the data for training and testing, the corpora and methods used for additional information (e.g., when building word representations or obtaining relational features), and so forth. Each domain—biology, medicine and so on—adds its own peculiarities.

The MUC and ACE shared evaluation tasks (which will be discussed in Section 3.2.1), as well as the tasks at 2007 and 2010 SemEval (Section 3.2.2), were meant to provide a benchmark for relation classification. They have been instrumental in advancing research on relation classification and extraction, but their small-scale datasets and their methods have long been superseded. Many conclusions drawn from the results published earlier have been rendered obsolete by more recent developments.

There is also a variety of evaluation measures, depending on the task. Precision, recall, F-score and accuracy are used in traditional relation classification tasks. In link prediction, in particular, the most commonly used measures are mean reciprocal rank (MRR), HITS@k (a precision measure computed on the first k ranked predictions), and mean average precision (MAP). Furthermore, summary results on a dataset hide the behavior on individual relation types. Good performance on one type does not ensure high performance overall.

To be blunt: a synoptic view of such heterogeneous results might be misleading rather than informative. An intrinsic evaluation of the extracted knowledge may also not be desirable. Relation extraction is not an end task. Its purpose is to build resources for use in other NLP and AI applications.

On the other hand, the NLP community (much like other scientific communities) exhibits a strong bias toward publishing positive results. This ensures that any published method has in some way improved on those it builds upon. It could be relatively easy to decide which methods perform better.

There is a more positive trend in the NLP community's publishing habits. The experimental data *and* the code are more and more often made public. That offers up a wide variety of handy methods which should be relatively easy to try out, especially on new but similar data. And even more helpfully, ML and NLP methods have been employed to gather and extract results from scientific publications. Papers with Code,[11] one of those wonderfully useful initiatives, group papers, code and results for specific tasks, and show the state-of-the-art for each of them.[12]

We encourage the reader to absorb the explanations about features and learning methods presented in the book, and then—guided by their own requirements—choose the most appropriate starting point and innovate from there.

1.5   ORGANIZATION OF THE BOOK

This brief chapter has explained why we found it worthwhile to write a book about recognizing semantic relations between nominals, what applications those recognized relations can facilitate, what the book does and what it does not discuss.

Chapter 2 recalls the history of the evolution of semantic relations in two separate but eventually intertwined threads: as relations in knowledge repositories, serving to organize our knowledge, and as connections we perceive between concepts and ideas expressed in texts. We show the progress of research on the design of lists of semantic relations, the change in understanding what a semantic relation is, and the lessons learned from that long-lasting enterprise.

Chapter 3 presents the supervised learning perspective: from annotated data sets, to features, to machine-learning formalisms employed to make the most of the available, and sometimes complex, features. We focus on methods of relation learning which can successfully build models from small, annotated datasets.

Chapter 4 goes to the other end of the learning and data spectrum. It surveys the unsupervised and distantly supervised learning of semantic relations, and shows how they can take advantage of large (unstructured) textual data. The early unsupervised methods have proved surprisingly robust and resilient. They have led to variations applied successfully even now. Distant supervision, which links unsupervised and supervised methods, has been the source of numerous ideas for producing large-scale training data from sometimes surprising sources.

---

[11]paperswithcode.com

[12]See paperswithcode.com/area/natural-language-processing/relation-extraction for the state-of-the-art in several benchmarking datasets.

Chapter 5, new to this edition, restates—in the context of deep learning—the matters discussed in Chapters 3 and 4. Neural networks date back to the 1940s but they have only quite recently shown their huge potential in NLP tasks, once their powerful mathematical basis could be backed up by an equally powerful (soft and hard) computational support. The adoption of this paradigm has opened up new avenues of research in semantic relation learning.

Chapter 6 wraps up the book with a look back at the landscape we have sought to describe. We re-emphasize the connections between the various ideas and techniques presented here. The goal is to leave the reader with a coherent, clear and informative picture of semantic relations between nominals.

CHAPTER 2

Relations Between Nominals, Relations Between Concepts

2.1 INTEGRATION OF KNOWLEDGE AND TEXTS IN TWO THOUSAND YEARS

Semantic relations describe interactions. A relation may connect nominals in a text or concepts in knowledge representation, depending on the level at which an interaction is perceived. It seems artificial to separate relations just because of this distinction, especially if one notes that the knowledge is ultimately expressed by words, and entities in particular are expressed by nominals. Indeed, we are at a stage in NLP when large amounts of textual data can help identify pairs of interacting entities. In the end, this information can be gathered and formalized to build large-scale knowledge repositories. Early work on understanding the nature of knowledge relied on contemplating the world and the objects within it, and on applying certain organizational principles to the structuring of the insights about the relations between objects in the world. Work on the study of language and the way it conveys meaning has been evolving separately until the 20th century.

The attempts of philosophers to capture and describe our knowledge about the world go back to the Antiquity. Aristotle's *Organon*, a posthumous collection assembled by his students, includes a treatise on *Categories* which presents criteria for organizing objects [Studtmann, 2008]. This endeavor must inevitably deal with language, given that world knowledge and language are intertwined. Objects in the natural world are put into categories called τὰ λεγόμενα (*ta legomena*, things which are said), and their organization is based on the relation of class inclusion.

For two millennia following Aristotle, contemplation on the nature of knowledge and on the principles of knowledge organization has been the domain of philosophers—and occasionally botanists or zoologists who would put living things into taxonomies. Let us fast-forward over centuries of hot philosophical debate, coloured by changing ideas about what concepts are and how they relate to the real world [Margolis and Laurence, 1999]. In the 1970s came a realization that a robust AI system needs the same kind of knowledge as what humans have. This revelation has spurred a concerted effort to capture and represent knowledge in a machine-friendly format, and at that point the intermingling with language became inevitable.

We now return to the Antiquity to pick up the language analysis thread and follow it to this intermingling point. During the second half of the first millennium BCE, scholars of the

Indian linguistic tradition (*vyākaraṇa*) developed a highly refined theory of language. It covered what we would now describe as morphology, syntax and semantics. The seminal document of this tradition was written by the celebrated scholar Pāṇini, often considered "the father of linguistics". The *Aṣṭādhyāyī* is an eight-volume collection of aphoristic rules which describe the process of generating a Sanskrit sentence from what would now be called a semantic representation. The latter is primarily conceptualized in terms of *kārakas*, semantic relations between events and participants—that is now studied under the name of *semantic roles*. The *Aṣṭādhyāyī* covers noun-noun compounds comprehensively from the perspective of word formation but only refers in passing to the semantics of such compounds. Subsequent commentators such as Kātyāyana and Patañjali expand on these semantic issues; they point out, for example, that compounding is only supported by the presence of a semantic relation between entities [Joshi, 1968].

Much closer to the modern day, early in the 20th century, Ferdinand de Saussure proposed a hugely influential *Course in General Linguistics* [de Saussure, 1959]. He distinguished between syntagmatic and associative relations, which *"correspond to two different forms of mental activity, both indispensable to the workings of language"*. A syntagmatic relation holds between two or more terms in a sequence *in praesentia*, in a particular context: *"words as used in discourse, strung together one after the other, enter into relations based on the linear character of languages—words must be arranged consecutively in spoken sequence. Combinations based on sequentiality may be called syntagmas."* Associative (paradigmatic) relations, on the other hand, come from accumulated experience and hold *in absentia*: *"Outside the context of discourse, words having something in common are associated withgether in the memory. [...] All these words have something or other linking them. This kind of connection is not based on linear sequence. It is a connection in the brain. Such connections are part of that accumulated store which is the form the language takes in an individual's brain."* Word associations can be morphological, phonological, grammatical or semantic.

Syntagmatic and associative relations interact in the understanding of text: word associations are summoned for the interpretation of a *syntagma*. Without the associations, a *syntagma* would have no meaning of its own. Interestingly, de Saussure's *Course* did not propose any list of relations. Harris [1987] observed that frequently occurring instances of syntagmatic relations may become part of our memory, and so turn paradigmatic. This parallels Gardin's [1965] proposal: that instances of paradigmatic relations be derived from accumulated syntagmatic data. By the way, this reflects current thinking on relation extraction from open texts.

From the point of view of structure, ontologies and texts sit at the two ends of the spectrum. The rise of formal semantics at the end of the 19th century began to bridge this gap. Starting with the work of Gottlob Frege [Frege, 1879], predicate logic and its extensions [L. T. F. Gamut, 1991] have been the standard analytical toolkit for philosophers of language. Predicate logic is an inherently relational formalism. A predicate takes one or more arguments; when modelling language, predicates which take multiple arguments usually encode semantic relations. Here is how a simple logical representation of the sentence `Google buys YouTube` might look:

$$buy(\texttt{Google}, \texttt{YouTube})$$

A representation like this is still commonly used in presentations of computational models. In another representation, sometimes called *neo-Davidsonian* after the philosopher Donald Davidson, additional variables represent the event or relation as something that can be explicitly modified and subject to quantification, for example:

$$\exists e \; InstanceOfBuying(e) \wedge agent(e, \texttt{Google}) \wedge patient(e, \texttt{YouTube})$$

or perhaps

$$\exists e \; InstanceOf(e, Buying) \wedge agent(e, \texttt{Google}) \wedge patient(e, \texttt{YouTube})$$

Charles Sanders Peirce was one of the great thinkers to whom people could turn for inspiration for representing knowledge and relations. His accomplishments include the *existential graphs*, which rely on the notion of an *existential relation R* [Peirce, 1909]: "anything that is *R* to *x* (where *x* is some particular kind of object) is nonexistent in case *x* is nonexistent. Thus, lovers of women with bright green complexions are nonexistent in case there are no such women."

From a mathematical point of view, relations had a dual nature. In logic, they served as predicates; in graphs (later known as semantic networks), they labelled arcs between vertices which represented concepts. AI chose the representation in logic to support knowledge-based agents and inference; the idea of a graph of concepts has been adopted to represent factual knowledge, prevalent in NLP [Russell and Norvig, 2020, chapter 10]. The latter has had a strong effect on the type of relations represented. In graphs, it is quite natural to represent binary relations. Binary relations have become the *de facto* norm in ontologies built from texts, and are by far the majority of relations which NLP targets for extraction.

The advent of the computer has brought about an interest in putting this new tool to the kind of tasks which people do, and thus the field of AI began. John McCarthy was the first to describe a complete, even if hypothetical, AI program [McCarthy, 1958]. Designed to apply general world knowledge in search of solutions to a problem, the program relied on two separate components, one for knowledge represented as rules and one for reasoning mechanisms. As a logic-based system, it already built upon relational information, but it was not directly concerned with language.

Linguistically oriented AI systems soon followed. Work such as Winograd's [1972] ground-breaking interactive English dialogue system or Charniak's [1972] study on understanding children's stories demonstrated that semantic knowledge about a variety of topics is essential to computational language comprehension. That was a conceptual shift from the "shallow" architecture of primitive conversation systems such as ELIZA [Weizenbaum, 1966] and first-generation machine translation systems. The need for storehouses of background knowledge to support reasoning systems has led in several directions; one of them was the creation of large-scale hand-crafted ontologies such as Cyc [Lenat and Guha, 1990]. A more recent, and perhaps more fruitful, direction was the acquisition of collections of propositional facts about the world via volunteer contributions over the Web; this trend began with OpenMind Common Sense [Singh et al., 2002], and MindPixel,[1] and has reached truly large scale with Freebase.[2]

At the crossroads between knowledge and language, we encounter interconnected systems in which knowledge about words and their various meanings is expressed in terms of their relations to other words. The idea of defining the meaning of a word by its connections to other words is familiar to any user of a dictionary. Spärck Jones [1964] suggested that the kind of lexical relations found in a dictionary could be formalized and learned automatically from text. Around the same time, Quillian [1962] proposed the *semantic network*, a graph in which meaning is modelled by labelled associations between words. The vertices of the network are concepts onto which one maps the words in a text, and then connections—relations between concepts—are established on arcs linking some of the words.

The network-based style of representation has remained very influential. It informs large-scale lexical resources such as WordNet [Fellbaum, 1998], a network whose latest active version—now over a decade old—had over 155,000 words (nouns, verbs, adjectives, adverbs) and over 117,000 groups of near-synonyms called *synsets*.[3] WordNet represents over twenty semantic relations between synsets, including synonymy, antonymy, hypernymy (a *sandwich* is a kind of *snack food*), hyponymy (*snack food* has a *sandwich* among its kinds), meronymy (*bread* is part of a *sandwich*) and holonymy (a *sandwich* has *bread* as a part). Section 2.2.2 will revisit WordNet's relations as examples of relations between concepts.

The early work on manual knowledge acquisition has quickly made it apparent that the process must be automated.[4] Luckily, work on text analysis has revealed that much of the knowledge we wish to extract is contained in texts. In parallel, methods of finding the structure in free-form texts—in the shape of part-of-speech and grammatical parsing—have been developed to fill in more of the gap between structured ontologies and unstructured texts. Work on the automatic construction of KBs from text collections took off with Hearst's [1992] pioneering research. At the beginning, the focus was on the relations which are the backbone of ontologies, Hearst's *is-a* and Berland and Charniak's [1999] *part-of*. The bootstrapping techniques developed for these relations were then applied to other relations; see for example Ravichandran and Hovy [2002] and Patwardhan and Riloff [2007].

One can observe that having specific targets for relation extraction may cause the omission of a wealth of information in texts. This has led to open information extraction. In this paradigm, one begins by hypothesizing about how a relation may be expressed, e.g., as a pattern over parts of speech [Fader et al., 2011], a path in a syntactic parse tree [Ciaramita et al., 2005], or a sequence of high-frequency words [Davidov and Rappoport, 2008b]. Next, all matching instances are

---

[1]The project has been dormant since 2005. See en.wikipedia.org/wiki/Mindpixel for a bit of history.
[2]Freebase was frozen in 2016.
[3]See wordnet.princeton.edu, in particular the WordNet 3.0 statistics at wordnet.princeton.edu/documentation/wnstats7wn.
[4]We accept the descriptor "manual", prevalent when the NLP literature talks about people creating language resources. But: the word means something *worked or done by hand and not by machine* (www.merriam-webster.com/dictionary/manual). Ontology creation, rule design, knowledge acquisition and text annotation are *intellectual* activities, not handiwork.

extracted as candidate relation instances. The downside of such methods is the high variability in relation expressions; a mapping onto a set of "canonical" relation expressions is the subject of ongoing work.

2.2   A MENAGERIE OF RELATION SCHEMATA

The two threads of parallel work, on the organization of knowledge and on texts, have led to two perspectives on relations. A relation manifests itself in text at the word level, and arises from the particular context in which it appears; we look at how relations between nominals have attained prominence in NLP research. In ontologies and other taxonomies, relations connect concepts, expressing facts considered (believed) to be true in view of the current state of our collective understanding of the world; we look at relations in a few of the knowledge repositories which have been applied in NLP, and at the trouble semantic relations may cause when they are used in ontologies. The next two sections briefly survey these two perspectives, and the different ways in which they have been turned into practice.

2.2.1   RELATIONS BETWEEN NOMINALS

Standard lexical-semantic literature discusses semantic relations at great length. We recommend that the interested reader consult Geeraerts's [2010] comprehensive monograph and the citations therein to all the classic publications. This section shows the evolution of work on determining, or building, a list of relations with coverage wide enough for text analysis—complete coverage, if at all possible. The work has first concentrated on people, trying to find out what kind of connections they perceive between various word combinations. Later, the focus shifted to data in attempts to design a list of relations which covers all the connections perceived in the texts under consideration. Then the nature of the texts changed—from general-purpose news texts or literature to texts in specialized domains like biology or medicine—and that caused another shift in perspective.

Casagrande and Hale [1967] attempted to build a *list* of semantic relations by asking native speakers of an exotic language to give definitions for a predetermined list of words. They analyzed the definitions into declarative sentences which state simple facts, and determined the relations expressed in those sentences. The result, a list of 13 relations not only between nominals, appears in Table 2.1.

Chaffin and Herrmann [1984] presented an exercise in the analysis of relations themselves, and of their distinguishing properties. They explored human perception of similarities and differences between relations via an exercise in grouping instances of 31 semantic relations. The results of the experiment showed that the subjects perceived five classes of semantic relations—see Table 2.2. Instances of these five classes can be distinguished by three properties: contrasting/non-contrasting, logical/pragmatic, and inclusion/non-inclusion.

Much of the debate on the correct representation of semantic relations has played out with regard to characterizing the interpretation of noun compounds. A noun compound is a sequence

Table 2.1: Casagrande and Hale's [1967] relations

Relation	Example	Relation	Example
attributive	toad–small	*contingency*	lightning–rain
function	ear–hearing	*spatial*	tongue–mouth
operational	shirt–wear	*comparison*	wolf–coyote
exemplification	circular–wheel	*class inclusion*	bee–insect
synonymy	thousand–ten hundred	*antonymy*	low–high
provenience	milk–cow	*grading*	Monday–Sunday
circularity	X is defined as X		

Table 2.2: Chaffin and Herrmann's [1984] relations

Relation	Example
constrasts	night–day
similars	car–auto
class inclusion	vehicle–car
part–whole	airplane–wing
case relations—agent, instrument	

of two or more nouns which functions as a single noun, e.g., `space shuttle` or `space shuttle mission`. Compounding is a frequent and productive process in English:[5] any text will contain numerous compounds, and many of these will be infrequent. Semantic interest in the special case of two-word noun compounds, or noun-noun compounds, is due not just to their ubiquity but also to the fact that they can encode a variety of relations. For example, a *taxi driver* is a driver who drives a taxi, while an *embassy driver* is a driver who is employed by / drives for an embassy, and an *embassy building* is a building which houses, or belongs to, an embassy.

The main questions about representation which arise in the study of compounds reflect broader questions relevant to any attempt at formalizing semantic relations in general. Noun compounds can therefore be viewed as an informative case study or microcosm. There is a voluminous literature on the semantics of compounds, from the perspective of both linguistics and NLP.[6] In linguistics, the primary aim is to find the most comprehensively explanatory representation. In NLP, it is to select the most useful representation for a particular application: this should have the right trade-off between generality and specificity to be computationally tractable and to give informative output to downstream systems. The two perspectives are complementary.

---

[5]Compounding is a feature of many other languages; see [Bauer, 2001] for a comprehensive cross-linguistic overview.
[6]See www.cl.cam.ac.uk/~do242/Resources/compound_bibliography.html for a long list.

Table 2.3: Warren's [1978] major semantic relations

Relation	Example
Possession	family estate
Location	water polo
Purpose	water bucket
Activity-Actor	crime syndicate
Resemblance	cherry bomb
Constitute	clay bird

Here is an important question: can the relational semantics of compounding be explained by a concise listing of possible semantic relations? Or is the set of distinguishable relations in practice boundlessly large? In linguistics, the former assumption has led to the compilation of relation inventories, starting with early descriptive work [Grimm, 1826, Jespersen, 1942, Noreen, 1904] and continuing through to the age of generative linguistics [Levi, 1978, Li, 1971, Warren, 1978].

For example, Warren proposed an inventory of relations informed by a comprehensive study of the Brown Corpus [Kučera and Francis, 1967]. The inventory consists of six *major* semantic relations, each of them further subdivided according to a hierarchy of up to four levels. Table 2.3 shows the major relations. As an example of further division, the relation *Time*—a direct child of the major relation *Location*—is specialized into *Time-Animate Entity* (weekend guests), *Time-Concrete, Inanimate Entity* (Sunday paper) and *Time-Abstract Entity* (fall colors).

Levi [1978] proposed a set of relations (for theory-internal reasons called "recoverable deletable predicates" or RDPs), which she claimed underlie all compositional non-nominalized compounds in English. They appear in Table 2.4. The *Role* column shows the modifier's function in the corresponding paraphrasing relative clause: when the modifier is the subject of that clause, the RDP is marked with the index 2.

In Levi's theory, nominalizations such as taxi driver are accounted for by a separate procedure because they are assumed to be derived from a different kind of deep representation. For those who are not committed to the transformational view of syntax and semantics, this separation is unnecessary and only leads to spurious distinctions (horse doctor would be labelled *for* but horse healer would have another relation label, *agent*). Levi deems the degree of ambiguity afforded by 12 relations to be sufficiently restricted for a hearer to identify the relation intended by a speaker by recourse to lexical or encyclopaedic knowledge, while still allowing for the semantic flexibility of compounding.

Levi's relations have influenced further proposals of relation inventories. One example is Ó Séaghdha and Copestake's [2007] work. They started from Levi's set of relations, and followed a set of principles based on empirical and theoretical considerations:

Table 2.4: Levi's [1978] relations

RDP	Example	Role	Traditional Name
$CAUSE_1$	tear gas	object	causative
$CAUSE_2$	drug deaths	subject	causative
$HAVE_1$	apple cake	object	possessive/dative
$HAVE_2$	lemon peel	subject	possessive/dative
$MAKE_1$	silkworm	object	productive/composite
$MAKE_2$	snowball	subject	productive/composite
USE	steam iron	object	instrumental
BE	soldier ant	object	essive/appositional
IN	field mouse	object	locative
FOR	horse doctor	object	purposive/benefactive
FROM	olive oil	object	source/ablative
ABOUT	price war	object	topic

   i. the inventory of relations should have good coverage;

   ii. relations should be disjoint, and each relation should describe a coherent concept;

  iii. the class distribution should not be too skewed or too sparse;

  iv. the concepts underlying the relations should generalize to other linguistic phenomena;

   v. the guidelines should make the annotation process as simple as possible;

  vi. the categories should provide useful semantic information.

The result was an inventory of eight relations. Four of Levi's relations (*about*, *be*, *have*, *in*) were kept, and *for* was replaced with *agent* and *inst* (instrument). Ó Séaghdha and Copestake introduced *rel* for compounds which encode non-specific relations, and *lex* for compounds which are idiomatic.

In contrast with the comprehensive view, Zimmer [1971] pointed to the great variety of English compounds. He concluded that it may be simpler to categorize the semantic relations which cannot be encoded in compounds than those which can. Downing [1977] cited compounds such as *plate length* ("what your hair is when it drags in your food") in order to argue: "The existence of numerous novel compounds like these guarantees the futility of any attempt to enumerate an absolute and finite class of compounding relationships." A complementary argument holds that simple relations chosen from a discrete set do not suffice to capture the richness of relational meaning, and that the meaning of word combinations arises from the interaction between necessarily complex representations of events and entities. This view received a detailed treatment in Coulson's [2001] work on frame semantics.

While this debate has arisen from theoretical linguistic concerns, the tension between parsimony and expressiveness in semantic representation is also a fundamental concern for computational linguists. The inventory approach has been popular in NLP because it is computationally suited to both rule-based and statistical classification methods. Su [1969] was, as far as we know, the first researcher to report on noun compound interpretation from a computational perspective. He described 24 semantic categories for use in producing paraphrase analyses of compounds. These categories contain many relations familiar from linguistically motivated inventories: *Use*, *Possessor*, *Spatial Location*, *Cause*, and so on. Other inventories proposed for noun compound analysis include those of Girju et al. [2005], Leonard [1984], Vanderwende [1994] and Ó Séaghdha [2008]. A large inventory, later used by a number of researchers, appeared in Nastase and Szpakowicz [2003]: 30 relations were grouped into 5 categories—see Table 2.5.

The example inventories presented here should make it clear that these alternative accounts have much in common. They all have categories for locative relations, for possessive relations, for purposive relations, and so on. Tratz and Hovy [2010] proposed a new inventory of 43 relations in 10 categories, developed in an iterative crowd-sourcing process to find a scheme which maximizes agreement between annotators. The relations appear in Tables 2.6–2.7. Tratz and Hovy performed meta-analysis of the most notable previous proposals; it has shown that they all cover essentially the same semantic space, although they differ in how exactly they partition that space.

Every representational framework considered in this section thus far has assumed that semantic relations are abstract constructs which correspond to logical predicates rather than to lexical items. In another take on meaning, semantic relations can be expressed by paraphrases. The relation in *weather report* can be attributed to the abstract predicate named *about* or *topic*; or the same relation can be described by saying that a *weather report* is "a report about the weather" or "a report forecasting the weather". Lauer [1995] proposed a widely cited analysis of noun compounds as paraphrases. He cast the task of interpreting compounds as that of choosing a prepositional paraphrase from the following set of precisely eight prepositions: *of*, *for*, *in*, *at*, *on*, *from*, *with*, *about*. For example, olive oil could be analyzed as OIL *from* OLIVES, night flight as a FLIGHT *at* NIGHT, and odour spray as a SPRAY *for* ODOURS. From a computational point of view, paraphrasing is attractive because a predictive model can be built by identifying noun-preposition co-occurrences in a corpus or even on the Web [Lapata and Keller, 2004].

On the other hand, the lexical nature of Lauer's relations has disadvantages. Prepositions themselves are polysemous, and the assignment of a prepositional paraphrase to a compound does not unambiguously identify the compound's meaning. In other words, once a compound has been identified as, say, an *of*-compound, there remains a question: what kind of relation does *of* indicate? The paraphrases *school of music*, *theory of computation* and *bell of (the) church* do not describe the same kind of semantic relation. Furthermore, the assignment of different categories does not necessarily entail a difference in semantic relations. The categories *in*, *at* and *on* have a significant overlap. The lexical distinction between prayer in (the) morning,

Table 2.5: Nastase and Szpakowicz's [2003] relations. *H* stands for *head*, *M* stands for *modifier*.

Relation Group	Examples	Paraphrase
Causality		
Cause	flu virus	H causes M
Effect	exam anxiety	M causes H
Purpose	concert hall	H is for M
Detraction	headache pill	H opposes M
Participant		
Agent	student protest	M performs H
Beneficiary	student discount	M benefits from H
Instrument	laser printer	H uses M
Object	metal separator	M is acted upon by H
Object_Property	sunken ship	H underwent M
Part	printer tray	H is part of M
Possessor	national debt	M has H
Property	blue book	H is M
Product	plum tree	H produces M
Source	olive oil	M is the source of H
Stative	sleeping dog	H is in a state of M
Whole	daisy chain	M is part of H
Quality		
Container	film music	M contains H
Content	apple cake	M is contained in H
Equative	player coach	H is also M
Manner	stylish writing	H occurs in the way indicated by M
Material	brick house	H is made of M
Measure	expensive book	M is a measure of H
Topic	weather report	H is concerned with M
Type	oak tree	M is a type of H
Spatiality		
Direction	outgoing mail	H is directed towards M
Location	home town	H is the location of M
Location_at	desert storm	H is located at M
Location_from	foreign capital	H originates at M
Temporality		
Frequency	daily experience	H occurs every time M occurs
Time_at	morning exercise	H occurs when M occurs
Time_through	six-hour meeting	H existed for the duration of M

Table 2.6: The relations from Tratz and Hovy [2010] (part I). The *Approximate Mappings* column shows the mapping of the proposed relation to a relation from [Barker and Szpakowicz, 1998] (B), [Girju et al., 2005] (G), [Levi, 1978] (L), [Nastase and Szpakowicz, 2003] (N), [Vanderwende, 1994] (V) and [Warren, 1978] (W).

Category Name	Example	Approximate Mappings
Causal Group		
communicator of communication	court order	BGN: Agent, L: act$_a$+Product$_a$, V: Subj
performer of act/activity	police abuse	BGN: Agent, L: Act$_a$+Product$_a$, V: Subj
creator/provider/cause of	ad revenue	BGV: Cause(d-by), L: Cause$_2$, N: Effect
Purpose/Activity Group		
perform/engage in	cooking pot	BGV: Purpose, L: For, N: Purpose, W: Activity, Purpose
create/provide/sell	nicotine patch	BV: Purpose, BG: Result, G: Make-Produce, GNV: Cause(s), L: Cause$_1$, Make$_1$, For, N: Product, W: Activity, Purpose
obtain/access/seek	shrimp boat	BGNV: Purpose, L: For, W: Activity, Purpose
modify/access/change	eye surgery	BGNV: Purpose, L: For, W: Activity, Purpose
mitigate/oppose/destroy	flak jacket	BGV: Purpose, L: For, N: Detraction, W: Activity, Purpose
organize/supervise/authority	ethics board	BGNV: Purpose/Topic, L: For/About$_a$, W: Activity
propel	water gun	BGNV: Purpose, L: For, W: Activity, Purpose
protect/conserve	screen saver	BGNV: Purpose, L: For, W: Activity, Purpose
transport/transfer/trade	freight train	BGNV: Purpose, L: For, W: Activity, Purpose
traverse/visit	tree traversal	BGNV: Purpose, L: For, W: Activity, Purpose
Ownership, Experience, Employment and Use		
possessor + owned/possessed	family estate	BGNVW: Possess*, L: Have$_2$
experiencer + cognition/mental	voter concern	BNVW: Possess*, G: Experiencer, L: Have$_2$
employer + employee/volunteer	team doctor	BGNVW: Possess*, L: For/Have$_2$, BGN: Beneficiary
consumer + consumed	cat food	BGNVW: Purpose, L: For, BGN: Beneficiary
user/recipient + used/received	voter guide	BNVW: Purpose, G: Recipient, L: For, BGN: Beneficiary
owned/possessed + possession	store owner	G: Possession, L: Have$_1$, W: Belonging-Possessor
experience + experiencer	fire victim	G: Experiencer, L: Have$_1$
thing consumed + consumer	fruit fly	W: Obj-SingleBeing
thing/means used + user	faith healer	BNV: Instrument, G: Means, Instrument, L: Use, W: MotivePower-Obj
Temporal Group		
time (span) + X	night work	BNV: Time(At), G: Temporal, L: In$_c$, W: Time-Obj
X + time (span)	birth date	G: Temporal, W: Obj-Time
Location and Whole + Part/Member of		
location/geographic scope of X	hillside home	BGV: Locat(ion/ive), L: In$_a$, From$_b$, B: Source, N: Location(At/From), W: Place-Obj, PlaceOfOrigin
whole-part/member of	robot arm	B: Possess, G: Part-Whole, L: Have$_2$, N: Part, V: Whole-Part, W: Obj-Part, Group-Member

Table 2.7: The relations from Tratz and Hovy [2010] (part II). The *Approximate Mappings* column shows the mapping of the proposed relation to a relation from [Barker and Szpakowicz, 1998] (B), [Girju et al., 2005] (G), [Levi, 1978] (L), [Nastase and Szpakowicz, 2003] (N), [Vanderwende, 1994] (V) and [Warren, 1978] (W).

Category Name	Example	Approximate Mappings
Composition and Containment Group		
substance/material/ ingredient + whole	plastic bag	BNVW: Material*, GN: Source, L: From$_a$, L: Have$_1$, L: Make$_{2b}$, N: Content
part/member + collection/config/series	truck convoy	L: Make$_{2ac}$, N: Whole, V: Part-Whole, W: Parts-Whole
X + spatial container/location/ bounds	shoe box	B: Content, Located, L: For, L: Have$_1$, N: Location, W: Obj-Place
Topic Group		
topic of communication/imagery/info	travel story	BGNV: Topic, L: About$_a$, W: SubjectMatter, G: Depiction
topic of plan/deal/arrangement/rules	loan terms	BGNV: Topic, L: About$_a$, W: SubjectMatter
topic of observation/study/evaluation	job survey	BGNV: Topic, L: About$_a$, W: SubjectMatter
topic of cognition/emotion	jazz fan	BGNV: Topic, L: About$_a$, W: SubjectMatter
topic of expert	policy wonk	BGNV: Topic, L: About$_a$, W: SubjectMatter
topic of situation	oil glut	BGNV: Topic, L: About$_a$
topic of event/process	lava flow	G: Theme, V: Subj
Attribute Group		
topic/thing + attrib	street name	BNV: Possess*, G: Property, L: Have$_2$, W: Obj-Quality
topic/thing + attrib value charac of	earth tone	
Attributive and Coreferential		
coreferential	fighter plane	BV: Equative, G: Type, IS-A, L: Be$_{bcd}$, N: Type, Equality, W: Copula
partial attribute transfer	skeleton crew	W: Resemblance, G: Type
measure + whole	hour meeting	G: Measure, N: TimeThrough, Measure, W: Size-Whole
Other		
highly lexicalized/fixed pair	pig iron	
other	contact lens	

`prayer at night` and `prayer on (a) feast day` does not signal different relations. There is another problem. Many noun-noun compounds which cannot be paraphrased using prepositions (*woman driver*, *taxi driver*) are excluded from the model. Other compounds admit only unintuitive paraphrases: should *honey bee* really be analyzed as *bee for honey*?

Nakov [2008a] and Butnariu et al. [2010] depart from the assumption that a handful of phrases can characterize a semantic relation. They consider a relation to be expressed by any combination of verbs and prepositions which occur in texts: `olive oil` can now be interpreted as, e.g., OIL *that is extracted from* OLIVES or OIL *that is squeezed from* OLIVES. Such paraphrases—more informative than Lauer's OIL *from* OLIVES or Levi's *from* (OIL, OLIVES)—come closer to the richness demanded by Downing's [1977] linguistic arguments. A semantic relation is represented as a distribution over multiple paraphrases, and this allows comparisons. Two compounds may be similar in some ways (`olive oil` and `sea salt` both match the paraphrase `N1 is extracted from N2`) and different in others (salt is not *squeezed from* the sea).

2.2.2   RELATIONS BETWEEN CONCEPTS

Machine-readable knowledge is usually stored in ontologies, KBs or KGs. Relations in such repositories connect concepts rather than words or phrases. Concepts are unambiguous—a concept is represented by a unique name/label—and they refer to something particular evoked by that name or label. Relations in a knowledge repository also have specific characteristics: they should be unambiguous; different relation names/labels should refer to different types of connections; and they should capture some form of enduring knowledge, as in the example in Section 1.1: ENDEAVOUR *is a* SPACE SHUTTLE vs. ENDEAVOUR *is now being prepared* for DISPLAY.

To develop an ontology or a KB, one must choose which entities and relations between them to represent. Both these choices depend on the domain of the knowledge to be captured, and we will see further on that there is much variety. There is, however, some consensus. The backbone of an ontology is the *is-a* relation, and *part-of* is desirable as well. The consensus may break over granularity: even *is-a* and *part-of* can be further refined.

An instance of the *is-a* relation usually links a more specific and a more general concept. From the point of view of formalizing knowledge, there is a distinction between linking two generic concepts (CHOCOLATE *is-a* FOOD), and linking a concept instance and its superordinate concept (TOBLERONE *is-a* CHOCOLATE). The first formalizes *class inclusion*, while the second models *class membership*. Such a distinction was added to WordNet's hyponym/hypernym hierarchy in the form of the *instance hypernymy* relation [Hristea and Miller, 2006]. Further distinctions can be made. Wierzbicka [1984] refined *is-a* into five subrelations. The two most interesting for us are the *is-a-kind-of* relation, which she calls *taxonomic* (chicken–bird) and *is-used-as-a-kind-of*, called *functional* (adornment–decoration).

Meronymic (*part-of*) relations also can be refined, and in certain situations they should be. Winston et al. [1987] made a convincing case for six types of meronymy; they are listed along with examples in Table 2.8. This is motivated by the apparent contradictions in the transitivity

Table 2.8: Winston et al.'s [1987] fine-grained *part-of* relations

Relation	Example
component–integral object	pedal–bike
member–collection	ship–fleet
portion–mass	slice–pie
stuff–object	steel–car
feature–activity	paying–shopping
place–area	Everglades–Florida

of meronymic relations. The distinctions are explained by changes in three properties: the functionality of the relation between the part and the whole; the separability between the part and the whole; and the homeomery of the part and the whole (their having like/similar parts). For example:

1. Simpson's arm is part of Simpson['s body].
2. Simpson is part of the Philosophy Department.
3. *Simpson's arm is part of the Philosophy Department.

Transitivity fails in this case. The relation in the first sentence is an instance of *component - object*, while the second sentence contains an instance of *member - collection*. Gerstl and Pribbenow's [1995] inventory proposal contains three meronymic relations, *quantity - mass*, *element - collection*, and *component - complex*. They have also been adopted in WordNet [Fellbaum, 1998], where *meronymy* has three subtypes: *member*, *substance* and *part* meronyms (and there are the matching holonym counterparts). A representative selection of WordNet's relations appears in Table 2.9.

Nutter [1989] presented an overview of lexical-semantic relations from 15 studies on the topic. The result of this analysis is a rich five-level hierarchy of over 100 relations, comprising semantic, morphological, syntactic and factive relations. They come from work on English and Russian, and most of them have been found language-independent. Nutter notes that domains are likely to require specific relations, so there is no comprehensive list.

The Cyc project [Lenat and Guha, 1990, Matuszek et al., 2006] aims at the large-scale acquisition of common-sense knowledge.[7] According to the 2006 paper, Cyc featured 15,000 predicates, organized hierarchically. There is a distinction between class inclusion *genls*: (#$genls #$Tree-ThePlant #$Plant) and class membership *is-a*: (#$isa #$BillClinton #$UnitedStatesPresident). There are causal and meronymic relations, as well as many "encyclopedic" relations such as for example *capitalCity* (#$capitalCity #$France #$Paris), *basedInRegion* or *biologicalMotherOf*. The resource also includes rules, relations between relations (e.g., *implies*), definitions of relations, and relations between both entities and general concepts. Our example of the *is-a* relation

[7]www.cyc.com

Table 2.9: Selected relations among nouns in WordNet 3.0 (its Unix-based implementation). In the examples, we note the sense numbers of polysemous nouns. The bottom part of the table shows nouns related to other parts of speech.

Relation	Example
synonym	day (Sense 2) / time
antonym	day (Sense 4) / night
hypernym	berry (Sense 2) / fruit
hyponym	fruit (Sense 1) / berry
member-of holonym	Germany / NATO
has–member meronym	Germany / Sorbian
part-of holonym	Germany / Europe
has–part meronym	Germany / Mannheim
substance-of holonym	wood (Sense 1) / lumber
has–substance meronym	lumber (Sense 1) / wood
domain—TOPIC	line (Sense 7) / military
domain—USAGE	line (Sense 21) / channel
domain member—TOPIC	ship / porthole
attribute	speed (Sense 2) / fast
derived from	speed (Sense 2) / quick
derived from	speed (Sense 2) / accelerate

shows a downside of the manual acquisition of encyclopedic knowledge. Not only must new data be added, but existing data must be checked for consistency, because some relations have an expiration date.

The collaborative manner of knowledge-sharing has given rise to other sources of encyclopedic relations. There is a bonus: such relations emerge from the interaction of multiple users, and so they reflect a form of collective knowledge and organizational principles. Wikipedia is a very popular source of collaboratively obtained relations.[8] In structured sections of articles called infoboxes, the users include attributes of the entity to which the article corresponds, and assign the corresponding values, which often are entities themselves. This in effect produces instances of relations between entities. Freebase, where users explicitly added facts, was from our point of view a large repository of relation instances.[9] Wikipedia infoboxes and Freebase will be discussed in Section 3.2.5.

---

[8]www.wikipedia.org
[9]developers.google.com/freebase or web.archive.org/web/2013*/www.freebase.com.

2.2.3   NO FINAL WORD

A review of the literature has shown that almost every new attempt to analyze relations between nominals leads to a new list of relations. We also observe that a necessary and sufficient list of relations to describe the connection between nominals does not exist [Downing, 1977, Jespersen, 1942]. This observation applies both to relations between nominals in texts and to relations between concepts in an ontology. Murphy [2003] reviews several properties of semantic relations, among them *uncountability*, which basically marks relations as an open class. This stance has been embraced by researchers who work on relation extraction from open texts, where relation markers are verbs or verb phrases, a clearly open-ended set. The missing step, for now, is the mapping of such relation expressions onto canonical relation types. Resources built collaboratively on the Web offer a middle ground. In particular, Wikipedia, Freebase and Wikidata contain instances of relations which the (human) contributors consider salient.

2.3   DIMENSIONS OF VARIATION ACROSS RELATIONS

While there is no consensus on a list of semantic relations which would be necessary and sufficient for analyzing texts (in any domain) or for building ontologies, a good look at related work suggests certain shared properties of relations. Such properties, which we briefly present in this section, can help differentiate relations, and can be relevant to computational methods of work with semantic relations.

2.3.1   PROPERTIES OF RELATIONS

Ontological and Idiosyncratic Relations

Ontological semantic relations between nominals come up practically the same in many contexts (APPLE *is-a*FRUIT regardless of the context, and even without considering any context at all). That is to say, they are appropriate for insertion into an ontology. *Idiosyncratic* relations hold between nominals which appear together in texts and which the reader perceives as connected. Such relations are highly sensitive to context (APPLE and BASKET will only sometimes be in a *content-container* relation). This distinction mirrors the contrast between paradigmatic and syntagmatic relations first noted in de Saussure's [1959] *Course in General Linguistics*, and adopted in other studies of semantic relations [Khoo and Na, 2006, Murphy, 2003]. Paradigmatic relations cover a wide variety of associations between words, including morphological and phonetic associations, whereas syntagmatic relations cover words which occur close in a text.

A classification of semantic relations as ontological or idiosyncratic appears very attractive. Had there been a fool-proof test, we would have structured the remainder of the book along this dimension. This would have enabled a systematic and well-grounded automation of induction of KBs and ontologies from texts. As it is, however, we must be practical.

Automated acquisition of knowledge in general seems to split rather neatly into three major forms of machine learning—unsupervised, semi-supervised and supervised—but there is no clear mapping from methods to the learning of specific types of semantic relations. The same relation can be acquired by any of these methods (it is true, for example, of the *is-a* relation) or indeed by a combination of methods. Features which characterize relations, such as context patterns, may come from unsupervised corpus analysis, and go into more or less supervised models of individual relations. Idiosyncratic relations are inherently context-dependent, just as ontological relations are not, but they cannot be distinguished easily only by data support. The arguments of relations of both kinds (e.g., *is-a* and *cause-effect*, or *content-container*) can be characterized by features acquired from large corpora. We do expect, however, that idiosyncratic relations will benefit more from including features which represent the specific context of the instance.

These considerations explain the way in which we chose to organize the material. Chapter 3 focuses on supervised learning, applicable both to ontological and idiosyncratic relations. Data representation consists of features which describe the entities, their interaction and the context. Chapter 4 shows methods which require little or no supervision, and work with large amounts of data with hardly any manual annotations. Relation analysis in this framework relies mostly on redundancy and consistency across data, so the methods presented here work better for ontological relations. Chapter 5 covers the supervised-to-unsupervised spectrum of relation learning in the deep-learning formalism, with its new ways of modelling instances and relations, and of acquiring its own training data.

Binary and n-ary Relations

The focus on binary relations is quite common in analyzing the semantic interaction of entities in text, but this is not the only possibility. The semantic relations for a verb—which takes between one and several arguments—may be better represented by a *frame* [Minsky, 1975]. A frame encompasses all the required semantic arguments. For example, a *selling* event can be seen as invoking a frame which covers relations between the buyer, the seller, the object bought and the price paid. Such a frame-based perspective can make sense for nominals and their modifiers, especially if the nominal is verbal or deverbal (e.g., `selling` or `purchase`). Texts in biomedicine and chemistry also require n-ary relations between nominals because of the need to account for multiple participants in a reaction or a metabolic process. There may be other situations best described using n-ary relations.

Targeted and Emergent Relations

One of the considerations in comprehensive knowledge acquisition from texts is this: is the inventory of relations to be extracted open-ended? In such cases, the extraction process will first assume how relations may be expressed, for example, as patterns over parts of speech:

```
(V | V (N | Adj | Adv | Pron | Det)* PP)
```

This allows the extraction of relations such as *invented*, *is located in* or *made a deal with*. All instances which fit these pre-specified patterns and their arguments are collected and proposed for inclusion in the KB. Further processing may cluster together similar relation expressions, but relations in this situation remain largely anonymous, and are identified either by a set of phrases (which match the specified patterns) or by examples.

This contrasts with situations when the list of relations to be extracted is given in advance. A system either learns how to distinguish instances of the targeted relations from all others, or bootstraps to incrementally enlarge a given set of seed examples.

First-Order and Higher-Order Relations

We have thus far only considered first-order relations, whose arguments can only be entities. Higher-order relations can take relations as arguments. For example, John's belief that apples are fruits might be notated as *believes* (*John*, *is-a* (*apple*, *fruit*)). Higher-order phenomena can be expressed quite elegantly in a notation inspired by Peircean logic, namely *conceptual graphs* [Sowa, 1984],[10] in which the target of a relation can be another relation. Higher-order semantic relations have been relatively less studied in NLP, although they play a role in datasets for biomedical event extraction [Kim et al., 2009] and in semantic parsing [Liang et al., 2011, Lu et al., 2008].

Consider, for example, this fragment of a biomedical text: "In this study we hypothesized that the phosphorylation of TRAF2 inhibits binding to the CD40 cytoplasmic domain." It contains three events, E1, E2, and E3, with one, three and two arguments, respectively. E3 is a higher-order event which takes E1 and E2 as arguments:

- E1: phosphorylation(Theme: TRAF2),
- E2: binding(Theme1: TRAF2, Theme2: CD40, Site: cytoplasmic domain),
- E3: negative_regulation(Theme: E2, Cause: E1).

General and Domain-Specific Relations

Some relations are likely to be helpful in processing all kinds of text or in representing knowledge in any domain. Examples of such general relations are *location*, *possession*, *causation*, *is-a* and *part-of*. Other relations are only relevant to a specific text genre or to a narrow domain. A system for interpreting the language of biomedical documents may need to understand gene/protein events [Kim et al., 2009], relations between diseases and treatments [Rosario and Hearst, 2004], or other relations such as *Person afflicted* and *Defect* [Rosario and Hearst, 2001]. On the other hand, such very specific relations will be of very little use when processing reports about, say, sport fixtures.

2.3.2   PROPERTIES OF RELATION SCHEMATA

Coarser- and Finer-Grained Schemata

Contingent on the application, it may make sense to partition the space of relations into a small set of coarse-grained relations or a larger set of fine-grained relations. In the extreme, one can

---

[10]conceptualgraphs.org/

argue that every interaction between entities is a distinct relation with unique properties. This is not practical, however, because it precludes useful generalizations from data. At the other extreme, a scheme which consists of one universal relation is equally useless. The increasing number of relations in collaboratively built resources—like Freebase or Wikipedia infoboxes, which will be discussed in Section 3.2.5—shows that an equilibrium has not yet been reached, as new types of necessary relations keep being added.

Hierarchical and Flat Schemata

There is a compromise which shares the benefits of coarse-grained and fine-grained schemes: adopt a schema with a hierarchical organization, in which more numerous but narrower relations are grouped into coarser "super-relations". For example, Nastase and Szpakowicz's [2003] relation set has a two-level structure. Each of the 30 relations belongs to one of five categories. Warren's [1978] schema (Section 2.2.1) goes as deep as four levels. For example, *Possessor-Legal Belonging* is a subrelation of *Possessor-Belonging* which is a subrelation of *Whole-Part* which is a subrelation of a top-level relation *Possession*.

Open and Closed Schemata

The categorization into open and closed schemata reflects the distinction between emergent and targeted relations. Chapter 4 will review open information extraction (IE) methods, which aim for comprehensive relation extraction. The methods assume that the relations are an open class, and the list of relations represented in the analyzed corpus will be revealed in the course of processing. Such an assumption fits the unsupervised, or self-supervised, learning framework of open IE systems. Closed relation schemata allow for a deeper analysis and definition of specific relations, and for their supervised learning from annotated data.

2.4   SUMMARY

This chapter has briefly reviewed the parallel threads of semantic relations in the representation of knowledge and in texts, and how they have come together in the field of information extraction. We have considered several characteristics of semantic relations and semantic relation schemata. One important observation is that relations are an open class and, like concepts, can be organized into hierarchies. Different relation inventories and different levels of generality are appropriate in different contexts and domains. What remains constant across all these differences is the nature of relations. Some are ontological, and so represent a long-lasting, and largely context-independent, connection; others are idiosyncratic, and hold in a specific context. Today, when a mass of freely available text is both a tempting source of information for the automatic acquisition of knowledge and the target for "regular" text analysis, it is important to understand that there is a difference between the two types of relations. Such understanding can help acquire better and cleaner resources.

A more detailed analysis of semantic relations appears in Green et al. [2002], Murphy [2003] and Khoo and Na [2006]. For a textbook overview of lexical-semantic representations for NLP, we refer the reader to Jurafsky and Martin [2009].[11] For knowledge representation and usage in AI, we suggest Russell and Norvig [2020].

---

[11]The 3rd edition is under way—see web.stanford.edu/~jurafsky/slp3/.

CHAPTER 3

Extracting Semantic Relations with Supervision

3.1   THE SUPERVISED SETTING

In supervised learning of semantic relations, a predictive model is trained on data in which every data point, a relation instance, comes with its correct label, the relation. Such learning requires text annotated with the relations it expresses: the relation arguments, and the type of the relation which describes their interaction. Supervised learning performs very well if annotated data are available, but that can be a serious bottleneck. Learning good models also requires the design and acquisition of a representative set of features to describe every instance in the dataset. Useful datasets are available; we will discuss some of them, paying particular attention to how the relation arguments and the surrounding context are represented.

Supervised learning enables an in-depth exploration of a variety of characteristics of the arguments and the context so as to find those which help predict semantic relations. Such characteristics become *features* of varying levels of complexity, from simple symbolic categorial values through vectors to textual contexts with complex structure. To reach their full potential, such various types of features must be paired in a representation with the kind of machine learning formalism best equipped to take advantage of the information they encode. We will describe a few such formalisms capable of processing the rich structural and semantic information which a context can provide.

The techniques which this chapter presents are appropriate for the semantic analysis of individual texts. That is a scale small enough that one can afford to compute interesting features, and possibly to apply and test different models. The lessons learned in such small, controlled settings can usefully inform unsupervised and distantly supervised work on semantic relations. They show which features are so useful that they should be reproduced, perhaps with less depth, when tackling very large text corpora.

In the supervised set-up, the learning system gets a text (maybe as short as a sentence, often a single paragraph, and seldom more than a pageful). It must decide if the text contains instances of one or more semantic relations from a pre-specified fixed inventory. In the full relation classification task, the system must also identify the nominals which fill the argument roles in every detected relation instance.

The starting point in this task is an annotated dataset, perhaps like those presented in Section 3.2. A relation instance in this dataset is represented by features. Attributional features

(Section 3.3.1) capture the meaning of the arguments, relational features (Section 3.3.2) the nature of their interaction. The dataset represented in such a systematic manner is given to a machine learning system. The system learns a model which can generalize from the given instances and their descriptions, and make predictions on unseen data. Section 3.4 describes the most successful learning algorithms. We highlight the connection between the types of features and the algorithms which best take advantage of the information they get.

3.2   DATA

A number of datasets have been created for the supervised learning of semantic relations. They have different sizes, offer different types of information, and cover different relations. This section gives representative examples, ranging from small-scale to large-scale and from general-purpose to domain-specific.

3.2.1   RELATIONS BETWEEN ENTITIES: MUC AND ACE

The first large-scale datasets for relation classification were produced for the Message Understanding Conferences (MUC).[1] Grishman and Sundheim [1996] presented a brief history of the first six MUC events, mostly engaged in the automatic filling of scenario templates. MUC-7 introduced a relation extraction task, whose distinguishing feature was the focus on relations which hold between specific classes of entities, typically covering entity types common in news stories. In some cases, these are restricted to *named entities*, which can be referred to by proper nouns, numbers or time expressions. MUC-7 considered three kinds of entities—PERSON, ORGANIZATION, and LOCATION—as well as dates, times, percentages and currency amounts. There was a very limited set of three relations, each of them mapping an organization into an entity: *Employee_of*, *Product_of* and *Location_of*. That was sufficient in a task in which relation extraction was only a step in a more general process.

The MUC program was followed by a series of Automatic Content Extraction (ACE) shared tasks.[2] For example, ACE 2008 featured two languages (English and Arabic) and five kinds of named entities: FACILITY (FAC), GEO-POLITICAL ENTITY (GPE), LOCATION (LOC), ORGANIZATION (ORG), and PERSON (PER); see [ACE, 2008] for more details. The ACE 2008 annotation also considered six types of relations between entities of these five types, and each of these relation types had one or more subtypes; the full list appears in Table 3.1.

The definition for each relation type listed the entity types permitted as its arguments. For example, the first argument of an instance of *Employment* must be a PERSON, and the second argument must be either an ORGANIZATION or a GEO-POLITICAL ENTITY. The MUC-7 and ACE relation classification datasets consist of collections of documents in which every markable instance of a relation is labelled with its type and subtype. There are detailed guidelines for the

---

[1]ir.nist.gov/muc

[2]www.ldc.upenn.edu/collaborations/past-projects/ace and web.archive.org/web/2019*/www.itl.nist.gov/iad/mig/tests/ace/

Table 3.1: The inventory of relation types and subtypes in ACE-2008

Relation Type	Subtypes
Physical	*Located*
	Near
Part–Whole	*Geographical*
	Subsidiary
Personal–Social	*Business*
	Family
	Lasting–Personal
Organization–Affiliation	*Employment*
	Ownership
	Founder
	Student–Alum
	Sports–Affiliation
	Investor–Shareholder
	Membership
Agent–Artifact	*User–Owner–Inventor–Manufacturer*
General Affiliation	*Citizen–Resident–Religion–Ethnicity*
	Organization–Location–Origin

Employment(PERSON, ORGANIZATION):
```
<PER>He</PER> had previously worked at <ORG>NBC
Entertainment</ORG>.
```
Near(PERSON, FACILITY):
```
<PER>Muslim youths</PER> recently staged a half
dozen rallies in front of <FAC>the embassy</FAC>.
```
Citizen–Resident–Religion–Ethnicity(PERSON, GEO-POLITICAL ENTITY):
```
Some <GPE>Missouri</GPE> <PER>voters</PER> [...]
```

Figure 3.1: Example annotations for three ACE-2008 relations.

annotation procedure. In general, an entity is markable if it belongs to one of the specified entity classes. Relation *R* is markable if it holds between two markable entities mentioned in the same sentence, the sentence contains explicit evidence for *R*, and *R* is in one of the specified relation classes. Figure 3.1 shows example annotations.

The MUC-7 and ACE datasets have been constructed so they can be used for a multi-stage information extraction evaluation consisting of entity detection and relation detection. Researchers who only focus on the relation classification task often rely on gold-standard entity annotations. The task then becomes that of assigning a relation type/subtype label to each pair of annotated entities which appear in the same sentence. For many entity pairs, no semantic relation holds, so there also is a *None* label.[3]

3.2.2   RELATIONS BETWEEN NOMINALS IN AND OUT OF CONTEXT

The 2007 and 2010 SemEval workshops on semantic evaluation included semantic relation classification tasks. These tasks differed from what ACE was after: they dealt with very general relations, not restricted to specific classes of entities. Those relations can be expected to matter in semantic processing in various text genres and domains. The datasets for these tasks are also publicly available, with no restrictions on use.[4] The datasets attracted many participants to the shared tasks, and other researchers have used them in a number of subsequent studies [Davidov and Rappoport, 2008b, Nakov and Hearst, 2008, Nakov and Kozareva, 2011, Ó Séaghdha and Copestake, 2008, Socher et al., 2012].

SemEval-2007 Task 4 [Girju et al., 2009] gave the participants a dataset in seven parts, each corresponding to one relation from the list in Table 3.2. Every part has a training and a test section, and can be treated as defining a binary classification task. Relation instances have been collected via a search engine by submitting simple query patterns (e.g., "* in *" for the *Content-Container* relation). On the other hand, the resulting collection will contain many false positives which represent near-misses (e.g., exercise in the morning). A supervised classifier could be used to distinguish true instances from such near-misses. Figure 3.2 exemplifies the format of the dataset. It shows a positive and a negative instance of the *Content-Container* relation.

The arguments of the candidate *Content-Container* instance are given to the system, marked up with the <e1>...</e1> and <e2> ...</e2> tags. The annotation also includes manually disambiguated WordNet senses for each argument, and the query string used to retrieve the sentence from the Web. The system must predict a label "true" or "false" for each data item, i.e., make a binary classification judgment.

The follow-up Task 8 at SemEval-2010 [Hendrickx et al., 2010] changed the experimental design in a few ways.

1. Instead of a separate dataset and a separate binary classification task for each relation, there was a single multi-class dataset. Systems were to choose among all relations in the inventory to classify an instance, and had the option of choosing no relation (*None*).

2. The candidate arguments were still given, but systems had to determine the ordering of these entities with respect to the predicted relation's argument slots.

---

[3]We did not have access to these datasets, so we cannot give detailed statistics on the number of instances for each relation type they include.

[4]sites.google.com/site/semeval2007task4/   www.kozareva.com/downloads.html (SemEval 2010 Task #8).

Table 3.2: The seven relations considered in SemEval-2007 Task 4. Shown: positive examples and the statistics of their absolute and relative distribution—both for the training set and the test set.

Relation	Training		Test	
	Positive	Size	Positive	Size
Cause-Effect laugh [*Cause*] wrinkles [*Effect*]	52.1%	140	51.3%	80
Instrument-Agency laser [*Instrument*] printer [*Agency*]	50.7%	140	48.7%	78
Product-Producer honey [*Product*] bee [*Producer*]	60.7%	140	66.7%	93
Origin-Entity message [*Entity*] from outer-space [*Origin*]	38.6%	140	44.4%	81
Theme-Tool news [*Theme*] conference [*Tool*]	41.4%	140	40.8%	71
Part-Whole the door [*Part*] of the car [*Whole*]	46.4%	140	36.1%	72
Content-Container the apples [*Content*] in the basket [*Container*]	46.4%	140	51.4%	74
Average	**48.0%**	**140**	**48.5%**	**78**

3. WordNet senses and query strings were no longer supplied.

The dataset created for Task 8 was also much larger (over 10,000 annotated sentences); the set of relations was larger as well. The relation inventory is listed in Table 3.3. Figure 3.3 shows an example data item.

The SemEval-2010 Task 8 dataset presents a challenge: the relation inventory contains two groups of very close relations. The first group consists of *Component-Whole* and *Member-Collection*, both special cases of *Part-Whole*. The second group includes *Content-Container*, *Entity-Origin* and *Entity-Destination*; they are distinguished by considering if the situation described in the corresponding sentence is static or dynamic, as shown in the examples in Figure 3.4.

Several other datasets have been employed in two types of learning exercises: recognize hypernymy, meronymy, synonymy/antonymy and other common semantic relations; or distinguish between relations (for example, tell hypernymy from other relations). While not all these datasets provide a sentential context for the nominal pairs, they were produced with the expectation that they would be used together with large corpora from which relational features

Table 3.3: The 9+1 relations considered in SemEval-2010 Task 8. Shown: positive examples and the statistics of their absolute and relative distribution—both for the training set and the test set.

Relation	Training		Test	
	Positive	Size	Positive	Size
Cause-Effect radiation [*Cause*] cancer [*Effect*]	12.5%	1003	12.1%	328
Instrument-Agency phone [*Instrument*] operator [*Agency*]	6.3%	504	5.7%	156
Product-Producer suits [*Product*] factory [*Producer*]	9.0%	717	8.5%	231
Content-Container wine [*Content*] is in the bottle [*Container*]	6.8%	540	7.1%	192
Entity-Origin letters [*Entity*] from the city [*Origin*]	9.0%	716	9.5%	258
Entity-Destination boy [*Entity*] went to bed [*Destination*]	10.6%	845	10.8%	292
Component-Whole kitchen [*Component*] apartment [*Whole*]	11.8%	941	11.5%	312
Member-Collection tree [*Member*] forest [*Collection*]	8.6%	690	8.6%	233
Message-Topic lecture [*Message*] on semantics [*Topic*]	7.9%	634	9.6%	261
Other people filled with joy	17.6%	1410	16.7%	454
Total		8000		2717

```
"Among the contents of the <e1>vessel</e1> were a set of
carpenter's <e2>tools</e2>, several large storage jars, ceramic
utensils, ropes and remnants of food, as well as a heavy load of
ballast stones."

WordNet(e1) = "vessel%1:06:00::",
WordNet(e2) = "tool%1:06:00::",
Content-Container(e2, e1) = "true",
Query = "contents of the * were a"
-----------------------------------------------------
"<e1>Batteries</e1> stored in <e2>contact</e2> with one another
can generate heat and hydrogen gas."

WordNet(e1) = "battery%1:06:00::",
WordNet(e2) = "contact%1:26:00::",
Content-Container(e1, e2) = "false",
Query = "batteries stored in"
```

Figure 3.2: Annotated sentences showing a positive and a negative instance of the semantic relation *Content-Container* in SemEval-2007 Task 4.

```
The <e1>collision</e1> resulted in two more <e2>crashes</e2> in
the intersection, including a Central Concrete truck that was
about to turn left onto College Ave.
Relation = Cause-Effect(e1, e2)
```

Figure 3.3: An instance of the semantic relation *Cause-Effect* in SemEval-2010 Task 8.

Entity-Origin(e_1, e_2)
```
He removed the <e1>apples</e1> from the <e2>basket</e2> and put
them on the table.
```
Content-Container(e_1, e_2)
```
When I entered the room, the <e1>apples</e1> were put in the
<e2>basket</e2>.
```
Entity-Destination(e_1, e_2)
```
Then, the <e1>apples</e1> were put in the <e2>basket</e2> once
again.
```

Figure 3.4: Annotated sentences showing instances of the close relations *Entity-Origin*, *Content-Container* and *Entity-Destination* from the SemEval-2010 Task 8.

Table 3.4: Statistics of the datasets applied in recognizing or differentiating common semantic relations

Dataset	Relations	#Instances	Total Size
BLESS	*hypernym*	1,337	26,554
	meronym	2,943	
	coordination	3,565	
	event	3,824	
	attribute	2,731	
	random-n	6,702	
	random-v	3,265	
	random-j	2,187	
EVALution	*hypernym*	3,637	13,465
	meronym	1,819	
	attribute	2,965	
	synonym	1,888	
	antonym	3,156	
CogALex-V shared task (subset of EVALution)	*hypernym*	637	7,314
	meronym	387	
	synonym	402	
	antonym	601	
	random	5,287	
Lenci/Benotto	*hypernym*	1,933	5,010
	synonym	1,311	
	antonym	1,766	
Weeds	*hypernym*	1,469	1,928
	coordination	1,459	

were to be obtained. Table 3.4 shows the statistics of the datasets: BLESS [Baroni and Lenci, 2011],[5] EVALution [Santus et al., 2015],[6] CogALex-V shared task [Santus et al., 2016],[7] Lenci/Benotto [Benotto, 2015][8] and Weeds [Weeds et al., 2014].

3.2.3   RELATIONS IN NOUN-NOUN COMPOUNDS

This section presents datasets for relation extraction which focus on the special case of noun-noun compounds; some of them do not supply sentential context.

[5]sites.google.com/site/geometricalmodels/shared-evaluation
[6]github.com/esantus/EVALution
[7]sites.google.com/site/cogalex2016/home/shared-task
[8]github.com/SussexCompSem/learninghypernyms

Table 3.5: Statistics of Nastase and Szpakowicz's [2003] noun-modifier dataset at the coarse 5-class level, and examples of annotated instances at the fine-grained level. Abbreviations: nmr = noun-modifier relation, eff = effect, freq = frequency, inst = instrument, lfr = locationFrom, cont = container.

Relation Class	# Examples	Example
Causality	86	rel(nmr, wrinkle, [n, 1], laugh, [n, 2], eff)
Participant	260	rel(nmr, observation, [n, 1], radar, [n, 1], inst)
Temporality	52	rel(nmr, workout, [n, 1], regular, [a, 1], freq)
Spatiality	56	rel(nmr, material, [n, 1], cosmic, [a, 1], lfr)
Quality	146	rel(nmr, album, [n, 2], photo, [n, 1], cont)

Nastase and Szpakowicz [2003] made available a set of 600 base noun phrases (noun-modifier pairs) with two annotations at different granularity levels.[9] One annotation covered 35 relations, the other five more general relations. The 35 relations, together with examples, were shown in Section 2.2.1, Table 2.5. The dataset contains two kinds of base noun phrases: noun-noun pairs and noun-adjective pairs. These phrases cannot be fully interpreted out of context but they are annotated with part-of-speech information and WordNet 1.7 senses. Table 3.5 shows the statistics of the dataset at the coarse 5-class level, and examples of annotated instances in a Prolog-style format:

```
rel(nmr,    Head, [POS_Head, WNSense_Head],
            Modifier, [POS_Modifier, WNSense_Modifier],
            Relation).
```

The WordNet 1.7 sense corresponds to that particular word and part of speech.

Kim and Baldwin [2005] gathered 2169 noun-noun compounds (split into 1088 for training and 1081 for testing) from the Wall Street Journal section of the Penn TreeBank [Marcus et al., 1994]. Those were only common nouns, and they were not part of longer compounds. The annotations assigned the 20 relations presented in Table 3.6. Unlike other datasets where annotations are disjunct, Kim and Baldwin allowed multiple labels: 94 compounds in the training data and 81 in the test data were annotated with more than one semantic relation.

Ó Séaghdha and Copestake [2007] collected and annotated 1568 noun compounds from the British National Corpus,[10] either with one of the 8 relations presented in Section 2.2.1 (derived from Levi's list of recoverable deletable predicates), or with the relation *unknown*. Table 3.7 shows the data statistics.

Tratz and Hovy's [2010] annotated list of 17,509 noun compounds consists of common nouns from a large corpus and the Wall Street Journal. Details of the relations appear in Ta-

---

[9] www.eecs.uottawa.ca/~szpak/pub/noun_modifier_relations_600_instances.zip
[10] www.natcorp.ox.ac.uk/

Table 3.6: Statistics of Kim and Baldwin's [2005] noun compound dataset (N_1 = modifier, N_2 = head)

Relation	Definition	Example	# Test/# Training
agent	N_2 is performed by N_1	student protest	10/5
beneficiary	N_1 benefits from N_2	student price	10/7
cause	N_1 causes N_2	exam anxiety	54/74
container	N_1 contains N_2	printer tray	13/19
content	N_1 is contained in N_2	paper tray	40/34
destination	N_1 is destination of N_2	exit route	2/2
equative	N_1 is also head	payer coach	9/17
instrument	N_1 is used in N_2	electron microscope	6/11
located	N_1 is located at N_2	home town	12/16
location	N_1 is the location of N_2	lab printer	29/24
material	N_2 is made of N_1	gingerbread man	12/15
object	N_1 is acted on by N_2	engine repair	88/88
possessor	N_1 has N_2	student loan	32/22
product	N_1 is a product of N_2	automobile factory	27/32
property	N_2 is like N_1	elephant seal	76/85
purpose	N_2 is meant for N_1	concert hall	160/160
result	N_1 is the result of N_2	cold virus	7/8
source	N_1 is the source of N_2	chest pain	86/99
time	N_1 is the time of N_2	winter semester	26/19
topic	N_2 is concerned with N_1	safety standard	465/446

Table 3.7: Statistics of Ó Séaghdha and Copestake's [2007] noun compound dataset with six Levi-inspired relations and three lexical relations

Relation	Example	Distribution
be	steel knife	191
have	street name	199
in	forest hut	308
inst	rice cooker	266
actor	honey bee	236
about	fairy tale	243
rel	camera gear	81
lex	home secretary	35
unknown	similarity crystal	9

ble 2.6 in Section 2.2.1. The most frequent relations in this dataset are *perform/engage in* (13.24%), *create/provide/sell* (8.94%), *topic of communication/imagery/info* (8.37%), *location/geographic scope of* (4.99%), and *organize/supervise/authority* (4.82%).

3.2.4   RELATIONS IN MANUALLY BUILT ONTOLOGIES

The early attempts to build ontologies for use in NLP and AI relied on manual contributions of a small number of experts. Such reliance limits the size and range of the resource, and may affect its availability. Even so, ontologies offer a good deal of useful information, including many instances of various relation types. For years WordNet has been the most popular resource in NLP, surpassing all other resources by a large margin. But there are others, with more varied relations, for example Cyc. Section 2.2.2 briefly presented the relations in WordNet and in Cyc.

Manually built resources tend to contain data of high quality and usually in larger quantity than data annotated specifically for relation-learning purposes, but often outside a textual context. On the other hand, learning from such good data would be restricted to the relations present in the ontology. Hyponymy/hypernymy, WordNet's equivalent of the *is-a* relation, often supplies initial seeds or training data for relation extraction.

WordNet and Cyc are based on different principles, so they organize their taxonomies differently. WordNet has been developed as a lexical-semantic network, in which synsets (groups of near-synonymous words) are linked by several fundamental lexical-semantic relations. Cyc aims for the organization of world and common-sense knowledge. It is, then, the concepts and the way in which they are defined that inform the construction of the ontology. In particular, Cyc's concepts, defined intensionally, lead to a "property-driven" organization. Cyc's top THING collection (concept) is partitioned into TEMPORAL THING–ATEMPORAL THING, SPA-

TIAL THING–ASPATIAL THING, INTANGIBLE–PARTIALLY TANGIBLE and SET OR COLLECTION–INDIVIDUAL. WordNet's top node, ENTITY, has subclasses PHYSICAL ENTITY, ABSTRACTION, THING; ABSTRACTION is subdivided into ATTRIBUTE, PSYCHOLOGICAL FEATURE, GROUP, RELATION, and so on. Somewhat optimistically, either ontology may offer its particular advantages to the task of learning semantic relations between nominals. That is because generalization can run along different dimensions, and so exemplify the refinement of *is-a* relations discussed by Wierzbicka [1984].

Relation extraction turns more and more to specialized scientific domains, and extraction methods help add to knowledge repositories in such narrower fields. Scientific knowledge keeps growing: new concepts and relations arise all the time. It is not surprising, then, that those repositories are not quite ontologies in the traditional sense. A comprehensive concept and relation schema, the cornerstone of any ontology, appears infeasible no matter which domain, so what gets stored are often concepts and relations found immediately useful.

Specialized resources have played a role in the automatic extraction of semantic relations, notably in biomedicine. There is, for example, Gene Ontology,[11] with the backbone *is-a* and *part-of* relations, and with highly specialized relations which represent the interaction between genes, such as *regulates*, *negatively regulates* or *positively regulates*. The Human Protein Interaction Database [Han et al., 2004], another narrowly conceived resource, contains relations which have also been the subject of extraction tasks. Section 3.2.6 explores at a greater length the treatment of semantic relations in such specialized domains.

3.2.5   RELATIONS IN COLLABORATIVELY BUILT RESOURCES

The infeasibility of building ontologies or data repositories on a very large scale has sometimes been referred to as the *data acquisition bottleneck*. Once the Web began to be regarded as a platform for facilitating online collaborative projects, this became much less of an issue. Knowledge sharing, in a more structured or less structured format, has led to the construction of large-scale knowledge sources. Two such sources in particular, Wikipedia and Freebase,[12] have accumulated data of much interest to the analysis of semantic relations. They find less use in the type of learning described in this chapter than in a semi-supervised setting. After a brief introduction here, they will be revisited in Section 4.6, where we discuss their role in distant supervision.

Wikipedia Infoboxes

Wikipedia, the online encyclopedia, contains a wealth of information. Some of that information has a fixed structure and so is relatively easy to obtain.

---

[11]The site at geneontology.org says: "The Gene Ontology describes our knowledge of the biological domain with respect to three aspects: Molecular Function [...] Cellular Component [...] Biological Process [...]."

[12]Freebase has not been added to since 2016, and has in practice been supplanted by Wikidata. See www.wikidata.org/wiki/Help:FAQ/Freebase and [Pellissier Tanon et al., 2016].

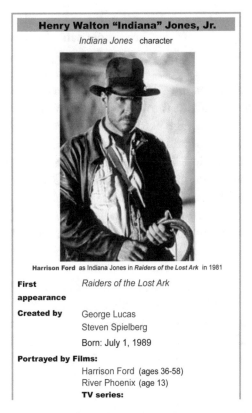

Henry Walton "Indiana" Jones, Jr.

Indiana Jones   character

Harrison Ford as Indiana Jones in *Raiders of the Lost Ark* in 1981

First appearance	*Raiders of the Lost Ark*
Created by	George Lucas
	Steven Spielberg
	Born: July 1, 1989
Portrayed by Films:	
	Harrison Ford (ages 36-58)
	River Phoenix (age 13)
	TV series:

Figure 3.5: Sample of the infobox for the article *Dr. Henry "Indiana" Jones*.

The information in *infoboxes* is especially interesting and useful for the analysis of semantic relations. As the example in Figure 3.5 demonstrates, an infobox contains attributes of the entity described in the surrounding Wikipedia article, and the values of those attributes, some of which are entities themselves. The attributes can be regarded as relations between the entity described by the article—that entity's name is the article's title—and those referenced in the infobox.

It is the contributors who select the attributes and their values for inclusion in the infobox. To make the content more consistent, infobox templates have been instituted. The contributors are encouraged to follow them, and that is meant to ensure (up to a point) that the attributes are consistent across multiple articles. For example, the birth date attribute is called *birth_date* across all articles which follow an infobox template referring to a person. There is still variation two decades on, but one can expect that in time schemata will converge.

There are approximately 195 infobox templates for persons alone, which share some (e.g., *birth_date, birth_place, nationality*) but not all attributes. For example, the motorcycle rider infobox contains attributes such as *current_team* and *bike_number*, specific to this template. Not every attribute value corresponds to a Wikipedia entry, customarily considered a concept. Some values, such as for example population size, are simple data. The remaining "true" relations still constitute a massive dataset.

These relation instances are very easily available, and in many languages; that makes them highly attractive to the NLP community. Because they appear in an article which includes also the information in the infobox in text form, one can establish the link between the two, and then both sources of information can be used together. Data of this kind have much success in seeding open information extraction; this will be explored further, especially in Section 4.4.

The well-structured information in Wikipedia infoboxes has been the source of DBpedia [Auer et al., 2007], a continuously growing resource. DBpedia grew around the DBpedia Ontology,[13] a shallow, cross-domain ontology built manually from the most commonly used infoboxes. DBpedia contains more than 6 million entities, connected by more than 9.5 billion RDF triples,[14] anchored in an ontology with 685 classes and 2795 properties. DBpedia is a substantial part of the Linked Open Data cloud,[15] a "switchboard" which connects numerous knowledge repositories.

YAGO,[16] a repository of general knowledge about people, cities, countries, movies, and organizations [Weikum et al., 2009], extracts article and category links from Wikipedia. It also extracts facts—representing relations of 100 types—from categories which provide relational information (1975 births), or categories which start with Countries in…, Rivers of…, and so on. Those categories provide instances of such relations as *bornInYear*, *locatedIn*, *politicianOf*, and so on. The 2017 version of YAGO represents over 10 million entities by more than 120 million facts about these entities.

WikiNet [Nastase and Strube, 2013] transforms Wikipedia into a multilingual concept network by exploiting category names, structural links and infoboxes. The network features approximately 450 relations; they arise from infoboxes or category names which express relations explicitly or implicitly. Explicit relations are expressed by verbs or participle+by combinations (e.g., *created by* from the category Characters created by Joss Whedon), relational nouns (e.g., *member* from the category Queen (band) members) or prepositions (e.g., *Spatial* from the category Chocolate in Belgium). Relations from infoboxes can be matched with category names, and then propagated in the network (e.g., *genre* from the infobox for the article on the novel *Ubik*, under the category Science fiction novels). WikiNet contains some 49 million relation instances.[17]

---

[13]wiki.dbpedia.org/services-resources/ontology
[14]www.w3.org/RDF/
[15]lod-cloud.net/
[16]yago.r2.enst.fr/
[17]The resource is available at www.h-its.org/software/wikinet-2/.

Freebase

Freebase is a large knowledge repository whose origin was a collaborative online knowledge base (KB). Its sources diversified in time, and combined contributions over the Web with facts sourced automatically. While its interface has since shut down,[18] the knowledge repository is still available,[19] and its various subsets have found much use in relation learning, link prediction, distant supervision and other related tasks. It consists of *topics* of various *types* connected by *properties*. Properties are close to what we call relations here. They are often expressed by a verb or a verb phrase, but also by relational nouns. The Freebase wiki explains:[20]

> Properties of a topic define a **HAS A** relationship between the topic and the value of the property, e.g., Paris {topic} has a population {property} of 2153600 {value}. In Freebase the value of a property can also be another topic, e.g., Apocalypse Now {topic} has a director {property} Francis Ford Coppola {value}.

In August 2012, Freebase contained more than 418 million facts, connecting almost 24 million topics with more than 8000 relation types (that is to say, properties). By the time the resource was closed for new input, it had reached 1.9 billion facts. Several subsets of Freebase have been built to help explore specific aspects of knowledge graphs (KGs); Section 5.5 presents the statistics of some of the most frequently applied subsets. Research based on these datasets is discussed throughout Chapter 5.

3.2.6   RELATIONS IN SPECIFIC DOMAINS

The development of methods and tools for extracting information from academic scientific literature has been one of the important applications of NLP technology. In particular, publications in biomedicine have been appearing at a rate impossible for human readers to keep up with. Researchers in this field have found great promise in the deployment of text-mining tools to automate or semi-automate tasks such as curating databases of extant knowledge [Cohen, 2010, Zweigenbaum et al., 2007].

A popular task, that of identifying *protein-protein interactions* (PPIs) in the abstracts or in the full text of biomedical publications, is conceptually similar to the standard relation classification task, and is generally amenable to similar methods [Hachey et al., 2011]. A variety of PPI classification datasets have been constructed for various task designs; Pyysalo et al. [2008] present an overview. In some cases, it is necessary to classify interaction types, while in others the task is simply to make a binary decision: is there an interaction? For example, the following sentence from Nédellec's [2005] PPI corpus expresses interactions between *SigK* and *ykvP* and between *GerE* and *ykvP*, but not between *SigK* and *GerE*:

---

[18]In May 2016—see en.wikipedia.org/wiki/Freebase_(database).
[19]developers.google.com/freebase
[20]We accessed this text on the Web in August 2012. The underlying page has disappeared.

Table 3.8: Semantic relations between treatments and diseases, proposed by Rosario and Hearst [2004]

Relation	# Examples	Example
Cure	810	Intravenous immune globulin for recurrent spontaneous abortion
Only DISEASE	616	Social ties and susceptibility to the common cold
Only TREATMENT	166	Flucticasone propionate is safe in recommended doses
Prevent	63	Statins for prevention of stroke
Vague	36	Phenylbutazone and leukemia
Side effect	29	Malignant mesodermal mixed tumor of the uterus following irradiation
No cure	4	Evidence for double resistance to permethrin and malathion in head lice
Irrelevant	1771	Patients were followed up for 6 months

Both SigK and GerE were essential for ykvP expression, and this gene was transcribed from T5 of sporulation.

The BioCreAtIvE challenge (Critical Assessment of Information Extraction Systems in Biology) is a community-wide effort to evaluate the applications of text mining and information extraction in biology.[21] The goal is to build, collect and offer the researchers a number of resources for data analysis in biology and biomedicine. The datasets cover various types of relations, e.g., relations which describe interactions between two proteins [Krallinger et al., 2008], between a chemical compound and a protein, and between a chemical compound and a disease [Li et al., 2016, Wei et al., 2016]. The relations in these datasets may cross sentence boundaries, or even span the complete article.

The PPI task follows the general trend in protein-protein datasets (such as MINT and BIND):[22] do not provide the type of protein-protein interaction. Still, some biomedical datasets include such information. For example, the manually curated HIV-1 Human Protein Interaction Database uses an inventory of 65 possible protein-protein interactions, including relations like *Binds*, *Inhibits*, and *Upregulates*. The ten most frequent among these relations were used in relation extraction from text [Rosario and Hearst, 2005].

Relations between genes and diseases, relations between treatments and diseases, and relations which deal with subcellular locations have also been of considerable interest in biomedicine. Table 3.8 shows the statistics of a dataset of 3495 relation instances of eight subtypes of the more general *Treatment-for-Disease* relation, taken from [Rosario and Hearst, 2004].

---

[21]biocreative.bioinformatics.udel.edu/
[22]MINT is currently part of IntAct (www.ebi.ac.uk/intact/). BIND is part of BioTools (bio.tools/bind).

Table 3.9: Semantic relations between the nouns in biomedical noun-noun compounds, proposed by Rosario and Hearst [2001]

Relation	# Examples	Example
Subtype	393	headaches migraine
Activity/Physical_process	59	virus reproduction
Produce_genetically	47	polyomavirus genome
Cause	116	heat shock
Characteristic	33	drug toxicity
Defect	52	hormone deficiency
Person_afflicted	55	AIDS patient
Attribute_of_clinical_study	77	headache parameter
Procedure	60	genotype diagnosis
Frequency/time_of	25	influenza season
Measure_of	54	relief rate
Instrument	121	laser irradiation
Object	30	bowel transplantation
Purpose	61	headache drugs
Topic	38	headache questionnaire
Location	145	brain artery
Material	28	aloe gel
Defect_in_location	157	lung abscess

There have been attempts to design and apply larger and more general relation inventories. For example, Rosario and Hearst [2001] annotated a set of 1551 biomedical noun-noun compounds with 18 relations; the data statistics appear in Table 3.9. There were 38 relations in the initial inventory; 20 of them had too few instances to be useful in supervised learning.[23]

The series of BioNLP Workshops and Shared Tasks has a long tradition.[24] The workshops have provided annotated biomedical data, at first for event extraction. They have later diversified and branched out. A relation extraction subtask has been first included in the 2011 edition.

ScienceIE is yet another SemEval task: Extracting Keyphrases and Relations from Scientific Publications. The 2017 edition covered the relations *hypernym-of* and *synonym-of*.[25] The Text

---

[23]The datasets can be found at biotext.berkeley.edu/data.html, along with other useful resources.

[24]For the 18th edition, see 2019.bionlp-ost.org/.

[25]scienceie.github.io/

Table 3.10: Annotation types, attributes, and relations statistics in a dataset of medical histories [Azab et al., 2019]

Annotation Type	Total
FT (family tree)	3,761
Name	2,865
Gender	1,480
Age	2,008
Illness	2,077
Cancer	774
Age at diagnosis	824
Age at death	362
Cause of death	705
Relations	20,774

Analysis Conference (TAC) tasks now also cover applications in medicine;[26] the extraction of instances of drug-drug interaction (DDI) targets relations such as *Boxed Warning*, *Clinical Pharmacology*, *Contraindications* and *Drug Interactions* [Demner-Fushman et al., 2018].

SciERC is a dataset which facilitates the identification of entities, relations and coreference clusters in scientific articles [Luan et al., 2018]. The dataset annotates generic entity types (such as task, method, metric or material) and generic relations (such as *Compare*, *Part-of*, *Feature-of* or *Used-for*) in scientific domains. The annotations are applied to 500 abstracts from research publications in AI.[27]

Gurulingappa et al. [2012] have built an annotated corpus of relations which describe the interaction between drugs and their side-effects.[28] In a collection of medical case reports, there are annotations of about 11,000 entities (*drugs*, their *adverse-effects* and *dosage*), and about 7,100 relations between them (*drug-adverse effect* and *drug-dosage*).

The dataset made available by Azab et al. [2019] represents a different type of relations in medicine.[29] The corpus contains medical histories, gathered via questionnaires prepared by medical professionals and administered in two ways: on Amazon's Mechanical Turk, and in an interaction with a genetic counselor. The data were annotated by professionals with a variety of family relations (e.g., *parent*, *sibling*), personal attributes (e.g., *age*, *gender*) and medical conditions (e.g., *illness*). Table 3.10 shows the statistics. The end result is a dataset of 4304 sentences of varying complexity, each containing at least one relation instance for a total of 20,774 instances.

[26]bionlp.nlm.nih.gov/tac2018druginteractions/, bionlp.nlm.nih.gov/tac2019druginteractions/
[27]nlp.cs.washington.edu/sciIE/
[28]github.com/davidsbatista/Annotated-Semantic-Relationships-Datasets/blob/master/datasets/ADE-Corpus-V2.zip
[29]lit.eecs.umich.edu/downloads.html

3.2.7   THE QUALITY OF DATA

The datasets we describe here, and those we will present in Section 5.5, were all built manually. There arises a natural question: how good are relation annotations in those sets? A useful answer should give the reader an idea about the difficulty of the annotation task—and possibly an upper bound on the performance of an NLP system using annotated data—as well as about the quality of annotated datasets.

Small datasets contain material for a specific experiment or task, and often arise from in-house effort which employs NLP specialists or domain experts. Inter-annotator agreement measured by some form of the kappa coefficient [Artstein and Poesio, 2008] is rather regularly reported in the resulting research papers. The agreement reported for the construction process for the surveyed datasets is between 0.6 and 0.9, depending on the relation; it turns out that some relations are easier to annotate. It is a challenge to compute agreement, because, as Hendrickx et al. [2010] note, chance agreement, required in the calculation of kappa, may be difficult to estimate. Agreement on the final versions of small datasets may be moot: they often contain only adjudicated items, or items on which all annotators agree; this has been discussed, e.g., by Girju et al. [2009] and Hendrickx et al.

Larger datasets are often the result of crowd-sourced annotation. Good annotations make for a good dataset. There are methods of measuring, and keeping track of, the quality of annotations. Some form of quality control is embedded in crowd-sourcing platforms such as Amazon Mechanical Turk or Figure Eight (formerly known as CrowdFlower). They allow the task organizers to evaluate candidate workers before and during the main annotation task. After reading the annotation guidelines, workers are tested on a small set of annotated instances, and those who score low can be rejected. Annotated instances can also be sprinkled throughout the task to monitor workers' performance. Information thus gathered goes into the reliability scores which accompany an annotator's work. Annotation task organizers can also plan their own quality control, for example by duplicating instances to help quantify the consistency of each rater's annotation.

Annotations obtained on a large scale from the public at large are only part of the solution. To build a reliable dataset from individual annotations is itself a complex problem [Qing et al., 2014]. Despite best effort, subsequent analysis may still uncover errors and inconsistencies. Alt et al. [2020] analyze the quality of relation labels in the TACRED dataset (we discuss it briefly in Section 5.5), and corrected instance labels in the development and test splits. They also show that such corrections affect model evaluation significantly.

And then there are repositories of collective knowledge, very large indeed. Annotation information for those datasets does not exist as such: they were built as repositories of collective knowledge, and not specifically (and perhaps somewhat narrowly) for scientific study. NLP adopted such datasets enthusiastically, but once they became the object of scientific study, their quality had to be assessed. Färber et al. [2018] present an in-depth analysis of Freebase, DBpedia, Wikidata, OpenCyc and YAGO, and give many references to additional work concerned with evaluating the quality of knowledge repositories. Based on a sample of instances, these resources are judged in terms of accuracy, trustworthiness, consistency and other such measures. Färber et al. also propose a framework for selecting the most suitable KG for a given setting based on the computed measures.

People who judge linguistics phenomena can rarely be in complete agreement. Even so, while a dataset may never be perfect, someone has built it in order to give the community a *reliable* resource. In the end, then, one must live with imperfect annotations, and factor their flaws into any honest analysis of research results.

3.3   FEATURES

The job of selecting features to represent relation instances adequately is an essential element of the task of learning semantic relations between nominals. In a typical incarnation, a relation instance appears in an annotated sentence with the two nominals marked, and such sentences must be mapped onto feature vectors. A larger context, perhaps a paragraph, may be called for, or an instance may just be the pair of nominals to be identified in texts automatically. In any event, a feature vector must contain enough distinctive information to make the relation classification problem at hand feasible. As always in supervised learning, the learning algorithm builds— trains—a model from annotated examples. The model's predictive power is then tested on new, previously unseen instances. Simply put, the process establishes similarities between relation instances, or between a relation instance and a relation model, as described by the features.

Many factors can affect the similarity between instances of semantic relations. Consider two pairs of relation arguments, (A, B) and (C, D). They may be instances of the same relation due to a combination of attributional and relational similarity [Turney, 2006b]. Figure 3.6 illustrates two extreme cases. The two instances of the *president_of* relation share attributional similarity, i.e., entity similarity between the corresponding arguments: BARACK OBAMA and FRANÇOIS HOLLANDE are similar because they are both presidents (also, politicians), while USA and FRANCE are similar because they are both countries (also, presidential republics). This is very different from the case of FELINE–TIGER and VEHICLE–MOTORCYCLE, where there is hardly any similarity between FELINE and VEHICLE or between TIGER and MOTORCYCLE.[30] In this case there is instead a parallel between the two instances, quantified by *relational similarity* between A and B and between C and D, perhaps because they have similar contexts. The degree to which relational and attributional similarity contribute to the similarity of two relation instances may vary depending on the relations, as the examples with *president_of* and *is-a* have shown.

3.3.1   ENTITY FEATURES

Entity features represent some of the meaning of the arguments of a relation instance. Many semantic representations are possible, and this is reflected in the various proposals of feature sets.

---

[30]One might argue for some highly metaphorical similarity between the latter two.

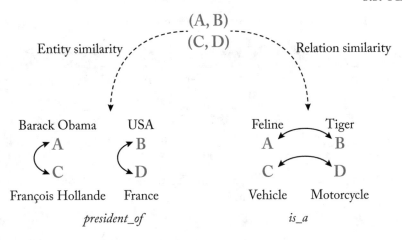

Figure 3.6: Types of similarities between instances of the same relation.

Basic entity features include the string value of every candidate argument and of the individual words which make up each of the arguments, possibly lemmatized or stemmed. In many cases, such features are informative enough for a good relation assignment, but unfortunately they also tend to be sparse.

Background entity features augment the basic features with syntactic or semantic information, possibly from a task-specific inventory such as the ACE entity types, or from a general lexical resource such as WordNet. They can also be learned in the form of automatically acquired word clusters. Such clusters help combat data sparseness by incorporating knowledge about the typical values of the arguments of the target semantic relation. A test-time candidate argument normally has not been seen in the training dataset. Even so, a classifier can make an informed prediction if it knows that the argument is semantically similar to previously seen fillers of the same argument slot of the target semantic relation.

Word clusters can be derived from word co-occurrences in a large text corpus. They easily allow tailoring to different domains and levels of granularity. For example, the *Brown clustering algorithm* [Brown et al., 1992] assigns each word in a training corpus to a position in a hierarchy of words, so that any two words can be compared by checking if they match at the first level of the hierarchy, at the second level, and so on. Brown cluster features have been shown to help in many NLP tasks, including ACE-style relation extraction [Chan and Roth, 2010, Sun et al., 2011]. Other clustering algorithms can also produce features, for example *Clustering by Committee* [Pantel and Lin, 2002] and *Latent Dirichlet Allocation* [Blei et al., 2003].

There is a complementary alternative to clusters learned from co-occurrence data: a direct representation of co-occurrence in the feature space. This allows the supervised relation classification system to identify the most relevant aspects of co-occurrence behaviour. Ó Séaghdha and Copestake [2008] observed that features based on coordination (*and*, *or*) can yield state-of-the-

Table 3.11: Distributional profile of the noun *paper* in the British National Corpus

Word	Syntactic Relation	Co-occurring Words
paper-n	coordination	pen-n:69, pencil-n:51, paper-n:32, glass-n:22, inkn: 20, . . .
	subject_of	say-v:86, make-v:39, propose-v:39, describe-v:31, set-v:30, . . .
	object_of	publish-v:147, read-v:129, use-v:78, write-v:62, take-43, . . .
	modified_by_adj	white-j:923; local-j:159, green-j:63, brown-j:56, non-stick-j:71, . . .
	modified_by_n	consultation-n:117, government-n:94, discussion-n: 84, tissue-n:71, blotting-n:59, . . .
	modifies_n	bag-n:150, money-n:44, cup-n:37, mill-n:36, work-n:34, . . .
	pp_with	number-n:6, address-n:3, title-n:2, note-n:2, word-n:2, . . .
	pp_on	reform-n:13, future-n:13, policy-n:10, environment-n:9, subject-n:8, . . .
	. . . . . .	

art performance for the SemEval-2007 Task 4, relation classification. The idea is that similar nouns tend to coordinate with other similar nouns, e.g., both *dog* and *cat* will often appear in coordinating constructions with other animals, especially pets, and so they will look similar in the feature space.

More generally, a *distributional representation* can pinpoint the meaning of a word by aggregating all its interactions found in a large collection of texts. Such descriptions can be either unstructured or grouped by grammatical relations. Table 3.11 shows an example of grammatically informed distributional representation for the noun *paper*. It comes from the British National Corpus,[31] and was parsed by the RASP system [Briscoe et al., 2006]. The representation includes semantically associated nouns such as *pen*, *ink* and *cardboard* obtained by coordination (*and/or*). The grammatical co-occurrences show what a paper can do, e.g., *propose* and *say*; what one can do with a paper, e.g., *read*, *publish*; some typical adjectival modifiers such as *white* and *recycled*; some noun modifiers such as *toilet* and *consultation*; nouns connected to the target via various prepositions, e.g., *paper on environment*, *paper for meeting*, *paper with a title*; and so on. Note that this representation mixes several senses of *paper*, so for example *ink* refers to the medium for writing, while *propose* refers to writing/publication/document.

A *relational semantic representation*, based on relations in a semantic network or in a formal ontology, is another way of finding semantic features which describe a relation's arguments. It is an important advantage of using semantic networks that they are usually organized around word senses rather than words. So, in a semantic network there would be one entry for *bank* as a "river bank", and another for "bank as a financial institution" (and possibly other senses, e.g., "bank as a building" or "to bank as to incline an airplane"). This is in contrast with distributional representations, which tend to ignore distinctions between word senses, assuming that such distinctions can be handled by the learning algorithm when necessary. In order to access this type of representation, however, one must be able to link the terms which express a relation's arguments with the appropriate nodes in the network. That is to say, one needs word-sense disambiguation (WSD)[32] to select the contextually correct sense for each argument. Provided that WSD has been performed or that the representation will merge and use all possible senses, the related concepts and their relations from the resource, as well as a concept's ancestors, can be extracted as entity features. Features of this kind have been used by Nastase and Szpakowicz [2003] and Girju et al. [2004] for general concepts, and by Rosario and Hearst [2001] for domain-specific concepts. Nastase et al. [2006] compared distributional representations from the British National Corpus (BNC) and relational semantic representations from WordNet; the goal was to find out how they represent nouns and their modifiers for relation learning in noun compounds. It turns out that word sense information is useful but if it is not available, then distributional representations are a better choice.

3.3.2 RELATIONAL FEATURES

Relational features characterize the relation directly, e.g., by modelling the text which serves as the context for instances. In principle, one could consider the entire document where the candidate arguments appear, but such a broad context is likely to include much irrelevant and spurious information and so to mislead the classifier. That is why it is usually assumed that only part of the context, e.g., in the vicinity of the candidate argument mentions, is relevant to the task of deciding if a given semantic relation holds between them. One well-liked option is to take the words between the two arguments, and maybe also the words from a fixed window of words on either side of the arguments, as a basic representation of context. Popular alternative representations include a dependency path from one mention to the other (a subgraph of a syntactic graph produced by a dependency parser from the context sentence); or the whole dependency graph ; or the smallest dominating subtree in a constituent parse tree. Figure 3.7 illustrates some of those popular context representations.

The extraction of relational features from the context typically involves enumerating substructures of the context representation. The exact nature of such substructures depends on the representation chosen; a bag of words naturally decomposes into words, a word sequence decomposes into n-grams, a parse tree decomposes into subtrees, and so on. Take the dependency parse tree of the sentence *Google bought YouTube in 2006*, shown in Figure 3.7. A system could extract a set of dependency triples:

$$\{(bought \xrightarrow{\text{nsubj}} Google), (bought \xrightarrow{\text{dobj}} YouTube),$$

---

[32] See [Ide and Véronis, 1998] for an early survey and [Navigli, 2009] for a more up-to-date overview of WSD.

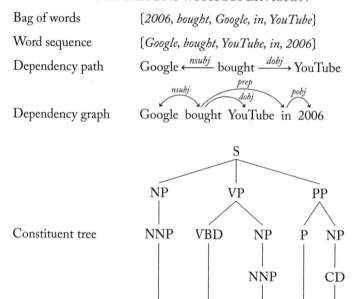

Figure 3.7: Context representations for the sentence *Google bought YouTube in 2006*.

$$(in \xrightarrow{\text{pobj}} 2006), (bought \xrightarrow{\text{prep}} in)\}$$

or more complex paths such as

$$(Google \xleftarrow{\text{nsubj}} bought \xrightarrow{\text{dobj}} YouTube)$$

or even the entire dependency tree, though larger structures will tend to be sparse and so less useful in learning. The number of subtrees or subgraphs can be exponential in the depth of the structure, so it may be necessary to restrict the features to substructures of up to certain maximal size, or to count only substructures complete in some way. It may also be beneficial to consider multiple representations to exploit the complementary strengths of syntax-based and adjacency-based features, or of different parsing styles. One can even adopt a hybrid representation, with syntax and sequential order both exhibited in a shared graph, and hope to capture distinctive features which combine syntactic and sequential information [Jiang and Zhai, 2007]. Such structural features can be useful even when the candidate relation instance crosses sentence boundaries. In such cases, discourse and sequential relations can link consecutive sentences into a.larger connected structure [Swampillai and Stevenson, 2011].

Background relational features attempt to encode knowledge about how entities typically interact in texts beyond the immediate context. Given a pair of nominals ($N1, N2$), such features

Table 3.12: Paraphrasing verbs, prepositions and coordinating conjunctions which link *committee* and *member*, extracted from the Web [Nakov and Hearst, 2007]

Frequency	Pattern	POS	Direction
2205	of	P	2 → 1
1923	be	V	1 → 2
771	include	V	1 → 2
382	serve on	V	2 → 1
189	chair	V	2 → 1
189	have	V	1 → 2
169	consist of	V	1 → 2
148	comprise	V	1 → 2
106	sit on	V	2 → 1
81	be chaired by	V	1 → 2
78	appoint	V	1 → 2
77	on	P	2 → 1
66	and	C	1 → 2
66	be elected	V	1 → 2
58	replace	V	1 → 2
48	lead	V	2 → 1
47	be intended for	V	1 → 2
45	join	V	2 → 1
...	...	...	...

can be extracted by querying a Web search engine with suitable patterns. This results in a *distributional* representation of a relation type.

A target relation can be represented with a vector whose coordinates correspond to fixed patterns. Turney and Littman [2005] characterize the relationship between two words as a vector with coordinates corresponding to the Web frequencies of 128 fixed phrases like "X for Y" and "Y for X", instantiated from a fixed set of 64 joining terms such as *for, such as, not the, is *.

Nakov and Hearst [2007] took exact-phrase queries of the form "N1 that * N2", "N2 that * N1", "N1 * N2" and "N2 * N1" to extract the verbs, prepositions and coordinating conjunctions which connected *N1* and *N2*. Table 3.12 shows an example. *V* stands for verb (possibly +preposition and/or +particle), *P* for preposition and *C* for coordinating conjunction. $1 \rightarrow 2$ means *committee* precedes the feature and *member* follows it; $2 \rightarrow 1$—the other way around.

Such features can be also extracted from the Google Web 1T Corpus [Parker et al., 2011];[33] a search engine is not necessary [Butnariu and Veale, 2008]. Background relational features need not be restricted to any part of speech: just about any pattern is fine, even patterns which contain placeholders. For example, Turney [2006a] mines from the Web patterns such as `"Y * causes X"` for *Cause* (e.g., *cold virus*) and `"Y in * early X"` for *Temporal* (e.g., *morning frost*).

The vector representation of relational features can assist classification directly. It can also be further mapped to vectors of lower dimensionality so as to help mitigate the effect of sparseness.

Clustering can be a solution. The classifier can then leverage training examples with similar but not identical contexts. Assume, for example, that *CEO* and *company* are often mentioned together in contexts which indicate relation *employed-by*. A new occurrence of *CEO* and *company* is also likely to describe this relation, even when the context is rather vague (e.g., *the company's CEO*).

Phrase patterns can be clustered, and transformed into features, in many ways. Davidov and Rappoport [2008b] use relation pattern clusters built during their work on unsupervised relation extraction on a corpus D of documents [Davidov and Rappoport, 2008a]; the work will be discussed in Section 4.4.3. This supplies features for a supervised model. The clustering begins with a set of patterns for each argument pair which corresponds to a potential relation instance. Shared patterns drive the clustering of sets of patterns for different argument pairs. A *core* pattern in a cluster is shared by multiple sets of patterns placed in that cluster; other patterns are called *unconfirmed*. Each final cluster will contain core and unconfirmed patterns, and will correspond to one relation type. The core patterns will have been shared by multiple potential instances of this relation type. The method works with pairs of nominals from a training dataset. It constructs pattern clusters C_i, each with n_i core patterns P^i_{core} and m_i unconfirmed patterns P^i_{unconf}. For one (w_1, w_2) potential relation instance, each cluster C_i will be a feature relative to the corpus D; its value is the affinity of the training instance to the patterns in the cluster:

$$HITS(C_i, (w_1, w_2)) = \frac{|\{p \mid p \in P^i_{core} \text{ and } (w_1, p, w_2) \text{ appears in } D\}|}{n_i} + \alpha \frac{|\{p \mid p \in P^i_{unconf} \text{ and } (w_1, p, w_2) \text{ appears in } D\}|}{m_i} \qquad (3.1)$$

The value of the parameter α adjusts the contribution of unconfirmed patterns. This style of data representation allows a system to work with information derived from relation patterns which occur in a large unstructured text corpus.

The relation patterns can also be mapped into a lower-dimensional space following dimensionality reduction strategies. The relation classification system learns to map the vector representations onto relation types. Turney [2006b] applies Singular Value Decomposition (SVD) to relations represented in the space of 128 fixed patterns. Wang et al. [2011] generate "relation

---

[33] catalog.ldc.upenn.edu/LDC2011T07

topics" by applying the diffusion wavelets algorithm [Coifman and Maggioni, 2006] to the set R of relations r_k with a similarity metric s. r_k is represented as a vector $[p_k^1 \ldots p_k^{|P|}]$. p_k^i is the frequency of occurrence of pattern p^i for relation r_k. The diffusion operator, which works on R, is defined as $T = S/\lambda_{\max}(S)$. S is the matrix of similarities between relations:

$$s_{ab} = \cos([p_a^1 \ldots p_a^{|P|}], [p_b^1 \ldots p_b^{|P|}]) \qquad (3.2)$$

$\lambda_{\max}(S)$ is the highest eigenvalue of S.

Multiscale diffusion analysis uses diffusion wavelets to learn the diffusion scaling functions of T. The initial orthonormal basis functions ϕ_0 are the k-dimensional space of T, so $\phi_0 = I$, the identity matrix. At each level $j = 0..J$, the matrix $[T^{2^j}]_{\phi_j}^{\phi_j}$ is computed as the projection of the columns and rows of matrix T^{2^j} into the space defined by the bases ϕ_j.[34] The matrix undergoes a QR-decomposition into an orthogonal matrix Q and a triangular matrix R: $[T^{2^j}]_{\phi_j}^{\phi_j} \approx QR$. Q's columns will be the new orthonormal basis functions $[\phi_{j+1}]_{\phi_j}$, represented in the space with the bases ϕ_j. The representation of the new bases with respect to the original space ϕ_0 is $[\phi_{j+1}]_{\phi_0} = [\phi_{j+1}]_{\phi_j}[\phi_j]_{\phi_0} = \prod_{x=0}^{j}[\phi_{x+1}]_{\phi_x}$. The repeated multiplication of T leads to the filtering of noise, and so to fewer basis functions at higher levels.

The method has interesting advantages. The topics are hierarchical, and are organized by the level at which they were obtained. The number of levels and the number of topics at each level are determined by the data, by the diffusion operator whose rank decreases with each level.

The mapping of relation patterns onto a lower-dimensional representation cannot only help provide a new way of representing relational features but explore correlations between existing relations and detect new relations.

3.4   LEARNING SEMANTIC RELATIONS

This section discusses supervised methods of relation classification. Chapter 4 will describe semi-supervised, unsupervised and self-learning methods. We first refresh the reader's memory on the algorithms of supervised machine learning in general, and then talk in more detail about the algorithms most successful in the learning of semantic relations.

3.4.1   SUPERVISED MACHINE LEARNING

Supervised classifiers are a robust and generally applicable tool for the task of semantic relation classification. In effect, such classifiers learn from labelled training data how to weigh up the evidence for a given target relation mention; to do it, they evaluate the contributions of multiple features.

The training data are given as a set of d-dimensional feature vectors $X = \{x_i = [x_{i1}, x_{i2}, \ldots x_{id}]\}$ paired with labels $Y = \{y_i\}$. A supervised classification model learns a *decision function* f which predicts a label for a feature vector x'. In principle, f can take any form

---

[34] J is an optional upper bound for the level, as the compression of matrix T at each step eventually leads to a 1×1 matrix.

but in practice each learning algorithm imposes a particular formula. One standard form is that of a linear decision function, parameterized by a real-valued vector $w \in \mathbb{R}^d$; w_i represents the weight of feature i and is learned from the training data:

$$f(x') = \langle w, x' \rangle \tag{3.3}$$

Equation 3.3 shows that the linear decision function takes the inner product of the weight vector and the feature vector x'. The vectors are often assumed to be points in an Euclidean space, so the inner product in Equation 3.3 becomes the dot product:

$$f(x') = \sum_{j=1}^{d} w_j x'_j \tag{3.4}$$

When the task is to predict a binary label $y' \in \{-1, 1\}$, the sign function is applied to $f(x')$. This is equivalent to putting the point x' on one of two sides of a hyperplane defined by w. If there are more than two labels, it is usual to decompose the problem into multiple binary classification tasks [Hsu and Lin, 2002].

Popular linear classifiers include the perceptron and the linear kernel Support Vector Machine (SVM). A related form of classification function is a log-linear model. It directly estimates the probability that a data point x' has a label y':

$$p(y'|x') = \frac{\exp(\sum_{j=1}^{d} w_{y'j} x'_j)}{\sum_{y'' \in Y} \exp(\sum_{j=1}^{d} w_{y''j} x'_j)} \tag{3.5}$$

There are numerous types of log-linear classifiers: logistic regression, maximum entropy or MaxEnt classifiers [Manning and Schütze, 1999, Part IV]. Among many other kinds of classifiers there are Naïve Bayes, decision trees and k-nearest-neighbours [Bishop, 2006, Mitchell, 1997, Witten et al., 2016]. In our experience, SVM and logistic regression models are reliably good choices for most practitioners.

3.4.2 LEARNING ALGORITHMS

Early work on relation extraction from text relied on manually crafted rules, which could often reach very high precision but suffered from low recall. FASTUS [Hobbs et al., 1997] was a classic rule-based system at MUC. It achieved high speed by means of cascaded, non-deterministic finite state transducers. Systems of this kind are outside the remit of our survey. From now on, we will focus on machine learning.

Supervised machine learning automatically constructs models which capture the essence of a phenomenon. The construction relies on the analysis of (usually many) instances of this phenomenon, represented by salient and relevant features. Computers outperform people by a huge margin when it comes to processing very much data very fast, so many regularities and correlations between the features and the targeted phenomenon can be found. Small sets of manually crafted rules can thus give way to automatically built models which are often more complex and more comprehensive. The user who wants to put machine learning to work on a problem must find a good description of the problem instances by features, and choose an appropriate learning algorithm.

We already saw how entity features or relational features can drive the recognition and acquisition of semantic relations. Such features represent data in a manner agreeable to many learning techniques. Depending on the characteristics of the features themselves and of the phenomenon in question, some methods may be more appropriate or useful than others. This section discusses in more detail two classes of learning methodologies: kernel methods and sequential labelling methods. We explain which characteristics make these methods particularly apt for the task of classifying semantic relations.

Classification with Kernels

In a typical relation classification problem, heterogeneous information sources are combined, and information from structures such as strings and parse trees is extracted. For example, relational features (Section 3.3.2) convey the interaction between two entities by extracting a syntactic graph from a parse tree, or a sequence of words from a sentence. In both cases, the representation has internal structure which would be ignored if it were treated as an atomic feature value. In particular, two syntactic representations of context can look quite different while sharing some substructures and some elements of meaning. At the same time, it may be desirable to combine entity features (Section 3.3.1) with relational information. Kernel methods are a class of machine learning methods which elegantly handle both concerns, and have been applied in many systems which learn semantic relations.

Kernel methods are based on the idea that the similarity of two instances can be computed in a high-dimensional feature space without necessarily having to enumerate the dimensions of that space. Consider again the case of learning to classify semantic relations using parse trees as the input representation. A feature mapping which expands a tree into a large set of subtrees can be chosen. The calculation of the distance between two instances with different parse trees will compare not only the trees but the subtrees, and so uncover "hidden" shared structure. Dynamic programming can help avoid the prohibitive computational expense of a naïve expansion. We will now outline how this can be incorporated in the learning method.

The similarity between instances is computed by a function known as the *kernel function* or simply *kernel*. It must be a *positive semi-definite* function: it must correspond to an inner product in some vector space.

$$k(x, x') = \langle \phi(x), \phi(x') \rangle \tag{3.6}$$

The embedding function ϕ maps data items from the input space $\mathcal{X}$ onto a feature space $\mathcal{F}$ in which the inner product is applied. $\mathcal{X}$ and $\mathcal{F}$ may be the same, and then learning is similar to that in the standard feature-vector method. $\mathcal{X}$ and $\mathcal{F}$ may also be qualitatively different, as when $\mathcal{X}$ is not a vector space or $\mathcal{F}$ has a dimensionality much higher (maybe exponentially higher) than $\mathcal{X}$. The feature space may account for interactions between features, as in the polynomial kernel $k(x, x') = (x^\top x' + a)^d$ where the dimensions of $\mathcal{F}$ correspond to degree-d polynomials of the features in $\mathcal{X}$. Shawe-Taylor and Cristianini [2004] give a comprehensive overview of kernels and kernel-based algorithms.

Kernels offer a significant advantage: it may be more practical to compute a kernel function k than a large (or even unbounded) feature mapping $\phi(x)$. For example, the Gaussian kernel $k(x, x') = \exp(\gamma \, ||x - x'||^2)$ corresponds to an inner product in a feature space of unbounded dimensions, with a straightforward calculation. This is sometimes known as the "kernel trick". Another advantage: various inner product geometries may be swapped in without requiring a new learning algorithm. For example, the performance of many NLP tasks can improve if one works with kernels derived from well-established similarity measures, such as the Jensen-Shannon divergence instead of the Euclidean dot product [Ó Séaghdha and Copestake, 2008]. Finally, the class of valid kernel functions is closed under addition and pointwise multiplication,[35] and that makes it easy to combine different information sources in a principled way.

The most popular classification algorithm which works with kernel functions is the SVM [Cortes and Vapnik, 1995]. SVM classification with a kernel k replaces the linear classification (Equation 3.3) with

$$f(x') = \sum_{x \in T} \alpha_x \, k(x, x') \tag{3.7}$$

T is the set of training examples. Every training example x is associated with a weight α_x in training. Assume the linear kernel embedding $\phi(x) = x$. Equation 3.8 shows the relationship between the weights α_x and the per-feature weights w learned by a standard linear classifier.

$$
\begin{aligned}
f(x') &= \sum_{x \in T} \alpha_x \, k(x, \, x') \\
&= \sum_{x \in T} \alpha_x \, \langle x, \, x' \rangle \\
&= \sum_{x \in T} \alpha_x \sum_{j=1}^{d} x_j \, x'_j \\
&= \sum_{j=1}^{d} x'_j \sum_{x \in T} \alpha_x \, x_j
\end{aligned}
\tag{3.8}
$$

It follows that the corresponding feature weights are:

$$w_j = \sum_{x \in T} \alpha_x \, x_j \tag{3.9}$$

---

[35]In pointwise multiplication of matrices, also known as the Hadamard product, $(A \bullet B)_{i, j} = A_{i, j} * B_{i, j}$.

The relationship is more opaque for kernels with more complex feature mappings, e.g., the Gaussian kernel, but the intuition holds. The example weights learned by an SVM determine a set of feature weights from a representation in a higher-dimension feature space even when that space is not represented explicitly. The optimization task defined by the SVM problem selects the set of weights which maximizes the *margin*; it is, roughly speaking, the separating distance between the members of each class and the decision boundary. To maximize the margin is to find a distinction between classes: the members of each class are as far away as possible from the border between them.

Kernel methods and SVM classification have become very popular tools for relation classification, in particular as a way of integrating relation information about the context of a candidate relation mention. As in feature-based classification, one can select from a variety of context representations. The choice of representation affects the nature of the kernel function which is to map instances into the implicit feature space. There is a common core intuition: two contexts are considered similar (or dissimilar) if they share many (or few) subparts. This intuition is formalized in the framework of *convolution kernels* [Haussler, 1999]:

$$k_R(x, x') = \sum_{x_i \in R^{-1}(x)} \sum_{x'_j \in R^{-1}(x')} k_0(x_i, x_j) \qquad (3.10)$$

The function R^{-1} decomposes each structure belonging to the set $\mathcal{X}$ into the multiset of its substructures, and k_0 is a function on substructures. The simplest choice of k_0 is a function which takes value 1 when two substructures are identical and 0 otherwise; this leads to a kernel k_R which counts the number of shared substructures. It is also possible to define k_0 which gives fractional credit for partial matches. This definition is rather abstract, because it applies to many different classes of structures. In relation classification, the structures of interest are typically representations of context; so long as they can be decomposed into substructures (e.g., a tree decomposes into subtrees), the convolution kernel method works.

There are proposals of convolution kernels on such representations of linguistic structures as strings [Cancedda et al., 2003], dependency paths [Bunescu and Mooney, 2005], shallow parse trees [Zelenko et al., 2003], constituent parse trees [Collins and Duffy, 2001], dependency parse trees [Moschitti, 2006], and directed acyclic graphs [Suzuki et al., 2003]. Most of these kernels have also been applied to relation classification, particularly in the context of the ACE evaluation. Comparative studies [Nguyen et al., 2009] have suggested that different representations can have different strengths, and that combining them via kernel addition can improve performance. In the remainder of this section, we will work through treatments of string kernels and constituent tree kernels, which have been the most popular.

String kernels for relation classification represent context as ordered sequences of words. Formally, a string is a sequence $s = (w_1, \ldots, w_{|s|})$ of symbols from an alphabet Σ. Σ^l denotes the set of all strings of length l and Σ^* is the set of all strings, also called the *language*. A subsequence u of s is determined by a list of integer indices $i = (i_1, \ldots, i_{|u|})$ such that $1 \leq i_1 \leq \ldots \leq i_{|u|} \leq |s|$. (This formulation allows subsequences to be discontinuous.) The length of

u is calculated with respect to s, as $len(i) = i_{|u|} - i_1 + 1$, regardless of the possible gaps in u. For example, if s is the string *cut the bread with the knife*, the index list $i = (1, 4)$ identifies the substring $s[i] = (cut, with)$ with $len(i) = 4$.

An expressive kernel on strings, the *gap-weighted subsequence kernel* [Lodhi et al., 2002], is defined like this:

$$k_l(s, s') = \sum_{u \in \Sigma^l} \sum_{i, j: s[i]=u=s'[j]} \lambda^{len(i)+len(j)} \tag{3.11}$$

The positive integer l sets the length of the subsequences to be counted, and λ is a decay parameter between 0 and 1. The contribution of a discontinuous subsequence goes down as the value of λ goes down.

This kernel induces a feature embedding $\phi_l : \Sigma^* \to \mathbb{R}^{|\Sigma|^l}$ which maps a string s onto a vector of non-negative counts. The counts are usually not integers unless $\lambda = 0$ or $\lambda = 1$. Lodhi et al.'s efficient dynamic programming algorithm does not require an explicit representation of the feature vector $\phi_l(s)$ of all subsequence counts. While k_l is parameterized to count subsequences of a specified length l, it is straightforward to combine the contributions of multiple subsequence lengths via kernel addition.

Tree kernels apply the convolution kernel principle to the output of syntactic parsers [Collins and Duffy, 2001]. A tree kernel defines similarity between trees in terms of the number of shared subtrees:

$$k(T, T') = \sum_{S \in Subtrees(T)} \sum_{S' \in Subtrees(T')} k_0(S, S') \tag{3.12}$$

This definition leaves many degrees of freedom [Nguyen et al., 2009]: work with dependency trees or constituent trees; take the full parse of the sentence or the parse of the sentence fragment with the candidate arguments; have k_0 accept partial matches, e.g., by allowing mismatches between lexical items while requiring their parts of speech to match. The assumption of tree structure enables efficient computation of tree kernels by dynamic programming; see [Collins and Duffy, 2001] and [Moschitti, 2006] for details.

As may be apparent to the reader, the motivation for convolution kernels is similar to that for context feature extraction in a standard scenario of feature engineering. A context is broken into smaller pieces in order to learn a more generalizable model. The tree kernel computes similarity in a feature space where each dimension indexes a subtree, while the syntax-based context features described in Section 3.3.2 can also correspond to subtrees.

Given the appropriate feature specifications, one can get the same results with a tree kernel and with an explicitly represented subtree feature space used with a linear kernel (dot product) SVM. Summation in kernel functions corresponds to a concatenation of the corresponding feature spaces [Joachims et al., 2001]. The kernel representation is more memory-efficient, but the explicit feature vector representation can be more flexible. Ó Séaghdha and Copestake [2009] consider alternative inner product similarities in the space defined by a string kernel feature mapping. Pighin and Moschitti [2010] perform feature selection on an explicit representation of a tree kernel feature space.

Culotta and Sorensen [2004] take an augmented dependency tree as input to a tree kernel. The nodes of the dependency tree of a sentence have additional features, such as WordNet hypernyms, parts of speech and entity types. Zhou et al. [2007] build a context-sensitive convolution tree kernel. It is to be applied to a syntactic tree representation which augments the tree covering the shortest path with additional relevant contextual information. Zhou et al. also note that linear kernels which operate on "flat" features and tree kernels complement each other. A composite kernel which integrates all this information performs better than either individually. This reinforces Zhang et al.'s [2006] empirical study of a compositional kernel which combines an entity kernel for processing entity-related features, and a convolution parse tree kernel for processing the structured syntactic information.

Zhao and Grishman [2005] work with information from three levels: tokens, parse trees and dependency relations. Each level is represented by a kernel function, and combined via composite kernels which integrate and extend individual kernels. Qian et al. [2008] rely on a dynamically built syntactic parse tree; it keeps the nodes and their head children along the path which connects the two entities. They also combine semantic information—in particular, entity semantic features, such as head word or entity type—with the syntactic tree. That gives the tree kernel a more complex, richer structure. To build a robust model with good performance across domains without additional training data, Plank and Moschitti [2013] propose a tree kernel augmented with lexical similarity based on Brown clusters or on latent semantic analysis.

A note on practical implementation: convolution kernels should be normalized, so that larger structures are not assigned higher similarity values simply because they contain more substructures. For example, consider the strings $s =$ the dog runs and the dog jumps and $t =$ the dog runs. s shares three two-token subsequences with t while t shares only with itself, so $k_2(s, t) > k_2(t, t)$, but s also contains many subsequences *not* shared with t. Here is the standard normalization operation:

$$\bar{k}(s,\ t) = \frac{k(s,\ t)}{\sqrt{k(s,\ s)}\ \sqrt{k(t,\ t)}} \tag{3.13}$$

This is equivalent to normalizing the substructure count vectors $\phi(s)$ and $\phi(t)$ so they have unit lengths, or to taking the cosine between the count vectors (rather than the dot product). As a result, the normalized kernel $\bar{k}(s,t)$ has a maximal value of 1, which arises when s and t are identical.

Sequential Labelling Methods

The focus has thus far been on the task of relation extraction, assuming that the arguments are given. This is unrealistic for a practical system. It should first be able to identify the relation

arguments, and possibly assign them some semantic type, e.g., PERSON, ORGANIZATION, LO-
CATION, PROTEIN, DISEASE. Next, it should connect some of these arguments in a relation of a
specific type, e.g., *President-of*, *Born-in*, *Cause* or *Side-Effect*.

These tasks are typically executed in a pipeline: the system first finds potential arguments,
and then tries to connect them by relations. Evaluation exercises such as MUC, ACE and
BioNLP usually have subtasks to encourage research on these two elements: a named-entity
recognition (NER) subtask, and a relation extraction subtask in which the targeted relations
take named entities as arguments.

Argument identification usually relies on a sequence model. Hidden Markov Model
(HMM), Maximum Entropy Markov Model (MEMM) and Conditional Random Field (CRF)
have been shown to work very well on segmenting and labelling sequence data [Bikel et al., 1999,
Lafferty et al., 2001]. This is handy for arguments which can have different lengths and for which
the order of appearance might be important. CRFs, the most sophisticated of the three families
of models, have become almost a standard in the special NER task [McCallum and Li, 2003], so
they have been much used for NER at evaluations such as MUC, ACE, BioNLP, BioCreAtIvE
and CoNLL.[36]

Named entity mentions in text are usually identified by a sequence tagger. Each token is
labelled with a BIO tag [Ramshaw and Marcus, 1995], which indicates whether it begins (B),
is inside (I), or is outside (O) of a named entity mention.[37] It is further necessary to show the
type of named entity, e.g., person (PER), organization (ORG) or location (LOC). This yields
tags such as B-PER, I-PER, B-ORG, I-ORG, B-LOC, I-LOC, and O.[38] Here is an example
annotation of a sentence with three named entities, two persons and one location:

> *George*   *W.*   *Bush*   ,   *son* *of* *the* *Republican* *president* *George* *H.*   *W.*
> B-PER I-PER I-PER O   O   O   O   O   O   B-PER I-PER I-PER

> *Bush*   ,   *was* *born* *in*   *New*   *Haven*   ,   *Connecticut*   .
> I-PER O   O   O   O   B-LOC I-LOC   I-LOC   I-LOC   O

It is straightforward to extract the named entities from a BIO annotation. In a dynamic
sequence model such as CRF, the labels would correspond to hidden states, while the observations would be individual words. The words and the labels are used indirectly, in feature functions
defined over

    a. *words*: individual words, preceding/following two words, word substrings (prefixes, suffixes
       of various lengths), capitalization, digit patterns, and specialized lists (of days, months,
       honorifics, stopwords, known countries, cities, companies, and so on);

    b. *labels*: individual labels, preceding/following two labels;

    c. *combinations* of *words* and *labels*.

---

[36]www.conll.org

[37]Variations also include the tags L (last) and U/S (unit/singleton).

[38]Ratinov and Roth [2009] discuss some BIO tag variations and alternatives.

Sequence models can help not only in argument identification, but in relation extraction. In fact, relation extraction can, in special cases, be reduced to sequence labelling. For example, biographical texts such as encyclopedia articles discuss one principal entity, and many of the other entities mentioned in the text are related to that entity, as already noted in Section 3.2.5. When analyzing such texts, it is important to predict how, if at all, any mentioned entity is related to the principal entity [Culotta et al., 2006]. This task is easier than general relation extraction. It is not necessary to enumerate all pairs of entities in the document, since relations are binary and one of the arguments is already fixed. There is also no need for two passes through the data, one to identify the entities and their types, and another to assign the relation to the principal entity; this can be solved in one step as a labelling problem.

Here is an example annotation of the sentence about GEORGE W. BUSH, assuming that he is the principal entity:

George	W.	Bush	,	son	of	the	Republican	president	George	H.	W.
B-Target	I-Target	I-Target	O	O	O	O	B-Party	B-Job	B-Father	I-Father	I-Father

Bush	,	was	born	in	New	Haven	,	Connecticut	.
I-Father	O	O	O	O	B-BirthPlace	I-BirthPlace	I-BirthPlace	I-BirthPlace	O

In this example, the relations *Party*, *Job* and *Father* come sequentially in this order. Such sequences are common and likely to occur elsewhere; this gives a sequence model an advantage over simple non-sequence classifiers.

Another example where relation extraction can be treated as a sequence labelling task comes from biomedicine. In Entrez Gene,[39] many genes are functionally described by GeneRIF (Gene Reference Into Function) phrases.[40] Since the target gene is known, one can use CRFs to extract various relations which involve that gene, e.g., gene-disease interactions [Bundschus et al., 2008]. For example, the following GeneRIF for *COX-2* contains interactions between the target gene and two diseases: *endometrial adenocarcinoma* and *ovarian serous cystadenocarcinoma*.

> *COX-2* expression is significantly more common in *endometrial adenocarcinoma* and *ovarian serous cystadenocarcinoma*, but not in *cervical squamous carcinoma*, compared with normal tissue.

Note, however, that most relation extraction problems do not have one of the relation arguments fixed, and so cannot be easily treated as sequence labelling tasks. While one can still apply sequence models to general relation extraction, there usually is a more complex structure; the following two examples show such more complex dynamic models.

In Ray and Craven's [2001] work, an HMM incorporates syntactic information, subsequently encoded in complex hidden states which pair up a syntactic category with an argument type, e.g., NP with LOCATION. The observations for the HMM are also not over individual words but over sets of words spanned by the syntactic phrase, e.g., *cervical squamous carcinoma*.

---

[39]www.ncbi.nlm.nih.gov/gene
[40]www.ncbi.nlm.nih.gov/gene/about-generif

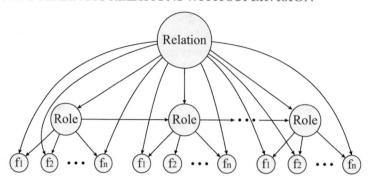

Figure 3.8: Dynamic graphical model for relation extraction [Rosario and Hearst, 2004].

Finally, there are separate HMM models for positive and negative examples. At test time, each sentence is scored against both models, and the model which assigns higher probability is selected.

HMMs and CRFs belong to a larger family of probabilistic models called *graphical models*. In such models, conditional dependencies between variables are represented as a graph. Rosario and Hearst [2004] work with a more complex *dynamic graphical model*. In addition to all hidden nodes, it has yet another node for the relation. Similarly to Ray and Craven's HMM, the hidden nodes in the graphical model do not represent labels over individual words but rather "roles" which can span sequences of words. For relations between treatments and diseases, e.g., the roles would be DISEASE, TREATMENT and NULL. The hidden node Relation represents the relationship in the sentence, e.g., *Cures, Does-not-cure, Prevents, Has-side-effect, No-relation*. It is assumed that a sentence contains no more than one instance of a relation of interest. There are links from the relation node to the role nodes, and optionally to the first word or to all words spanning these roles; words are decomposed as features, e.g., prefixes, suffixes, capitalization or digit patterns. Figure 3.8 shows the fully connected version of the model (it has also been found effective in the extraction of protein-protein interactions [Rosario and Hearst, 2005]). Just like Ray and Craven's HMM, this dynamic graphical model makes it possible to discover simultaneously the relation and its arguments. It is, however, more general, and it allows for multi-way relation classification, while Ray and Craven's model is limited to yes/no decisions about the presence of a relation.

3.4.3 DETERMINING THE SEMANTIC CLASS OF RELATION ARGUMENTS

Section 3.3.1 briefly discussed the mapping of relation arguments onto an ontology, and their description by features from an ontology. The motivation is to find an expression of a relation's arguments in terms of general concepts, in a manner similar to the argument types in the ACE relation definitions. There are various ways of determining the best level of generalization. If a description is based on ancestors in an ontology, then any learning algorithm can automatically determine the best generalization level [Nastase and Szpakowicz, 2003, Nastase et al., 2006]. The arguments of the collected instances can also be clustered [Girju et al., 2004]. The degree of generalization can be determined manually or automatically.

The descent or ascent of hierarchy   The *descent of hierarchy* was proposed by Rosario et al. [2002]. They were interested in the implicit relation between the two nouns in a noun-noun compound; for example, a KITCHEN KNIFE is a knife *used in* the kitchen. Rosario et al. were motivated by the assumption that head-modifier relations reflect the *qualia structure* [Pustejovsky, 1995] associated with the head noun. Under this interpretation, the meaning of the head determines what can be done to such a thing, what it is made of, what it is a part of, and so on. For example, a KNIFE can be in the following relations:

> *used-in*: KITCHEN KNIFE, HUNTING KNIFE
>
> *made-of*: STEEL KNIFE, PLASTIC KNIFE
>
> *instrument-for*: CARVING KNIFE
>
> *used-on*: MEAT KNIFE, PUTTY KNIFE
>
> *used-by*: CHEF'S KNIFE, BUTCHER'S KNIFE

Some relations are specific to narrow noun classes, while others, more general, apply to wider classes. Building on this idea, Rosario et al. [2002] proposed a semi-supervised characterization of the relation between the nouns in a noun-noun compound from bioscience. The characterization is based on the semantic category in a lexical hierarchy to which both nouns belong. Rosario et al. extracted all noun-noun compounds from a corpus of one million MEDLINE abstracts,[41] and made observations about which pairs of semantic categories the nouns tend to belong to. Based on these observations, they manually labelled the relations for a small subset of the compounds, and so avoided the need to decide on a particular set of relations in advance.

The work was based on the MeSH lexical hierarchy,[42] where each concept is assigned a unique identifier (e.g., *Eye* is D005123) and one or more descriptor codes corresponding to particular positions in the hierarchy.[43] Rosario et al. manually selected different levels of generalization, and then tested them on new data, reporting about 90% accuracy. For example, all compounds in which the first noun is in the A01 sub-hierarchy (*Body Regions*) and the second noun in A07 (*Cardiovascular System*) are hypothesized to express the same relation.[44]

Rosario et al. further found empirically that the majority of the observed noun-noun compounds fall within a limited number of semantic category pairs which correspond to the top

---

[41]www.nlm.nih.gov/bsd/medline.html

[42]Medical Subject Heading, www.nlm.nih.gov/mesh

[43]Those who require detailed examples need only consider the path A (*Anatomy*), A01 (*Body Regions*), A01.456 (*Head*), A01.456.505 (*Face*), A01.456.505.420 (*Eye*). By the way, the word is ambiguous, so it has another code: A09 (*Sense Organs*), A09.371 (*Eye*).

[44]Examples: *limb vein, scalp arteries, shoulder artery, forearm arteries, finger capillary, heel capillary, leg veins, eyelid capillary, ankle artery, hand vein, forearm microcirculation, forearm veins, limb arteries, thigh vein, foot vein.*

levels in the lexical hierarchy, e.g., A01–A07. Most of the remaining compounds require a descent of one level or two levels down the hierarchy for at least one of the nouns in order to arrive at the appropriate level of generalization of the relation. For example, the relation is not homogeneous when the modifier is in A01 (*Body Regions*) and the head is in M01 (*Persons*). It depends on whether the person is a patient, a physician, a donor, and so on. Making the distinction between different kinds of persons requires specialization for the head: going one level down the M01 hierarchy.

A01-M01.643 (*Patients*): *abdomen patients, ankle inpatient, eye outpatient*
A01-M01.526 (*Occupational Groups*): *chest physician, eye nurse, eye physician*
A01-M01.898 (*Donors*): *eye donor, skin donor*
A01-M01.150 (*Disabled Persons*): *arm amputees, knee amputees*

The idea of the descent of hierarchy is appealing and the accuracy is very high (about 90%), but there are limitations. First, the classification is not fully automated; human annotators decide where to cut the hierarchy. Second, the coverage is limited by the lexical hierarchy, most likely to narrow domains. Third, lexical and relational ambiguities cause problems. Finally, the technique does not propose explicit names for the assigned relations.

Iterative semantic specialization   Girju et al.'s [2003] system is similar but automated. It was applied to the *part-whole* relation. The training data, both positive and negative examples annotated with WordNet sense information, are first generalized by going from each positive/negative example up the WordNet hierarchy. Next, these generalizations are iteratively specialized whenever necessary, to make sure that they are not ambiguous with respect to the semantic relation assigned. Supervised learning then produces a set of rules from these examples.

Semantic scattering   Moldovan et al. [2004] implement an idea along the same lines. They rely on the training data to determine a boundary (essentially, a cut) in a hierarchy, in particular, in WordNet's hyponym/hypernym hierarchy. The boundary has the following property: the sense combinations in a noun compound which can be mapped onto this boundary are unambiguous with respect to the relation in the compound. Sense combinations found above the boundary may convey different relation types.

3.4.4   JOINT ENTITY AND RELATION EXTRACTION

Relation extraction is most often done on a dataset in which the potential relation arguments have already been annotated. Their variable length make argument identification a difficult task in itself. Keeping the two tasks separate also allows researchers to build upon previously developed resources for entity identification and classification.

The previous sections have shown that knowing the type of the arguments (e.g., Person, Location) can help identify the relation, and vice versa. Based on this observation, several systems perform joint extraction of entities and relations, allowing each piece of information to contribute to the final decisions.

Roth and Yih [2007] combine pieces of information from the local and global context in a linear programming setting, aiming to learn named entities and relations simultaneously. Their optimization problem sets out to minimize a combination of two costs: the assignment cost (the cost of deviating from the label assigned by the entity type classifier) and the constraint cost (the cost of breaking constraints between neighbouring nodes). Such a method applies to named entities and strongly typed relations (e.g., *work_for* requires a first argument of type Person and a second argument of type Organization), which do provide the necessary constraints.

Kate and Mooney [2010] take the entities in a sentence, and build from them a graph they call a "card-pyramid". The aim is to label this graph fully using card-pyramid parsing, an efficient dynamic-programming algorithm which resembles CYK parsing for context-free grammars [Jurafsky and Martin, 2009, Chapter 13]. The process relies on labels predicted by an entity type classifier and a relation classifier, and on mutual constraints.

Yu and Lam's [2010] probabilistic method works on Wikipedia articles. It detects the entities, their types and the relation between the principal entity in an article and the secondary entities mentioned in it. Yu and Lam's model, collective iterative classification (CIC), iteratively performs approximate inference to find the maximum *a posteriori* segmentation (for entity identification) and relation assignments. The first step, bootstrapping, predicts an initial label assignment to an unlabelled sequence given the trained model. The second step, iterative classification, performs multiple sampling to re-estimate the label assignment.

Singh et al.'s [2013] probabilistic graphical model classifies entity mentions into entity types, then clusters these mentions using coreference relations, and finally identifies the relations between them. Such a joint model has distinct benefits: constraints on the types of a relation's arguments can improve entity detection and classification, as well as coreference resolution. Ren et al. [2017] take entity type information from an external KB, and combine it with aggregated information from the context and relation-entity interactions.

In Li and Ji's [2014] work, a structured perceptron with beam search jointly recognizes entities and relations. The algorithm gradually builds all segments within the beam constraints. In the process, it associates entity types with subsequences (which are then treated as entity mentions), and relations with pairs of recognized entity mentions. The representation of these sequences combines local syntactic and semantic features with global features (coreference and neighbour coherence, constraints on relation combinations). A model is trained using a structured perceptron. The joint model identifies entity mentions better than a sequence labelling method using CRFs, an extended set of labels (BILOU: Beginning, Inside, Last, Outside, Unit), as well as syntactic and semantic features. The model also has better results than relation classification by the Maximum Entropy Markov Model (see Section 3.4.2).

Miwa and Sasaki [2014] apply history-based structured learning to relation extraction. They transform the task into a table-filling problem: build a word × word table, and fill it with labels

	Mrs.	Tsutayama	is	from	Kumamoto	Prefecture	in	Japan	.
Mrs.	B-PER								
Tsutayama	⊥	L-PER							
is	⊥	⊥	O						
from	⊥	⊥	⊥	O					
Kumamoto	⊥	⊥	⊥	⊥	B-LOC				
Prefecture	⊥	Live_in→	⊥	⊥	⊥	L-LOC			
in	⊥	⊥	⊥	⊥	⊥	⊥	O		
Japan	⊥	Live_in→	⊥	⊥	⊥	Located_in→	⊥	U-LOC	
.	⊥	⊥	⊥	⊥	⊥	⊥	⊥	⊥	⊥

Figure 3.9: Entity and relation table. The symbol ⊥ means "no relation" [Miwa and Sasaki, 2014].

which represent entity types and relation information. Entities are identified by the BILOU encoding scheme. Relations are defined on (head) words, since the span of entities is determined dynamically. Miwa and Sasaki explore various orders for traversing the table. Labels are assigned sequentially by a probabilistic method which combines local features (of the word itself) and global constraints (label assignment to previous cells).

3.4.5   N-ARY AND CROSS-SENTENCE RELATIONS

Binary semantic relations are by far the most widespread in NLP. There are, however, many interesting relations with more than two arguments. For example, one can define a *Purchase* relation with four arguments (PURCHASER, PURCHASED ENTITY, PRICE, SELLER) or a *Local_Sports_Team* relation with three arguments (TEAM, CITY, SPORT). The methods discussed in the preceding sections apply as well to *n*-ary relations. One can train supervised models to classify a candidate argument set of *n* entities in a given context as either positive or negative instances. Even so, the move to relations of higher arities is not free of complications.

First, it is not trivial to implement feature extraction based on the words between entity mentions, or the dependency path between mentions, or the least common subtree.

Second, a corpus often contains partial mentions where some but not all arguments of the relation appear. Take the sentences Sparks Ltd. bought 500 tons of steel from Steel Ltd. where the PRICE argument is missing, and Steel Ltd. bought 500 tons of coal where PRICE and SELLER are missing. Such examples cannot sensibly be presented in training as positive or negative. One can ignore all such partial mentions, but this limits the applicability of the trained system. One can also train separate models for every possible combination of arguments (one four-argument model, three three-argument models, six two-argument models), but this goes against the intuition that we are dealing in each case with the same relation.

One option is to decompose every instance with n entities into $\frac{n(n-1)}{2}$ binary instances. This allows an equal treatment of both full and partial mentions. Such a decomposition can also be the first step of a process; in a second step, the n-ary relation can be assembled from its binary components. McDonald et al. [2005] implement such a two-step process. They train a single classifier to predict if two entities are related to each other, and build a graph in which the entities in a text are linked by edges. The edges reflect the probability that the connected entities have a relation. The graph structure and the edge weights allow the detection of high-probability cliques in the graph; the cliques are then considered instances of n-ary relations. McDonald et al. apply their method to the extraction of genomic variation events—specific, one-time alterations at the genomic level—from biomedical texts. Such events are represented as ternary relations which connect the location, the initial state and the altered state. Take, for example, the sentence:

```
At codons 12 and 61, the occurrence of point mutations
from G/A to T/G were observed.
```

Two instances of the *point mutation* relation can be extracted:

$$(\textit{point mutation}, \text{CODON 12}, \text{G}, \text{T})$$
$$(\textit{point mutation}, \text{CODON 61}, \text{A}, \text{G})$$

The problem of identifying n-ary relations also arises in *semantic role labelling*. Palmer et al. [2010] published a monograph on the topic.[45]

Relations which cross sentence boundaries also complicate relation extraction/classification. Stevenson [2006] analyzed three information extraction evaluation corpora—MUC4, MUC6, MUC7—and noted that only approximately 60% of the n-ary relations (events in this case) have full matches in one sentence. Anaphora resolution can help mitigate this deficiency but the conclusion stands: many relations connect entities in different sentences.

Roberts et al. [2008] work with a corpus of oncology narratives, in which relations such as *has_indication*, *has_finding* and *has_target* link medical investigations and treatments with patient conditions and treatment results. Roberts et al. note that those relations' arguments are often separated by even more than nine sentences. In the dataset, 23% of the relations are inter-sentential. In the representation of these instances, most of the features characterize each argument by considering a surrounding window, and a few quantify the order and the distance between the arguments; the same features describe intra-sentential and inter-sentential relation instances. The relation models are learned with an SVM classifier. Roberts et al.'s analysis shows that the classifier performs worse for inter-sentential relations. What seems to be missing from this model are the relational features describing how the two arguments interact in the given context. When relations span multiple sentences, finding such features is problematic. Swampillai and Stevenson [2011] propose a remedy: they link the parse trees of the sentences

---

[45]The book (www.morganclaypool.com/doi/abs/10.2200/S00239ED1V01Y200912HLT006) remains the go-to survey of SRL but it is 10 years old. The advent of deep learning has brought about a new look at SRL, and thus a stream of publications. He et al.'s [2017] paper represents early work—early for neural NLP methods, anyhow.

containing the arguments via a common ancestor ROOT node. This makes it possible to produce both flat features, which describe the entities independently, and structured features. The latter are the shortest path tree (the shortest path between the entities), and the shortest path-enclosed tree (the shortest path augmented with all grammatical information for the nodes in the path). Swampillai and Stevenson's SVM uses a composite kernel which can process both types of information.

3.5   SUMMARY

This chapter gave an overview of supervised learning as applied to semantic relations between nominals, and presented several available datasets. They range from small, e.g., Nastase and Szpakowicz's [2003] set, to very large, e.g., all the Wikipedia infoboxes; from few relations, e.g., Rosario and Hearst's [2004] list, to very many, e.g., the Wikipedia infoboxes (again) and Freebase; from general-purpose, e.g., WordNet, to those specific to narrow domains, e.g., Rosario and Hearst's [2004] list (again). We reminded the reader the basics of supervised machine learning, and sketched a few popular techniques: kernel methods, sequence models and hierarchy-based methods. The chapter concluded with a brief discussion of the difficulties which arise when the learning problem is further complicated by applying it to relations with more than two arguments, or to relations which cross sentence boundaries.

Our collective experience has shown that supervised learning methods yield good results. Supervised learning, however, relies on annotated data, so it is limited to the semantic relations present in the annotation, and maybe to additional information such as WordNet senses, links to an ontology or textual context. This is a disadvantage.

The fact that learning is limited to the relations represented in the training data precludes the recognition of unexpected relations in a text. Changes in the training data—perhaps via the addition of new relations—require the derivation of new models. Transfer learning is seeking solutions to such problems [Thrun and Pratt, 2012]. In the meantime, various methods have been developed for semantic relations; those are methods better tailored to open-ended relation inventories, or to voluminous textual data. We investigate them in the next chapter.

On the positive side, supervised relation learning, in virtue of working in a controlled and information-rich environment, can help determine the characteristics of entities and relations useful in relation identification, and pinpoint learning formalisms which make the most of such characteristics.

A system's performance depends on all these factors: the nature and size of the data and of the relations to be classified, the way the data are represented, the learning algorithm applied. A few observations may help in the set-up of a new system.

- Favour learning algorithms with reliably high performance, such as SVM, logistic regression or CRF (the latter if the task makes sense as sequence labelling).
- Entity features and relational features are almost always useful.

- The value of background features will tend to vary according to the degree of world knowledge required to disambiguate the relation instances. For noun compound classification, the immediate context may not be useful while background knowledge plays a very important role.

Such lessons may give directions for future work. For example, the fact that sense information is very helpful may motivate work toward including (possibly coarser) sense information in open relation extraction on a large scale.

CHAPTER 4

Extracting Semantic Relations with Little or No Supervision

4.1 SEMANTIC RELATIONS IN VERY LARGE TEXTS

Before the year 2000, a few million tokens would have been a large text collection. Since then, there has been an explosion of available textual data; the Web scale has now been reached. This is a boon but also a concern. The avalanche of textual data makes it possible to build better language models which cover more phenomena that NLP methods aim to account for. On the other hand, such an amount of data precludes careful manual preparation: scalable, efficient automatic methods are urgently needed. For semantic relation analysis, this deluge of unstructured data means a richer source for building representations of meaning for the arguments and for gathering relational information. On the downside, it becomes necessary to reconsider how to define semantic relations and relation schemata, and how to find them without the benefit of the carefully and comprehensively annotated small texts.

Many arguments can be advanced in favour of developing unsupervised methods of relation extraction. There is a compelling motivation: such methods can help cope with the overwhelming amount of data available to scientists in *any* field. Without automation in the form of knowledge discovery, connections between entities or phenomena may go unnoticed. Swanson's [1987] pioneering work has shown the value of finding new connections between concepts in scientific literature. He combined relations extracted from various biomedical articles to discover previously unknown, but very important, connections between fish oil and constriction of blood vessels, and between magnesium and migraines. The hypotheses which Swanson discovered (with heavy manual intervention) were subsequently proven by medical professionals. The technique of connecting pieces of knowledge found in various sources, previously thought to be unrelated, has become known as *Swanson linking*, or *literature based discovery*. For example, one publication may show evidence that illness *A is caused by* chemical *B*, and another can report that drug *C reduces the amount of* chemical *B* in the body. Linking the two establishes a connection between illness *A* and drug *C*.

Another strong argument in favour of unsupervised methods is the reliance of language understanding on large-scale knowledge repositories. Manually created knowledge bases (KBs) are inevitably incomplete, even when they are created by a long-term and large-scale effort.[1]

---

[1]Consider Cyc (old.datahub.io/dataset/opencyc) and Freebase (developers.google.com/freebase).

Automatic population of a database or KB can, at the very least, assist the human builders. Even better, it can autonomously learn to find and extract more data from already encoded data.

Why cannot we simply deploy models learned from annotated data? A model is based on the information in the training data: the types of relations, their distribution in the data, and the features which represent them. Such information is often different from the information in large-scale text collections. Some relation types may not have been represented in the training data. Large-scale derivation of some deep features—e.g., sense information or dependency relations—may not be cost-effective (or even possible) on a large scale. Texts in different domains or genres have different characteristics, and that can also confound a model pre-learned on another domain. Transfer learning investigates ways of dealing with some of these concerns [Thrun and Pratt, 2012].

The unsupervised set-up requires new methods of discovering and learning semantic relations. The first steps in this direction—described in Sections 4.2–4.3—relied on hand-crafted patterns, on the assumption that those were unambiguous/precise clues which point to the existence of a semantic relation. Hearst [1992] has pioneered this line of research, with nine patterns very useful in discovering instances of the *is-a* relation. Her success inspired research into similar patterns for *part-of*. While such fixed lists of patterns can achieve high precision, recall is inherently limited because a relation instance can be expressed in a wide variety of ways. Coverage may also be limited because it is impractical, if at all possible, to devise high-precision patterns for all relations which might be of interest.

The methods which rely on hand-crafted patterns have evolved to a broader perspective: rather than starting with patterns, start with a small set of relation examples. Such examples can then be leveraged to find patterns, which in turn help discover more relation examples, and so on in a bootstrapping process. This is the subject of Section 4.3.1. Next, small sets of bootstrapping seeds were replaced with large sets of relation examples from knowledge repositories, and various methods were devised to help control the discovery of patterns and new relation instances. Self-supervised and distantly supervised methods grew out of the accumulated experience of combining texts with sample relation instances or patterns. This has led to large-scale training data for relation extraction in the form of automatically annotated sentences with relation examples from knowledge repositories; see Sections 4.5–4.6.

Bootstrapping and distant supervision are still limited because the targeted relations must be given—as patterns, or as sample instances for bootstrapping, or as automatically annotated (noisy) data for distant supervision. To deal comprehensively with large-scale (Web-scale), unstructured and open-ended data, one requires a different take on relation extraction. Instead of information about what relations to extract, a system gets information about what form relations have in text. Understanding how relations can be expressed has evolved: from considering only verbs and occasionally prepositions, through including nouns and relying on creative constraints to ensure cleaner extractions, to deriving more general relation-unspecific patterns and including conditions which modify a potential relation instance. Section 4.4.2 elaborates on this evolution.

This chapter takes an in-depth look at unsupervised relation extraction. After reviewing the evolution of the ever more scalable and robust methods, it wraps up in Section 4.7 with a brief overview of two projects which attempt to tame Web-scale data using very different relation extraction/classification ideas and methods.

4.2   MINING ONTOLOGIES FROM MACHINE-READABLE DICTIONARIES

The acquisition of ontological relations is a step in formalizing human knowledge so that it can be embedded in applications in NLP, and more generally in AI. In the 1970s and 1980s, when such work was first seriously contemplated, it was natural to turn for help to repositories of human knowledge. What was then available in machine-readable format were unilingual dictionaries, in particular Merriam-Webster and Longman's Dictionary of Contemporary English. The main focus were hyponymy and hypernymy—the subclass and superclass relations. We refer the reader interested in this early line of research to the work of Ahlswede and Evens [1988], Alshawi [1987], Amsler [1981], Chodorow et al. [1985], Ide et al. [1992] and Klavans et al. [1992].

Machine-readable dictionaries as an information source for relation mining offer certain clear advantages. Dictionaries contain short and focused definitions of concepts, they are written in somewhat standard language, and they tend to rely for the definitions on a limited vocabulary. All these characteristics simplify the mining task significantly. Still, there are difficulties. Consider, for example, the subset of interrelated senses of the following nouns: CLASS, GROUP, TYPE, KIND, SET, DIVISION, CATEGORY, SPECIES, INDIVIDUAL, GROUPING, PART and SECTION. The Merriam-Webster dictionary gives the following definitions (reproduced from [Amsler, 1981]):

> GROUP 1.0A—a number of <u>individuals</u> related by a common factor (as physical association, community of interests, or blood)
> CLASS 1.1A—a <u>group</u> of the same general status or nature
> TYPE 1.4A—a <u>class</u>, <u>kind</u>, or <u>group</u> set apart by common characteristics
> KIND 1.2A—a <u>group</u> united by common traits or interests
> KIND 1.2B—<u>CATEGORY</u>
> CATEGORY .0A—a <u>division</u> used in classification
> CATEGORY .0B—<u>CLASS</u>, <u>GROUP</u>, <u>KIND</u>
> DIVISION .2A—one of the <u>parts</u>, <u>sections</u>, or <u>groupings</u> into which a whole is divided
> *GROUPING <== W7—a <u>set</u> of objects combined in a group
> SET 3.5A—a <u>group</u> of persons or things of the same kind or having a common characteristic usu. classed together
> SORT 1.1A—a <u>group</u> of persons or things that have similar characteristics

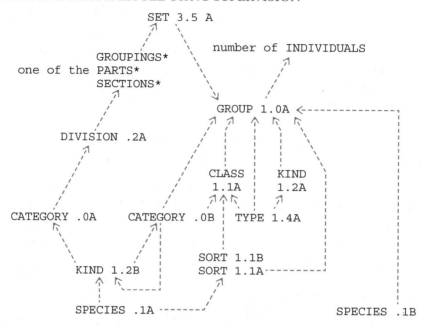

Figure 4.1: The GROUP concept and its relation to other concepts as extracted from a machine-readable dictionary [Amsler, 1981].

SORT 1.1B - <u>CLASS</u>
SPECIES .1A—<u>SORT</u>, <u>KIND</u>
SPECIES .1B—a taxonomic <u>group</u> comprising closely related organisms potentially able to breed with one another

One evident trouble is the circularity in definitions, depicted in Figure 4.1. It may cause problems for many applications which assume a tree-like, or at least acyclic, taxonomic structure.

There is another difficulty in the extraction of taxonomic relations from dictionary definitions: identifying the terms of interest. Chodorow et al. [1985] defined the keyword (the term of interest) as the head of a phrase, but this heuristic is not always appropriate. For example, in the definition of SET, group is the keyword in the noun phrase group of persons, whereas in the definition of GROUP 1.0A individuals should be the actual keyword in the syntactically parallel noun phrase number of individuals.

It is a challenge to build an ontology from text, even if the vocabulary and grammar are as controlled as they are in dictionary definitions. An ontology interconnects concepts (represented as strings), while a text contains words (also strings, but interpreted linguistically). Adding a relation extracted from text to an ontology implies mapping the relation's arguments onto ontology concepts and adding the corresponding edge. Mapping words in a text onto concepts in a hierarchy may require dealing with ambiguity, including polysemy and homography.[2] Information extraction often ignores such matters, because it remains at the text level: it extracts isolated relation instances with textual arguments.

Last but not least, dictionaries clearly have limited coverage. General dictionaries are shallow, specialized dictionaries are narrow. Either way, what they cover is small compared to what is potentially out there in open texts, and small compared to what has come to be expected of "real-world" NLP applications. Still, work on extracting knowledge from dictionaries, in particular comparing syntactic parsing and pattern matching [Ahlswede and Evens, 1988], has shown that patterns have much potential for relation extraction. They are computationally light compared to parsing, so they can be easily applied to very large text collections.

4.3 MINING RELATIONS WITH PATTERNS

The fundamental concept of a *relation pattern* underpins most relation extraction systems. It is an expression which, when matched against a text fragment, identifies a relation instance. Such patterns come in many forms; they can incorporate lexical items, wildcards, parts of speech, syntactic relations, and flexible rules such as those available in regular expressions. Hearst [1992] introduced a seminal inventory of patterns for the extraction of instances of the taxonomic *is-a* relation:

1. `NP such as {NP,}* {(or|and)} NP`
   e.g., ...*bow lute, such as Bambara ndang* ...
   → `(bow lute, Bambara ndang)`
2. `such NP as {NP,}* {(or|and)} NP`
   e.g., ...*works by such authors as Herrick, Goldsmith, and Shakespeare*
   → `(authors, Herrick); (authors, Goldsmith); (authors, Shakespeare)`
3. `NP {, NP}* {,} (or|and) other NP`
   e.g., ...*temples, treasuries, and other important civic buildings* ...
   → `(important civic buildings, temples); (important civic buildings, treasuries)`
4. `NP{,} (including|especially) {NP,}* (or|and) NP`
   e.g., ...*most European countries, especially France, England, and Spain* ...
   → `(European countries, France); (European countries, England); (European countries, Spain)`

These lexico-syntactic patterns are frequent across text genres, and have been shown to yield very high precision. It is, then, fairly safe to assume that any single match for a pattern is sufficient evidence for extracting a relation instance. Yet, *is-a* can be expressed in many other ways which

---

[2]Reminder: polysemy = same word, different but related senses (e.g., school as a building and as an institution), homography = same word, different unrelated senses (e.g., school as an institution and as a group of fish).

this limited set of patterns does not cover, so the recall is low. Recall can be improved thanks to the rapid increase in the size of available corpora and additional patterns; see Section 4.4.1.

It is unclear if such high-precision rules can be devised for *all* relations of interest. Even so, the matching of lexico-syntactic patterns has been attempted for many other relations. For example, Berland and Charniak [1999] proposed patterns which identify instances of the *part-of* relation. Similarly, early work on automatically identifying protein-protein interactions in biomedical journal articles has focused on searching for words from a predefined list which describe the noteworthy interactions [Blaschke et al., 1999, Pustejovsky et al., 2002]. To recognize instances of the *Inhibition* relation, one might search for patterns like N1 inhibits N2, N2 is inhibited by N1 and inhibition of N2 by N1. The detection of instances of the *Activation* relation might require looking for occurrences of specific verbs such as *activate* and of specific nominalizations such as *activation*.

4.3.1   BOOTSTRAPPING RELATIONS FROM LARGE CORPORA

Hearst's [1992] pattern-based search for relation instances originally ran on a corpus very small by today's standards. Grolier's American Academic Encyclopedia, with 8.6 million tokens, yielded instances of high quality, but there were merely 152 of them. Riloff and Jones [1999] later noted that the set of initial patterns can itself be further enlarged by using the extracted instances, and this new set in turn can lead to extracting more instances, and so on. This iterative learning framework is a form of *bootstrapping*. Experiments with this seemingly simple procedure have led to a few negative observations. In particular, noise in data can "infiltrate" the algorithm and steer it in a wrong direction. This phenomenon is called *semantic drift*. Systems which operate on large amounts of unstructured text should implement methods of avoiding semantic drift.

Bootstrapping begins with a small set of seed patterns, and each iteration adds patterns based on new matches found in the data. The procedure was developed to overcome the weakness of relation extraction via matching hand-crafted patterns: one cannot presume to have enumerated all the ways in which a relation might be expressed. That is why the system is allowed to discover new instances, and through them new patterns which indicate the relation of interest. Brin [1998] and Agichtein and Gravano [2000] demonstrated empirically the efficacy of this type of processing.

Algorithm 4.1 presents the process. The system is initialized with a small set of seeds in the form of high-precision patterns $\mathcal{P}$ or known instances $\mathcal{R}$ of the relation to be learned. No other supervision is required. For example, a system for extracting *is-a* relation instances could be initialized with Hearst patterns or with seed examples such as cat---animal, car---vehicle and banana---fruit. In the most typical scenario, the system will expand both the pattern set and the instance set. New patterns are collected by identifying candidates which co-occur with the set of known instances, while new instances are collected by matching the set of patterns against the corpus.

Algorithm 4.1 Bootstrapping with pattern and relation scoring for relation extraction. The set of seed patterns or the set of seed relation instances may be empty—but not both.

Require:
  $\mathcal{P}$—a set of seed patterns
  $\mathcal{R}$—a set of seed relation instances
  $\mathcal{C}$—a corpus
  N—maximum number of iterations
  rankInstances and *rankPatterns*—rank-and-select functions
Ensure: $\mathcal{R}$—a set of relation instances

  for $i = 1..N$ **do**
    $\mathcal{P}' = \{\}$
    $\mathcal{R}' = \{\}$
    for $p \in \mathcal{P}$ **do**
      match p in $\mathcal{C}$
      add matched pairs: $\mathcal{R}' = \{(np_i, np_j)\} \cup \mathcal{R}'$
    end for
    $\mathcal{R} = \mathcal{R} \cup Top_k(rankInstances(\mathcal{R}'))$
    for $(np_i, np_j) \in \mathcal{R}$ **do**
      match $np_i(.*)np_j$ in $\mathcal{C}$
      add matched pattern $(.*)$ to $\mathcal{P}'$
    end for
    $\mathcal{P} = \mathcal{P} \cup Top_k(rankPatterns(\mathcal{P}'))$
  end for
  return $\mathcal{R}$

To avoid adding noisy relation instances and patterns to the initial seed sets, extracted candidate instances $\mathcal{R}'$ and patterns $\mathcal{P}'$ are scored and ranked. The top k, or those with a score above a given threshold, are selected and added to $\mathcal{P}$ and $\mathcal{R}$ for use in the next iteration. Given enough text, this procedure can in principle be repeated indefinitely [Carlson et al., 2010a]. For a fixed corpus, however, it will naturally reach a point when no new patterns or instances can be harvested, while repeated iterations are not practical for a very large text collection. The solution is then to set an upper limit on the number of iterations.

Patterns produced by bootstrapping may comprise lexical items, syntactic categories and other easily identifiable textual items such as HTML markup [Brin, 1998]. Where entity categories such as LOCATION and ORGANIZATION are given in the data annotation or can be predicted automatically, they can help constrain the semantic types of a relation's arguments. For example, the Snowball system [Agichtein and Gravano, 2000] might generate these patterns if named-entity tags were available:

⟨ORGANIZATION⟩'s headquarters in ⟨LOCATION⟩
⟨LOCATION⟩-based ⟨ORGANIZATION⟩
⟨ORGANIZATION⟩, ⟨LOCATION⟩

Syntactic patterns in the form of dependency triples can improve the quality of bootstrapping for such relations as *Management_Succession* [Greenwood and Stevenson, 2006, Stevenson and Greenwood, 2005], exemplified by

COMPANY+*appoint*+PERSON
COMPANY+*elect*+PERSON
COMPANY+*promote*+PERSON
COMPANY+*name*+PERSON

On the other hand, syntactic representations require the parsing of the corpus, which may be completely impractical. Even shallow parsing takes a lot of time for the very large corpora one typically wishes to work with.

In principle, bootstrapping can help learn any semantic relation. In practice, the framework works best for ontological relations, which satisfy the assumption that the relation's arguments always interact in the same manner, regardless of the context. An idiosyncratic relation would tend to find contradictory evidence for a given set of arguments: one sport report might say "Manchester United defeated Chelsea", while the same newspaper might say six months later "Chelsea defeated Manchester United", referring to a different match.

A comparative study of relation types has shown that bootstrapping works better for specific relations such as *birthdate*, and has trouble with more generic or more heterogeneous relations such as *is-a* or *part-whole* [Ravichandran and Hovy, 2002]. This also depends on the granularity of the relations targeted. Suppose the goal is to extract Winston et al.'s [1987] six types of *part-whole* relations (*Component-Integral_Object*, *Member-Collection*, *Portion-Mass*, *Stuff-Object*, *Feature-Activity*, and *Place-Area*) instead of just one coarse-grained relation. Patterns will not be helpful: they will be shared across the six relations. As their names suggest, the difference between the relations is due mainly to the types of entities they connect.

4.3.2 TACKLING SEMANTIC DRIFT

One of the problems with bootstrapping is that, as it iteratively increases the seed set, it also increases noise which gets into the system. Such *semantic drift* [Curran et al., 2007] can be illustrated with the extraction of instances of the notion of *City* from a corpus; this is a kind of *is-a* relation extraction. While some of the patterns (such as `mayor of X`) are good, other patterns frequently encountered with cities (`lives in X`) often appear with other types of locations, such as countries, states or continents. In the next iteration, these ambiguous/deceptive patterns will bring in erroneous instances, which will bring more bad patterns, and so on.

Seeds		**Patterns**		**Added examples**
London		mayor of X		California
Paris	$\rightarrow$	lives in X	$\rightarrow$	Europe
New York		...		...

To counter semantic drift, one first scores the patterns and relation instances considered for addition to the expanding pattern set and relation instance set. Only the top scorers are eventually added, as shown in Algorithm 4.1.

One popular pattern-scoring function is the *specificity of patterns*:

$$specificity(P) = -\log(\Pr(X \in M_D(P))) \qquad (4.1)$$

P is the pattern to be scored, $M_D(P)$ is the set of tuples matching the pattern in the document set D, and X is a random variable uniformly distributed over the domain of the tuples of the target relation [Curran et al., 2007].

The idea is that patterns which match many contexts are probably too general, so they should be avoided. In practice, the specificity of a pattern is often measured by its length [Brin, 1998]; one assumes that longer patterns are more specific. Patterns of higher specificity are preferred since they are more likely to have high precision, and so less likely to cause semantic drift.

Agichtein and Gravano [2000] propose a precision-based measure, the *confidence of patterns*:

$$Conf(P) = \frac{P.positive}{P.positive + P.negative} \qquad (4.2)$$

P.positive and *P.negative* count the positive and negative matches for pattern P.

Agichtein and Gravano further define the *confidence of relation instances*:

$$Conf(I) = 1 - \prod_{k=0}^{|\mathcal{P}_I|} (1 - Conf(P_k)Match(c_k, P_k)) \qquad (4.3)$$

$\mathcal{P}_I = \{P_k\}$ is the set of patterns which can extract relation instance I, and $Match(c_k, P_k)$ is I's matching score for pattern P_k in context c_k.

Pantel and Pennacchiotti [2006] based the confidence of relation patterns on the *reliability* of patterns and relations, defined recursively:

$$r_\pi(P) = \frac{\sum_{I \in \mathcal{I}} \frac{pmi(I,P)}{\max_{I,P} pmi(I,P)} r_\iota(I)}{|\mathcal{I}|} \qquad (4.4)$$

$$r_\iota(I) = \frac{\sum_{P \in \mathcal{P}} \frac{pmi(I,P)}{\max_{I,P} pmi(I,P)} r_\pi(P)}{|\mathcal{P}|} \qquad (4.5)$$

$r_\pi(P)$ is the reliability of pattern P, and $r_\iota(I)$ is the reliability of relation instance I; $r_\iota(I) = 1$ for instances supplied initially as seeds; $\max_{I,P} pmi(I, P)$ is the maximum pointwise mutual information between all patterns and all instances. The pointwise mutual information $pmi(I, P)$ between pattern P and a binary relation instance $I = (x, y)$ is defined as follows:

$$pmi(I, \ P) = \log \ \frac{|x, \ P, \ y|}{|x, \ *, \ y| \, |*, \ P, \ *|} \tag{4.6}$$

$|x, \ P, \ y|$ is the number of times pattern P can be instantiated with relation instance $I = (x, \ y)$, $|x, \ *, \ y|$ is the number of times x and y co-occur, and $|*, \ P, \ *|$ is the number of times pattern P can be instantiated in the corpus.

These reliability measures lead to the *confidence of relation instances* calculated as follows:

$$S(I) = \sum_{P \in \mathcal{P}_R} S_P(I) \, \frac{r_\pi(P)}{T} \tag{4.7}$$

$S_P(I) = pmi(I, P)$, $\mathcal{P}_R$ is the set of reliable patterns extracted up until the previous iteration, and T is the sum of the reliability scores $r_\pi(P)$ for each pattern $P \in \mathcal{P}_R$. Instances whose score is higher than a given threshold are added to the set of extracted relations.

Paşca et al. [2006b] relied on word similarity to score candidate entities or relations. They calculated the similarity from a distributional representation of a word's meaning based on collocations extracted from a corpus.

Mutual bootstrapping, or mutual exclusion, extracts multiple categories of entities (or relation types) simultaneously [Riloff and Jones, 1999, Yangarber, 2003]. Categories are assumed to be disjoint, so patterns can be scored to favour those which extract instances of only one category:

$$score(P_i) = \frac{F_i}{N_i} \, \log_2(F_i) \tag{4.8}$$

F_i is the number of instances among those extracted with pattern P_i which belong to the desired category, and N_i is the total number of instances extracted with this pattern [Riloff and Jones, 1999]. In turn, instances extracted with high-scoring patterns are more highly scored, and will be retained for further iterations.

Argument type checking matches the entity type of a relation's argument with the expected type, and so filters erroneous candidates. Classifying a potential relation's arguments into fine-grained entity classes is error-prone and computationally inefficient for large-scale data. That is why type checking is done via a measure of word/term similarity based on collocations extracted from corpora [Paşca et al., 2006a], or by matching against coarse-grained classes for provided relation schemata, and against the given seeds [Rosenfeld and Feldman, 2007].

Coupled learning [Carlson et al., 2010b] combines constraints of various types to filter the list of candidate extractions. The method is based on the observation that the semi-supervised learning of relations in context (together with other relations) rather than in isolation yields

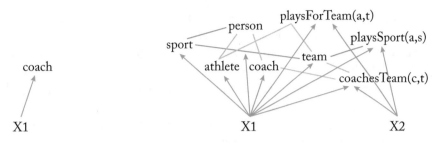

(a) A difficult semi-supervised
learning problem

(b) An easier semi-supervised
learning problem

Figure 4.2: Example of coupled relation learning [Carlson et al., 2010b].

better results. That is because constraints can lead to mutual disambiguation, and can help filter out bad candidates. Figure 4.2 illustrates. The system learns together relation extractors for multiple relations, and so takes advantage of constraints on categories (e.g., PERSON and SPORT are mutually exclusive) or on argument types (e.g., Blue Devils is a team).

4.3.3   BOOTSTRAPPING WITH LEARNED SEEDS

Instead of discovering and using textual patterns, one can also learn a model, deploy it on unlabelled data in the same manner as a newly discovered pattern, and so find more relation instances. This is in essence also a form of co-training, where one of the classifiers is a bootstrapping step.

For a learned model to replace patterns, one would require a sizeable training dataset, which is what bootstrapping was trying to avoid in the first place. When one has very little training data, successful relation classification depends on the quality of such data. Instances in good-quality data are representative of the phenomena accounted for, and of the number of interesting phenomena for a certain relation they cover. Good instances also have a distribution which reflects the distribution of relation types "in the wild". To build a robust relation classification model, it is crucial to select the appropriate set of seeds or patterns at each step of the bootstrapping process.

If a reasonable number of seed examples can be acquired, an initial model can be learned to distinguish good from bad patterns. In subsequent iterations, the model can be relearned using richer data. Zhang [2004] takes a Support Vector Machine (SVM) in lieu of the patterns in the bootstrapping process. The seed set to produce an initial good-pattern model is built by selecting data points at random.

Zhou et al. [2009] describe a method which, given a small amount of labelled data, can take advantage of a large amount of unlabelled data. In the first step, Zhou et al. apply bootstrapping in the automatic annotation of part of the unlabelled data. The data are represented by different subsets of features; on each of these representations, a model is built and used to classify the unlabelled data. The instances labelled as high-confidence (on which most models predicted the same label) are added to the training data, and used in the new iteration of bootstrapping. In the second step, the instances—both labelled and unlabelled—are represented as vertices in a graph, with arcs weighted by the similarity of the connected instances. Label propagation in this graph takes several iterations until convergence.

One method of getting high-quality seeds for bootstrapping is to select "good" candidates automatically, and to present them for manual annotation, in a form of active learning. To acquire such annotation candidates, Qian et al. [2009] assume that the distribution of relations is known, and use that as a guide in a stratified sampling strategy. The "true" distribution of relation types serves as a stratification variable. It is, however, unrealistic to assume that such knowledge about relations is available, so Qian and Zhou [2010] expand their previous work to propose a clustering-based stratified seed sampling. Unlabelled data are clustered, and each cluster represents a stratum. An intra-stratum sampling method selects a number of instances from each stratum/cluster, and these are annotated by an oracle to provide bootstrapping seeds.

4.4   UNSUPERVISED RELATION EXTRACTION

Bootstrapping relies on a small set of seed instances or patterns iteratively increased in multiple passes over a corpus. Unfortunately, in open information extraction, where the data support for relation extraction is the Web or a sufficiently large corpus, multiple passes over the data are computationally neither desired nor even feasible. Moreover, when extracting all relations which could be encountered, one simply cannot specify seed examples or patterns for each of those relations, particularly because it may not be known what different types of relations appear in the corpus. In such cases, relation extraction proceeds without a pre-specified list of relations, seeds or patterns.

4.4.1   EXTRACTING IS-A RELATIONS

The Distributional Inclusion Hypothesis

Relation mining and relation classification have been influenced by the adoption of the distributional representation of meaning for the relations' arguments. This type of representation can help identify *is-a* relations based on the distributional inclusion hypothesis: the set of contexts of a more specific term t should be a subset of the set of contexts of t's hypernym [Geffet and Dagan, 2005]. This approach was motivated by the task of textual entailment [Kotlerman et al., 2010].

Lenci and Benotto [2012] test several directional (asymmetric) similarity measures on a distributional semantic model. They conclude that the best results come from a measure which tells us if one term is semantically broader than another. Shwartz et al. [2017] test a comprehensive set of measures which combine distributional evidence in various ways, including the distributional inclusion hypothesis: hypernyms tend to appear in more general contexts (e.g., *eat*, *live*), while hyponyms appear in more specific ones (e.g., *bark*, *arrest*). The measures tested are similarity measures, inclusion measures and informativeness measures (hypernyms tend to be less informative than their hyponyms). Shwartz et al. also test the reversed hypothesis, using reversed inclusion measures. All these measures are supervised, and the parameters for some of them are trained on a small subset of the available data. The experiments on several datasets— BLESS [Baroni and Lenci, 2011], EVALution [Santus et al., 2015], Lenci/Benotto [Benotto, 2015] and Weeds [Weeds et al., 2014]—showed that no method or combination works best at identifying the hyponym/hypernym relation across all datasets. It gave, however, interesting insights into the metrics which distinguish hypernymy from other relations.

- Syntactic contexts distinguished best between hypernyms and meronyms—this reflects the fact that meronyms and holonyms often play different roles.
- Symmetric similarity measures using syntactic contexts distinguished best between hypernyms and attributes.
- Informativeness-based measures helped distinguish hypernyms from synonyms and antonyms, because synonyms and antonyms usually have a similar level of informativeness while hypernyms do not.
- The contrast between hypernymy and coordination showed no consistent pattern with respect to the measures applied to the various datasets.

Supervised learning with the results of these measures as features performs well. The individual measure results, however, have shown that they are sensitive to the distribution of data in the training set, and do not generalize well.

Hearst Patterns Revisited

Hearst published her patterns in 1992. Low recall was their weakness. Since then, corpora have grown by several orders of magnitude, and numerous methods have been developed to deal with the data sparseness inherent in any lexicalized model. Various techniques help increase the performance of methods which rely on Hearst-like patterns.

In Hearst's original experiments, the patterns were separately used to find new *is-a* relation instances, and the only *is-a* instances were those found in the corpus. Improvements could be achieved as follows: aggregate the set of Hearst patterns which occur with a candidate nominal pair, and take this as evidence for confirming the candidate as an *is-a* instance; and expand the decision from the directly found pairs to new ones.

Roller et al. [2018] implement such improvements using a slightly longer list of more flexible Hearst-like patterns on a very large corpus (Gigaword [Parker et al., 2011][3] and Wikipedia). They extract all potential *is-a* nominal pairs, and build from them a *word* × *word* matrix X, in

---

[3]catalog.ldc.upenn.edu/LDC2011T07

which a row and a column correspond to the two nominals in a pair. The element X_{ij} quantifies the pointwise mutual information of Hearst patterns for the nominal pair (i, j). From this matrix, Roller et al. obtain representations for the nominals in their dataset using singular value decomposition. The representations are then used to predict new *is-a* relation instances between nominal pairs not found together in the corpus. This leads to a higher rate of *is-a* relation detection than in systems inspired by the distributional inclusion hypothesis. These results suggest an important observation: patterns get information which disconnected contexts cannot (yet) get. Also, word representations obtained by a form of matrix decomposition enable a type of link prediction with matrix factorization; Chapter 5 elaborates on this in several places.

Clustering

In the case of a homogeneous cluster of closely related terms—such as *Apple, Google, IBM, Oracle, Sun Microsystems,* ...or *cat, mouse, dog,* ...—*is-a* relations can be automatically induced if the cluster can be named. Such a name might be *company* for *Apple* etc. and *animal* for *cat* etc. One can assume that the *is-a* relation holds between the name of the cluster and each of its members: *is-a*(*Apple, company*), *is-a*(Google, *company*), ... and *is-a*(*cat, animal*), *is-a*(*mouse, animal*), ...

Pantel and Ravichandran [2004] take this line of research. They work with noun clusters obtained by co-occurrence information and the method proposed by Pantel and Lin [2002]. The cluster, considered to represent a semantic class, is labelled with the hypernym of the elements in the cluster. For example, *company* would (ideally) be predicted for the automatically generated cluster of semantically related terms:

Apple, Google, IBM, Oracle, Sun Microsystems, ...

Finding this hypernym is a three-step process.

i. Represent the elements in the cluster with their grammatical collocates, and score those collocates.[4]

ii. Define a measure of representativeness for elements of the clusters, and extract the most representative elements which unambiguously describe the cluster.

iii. Extract the name of the class using the grammatical relations (e.g., apposition, nominal subjects, patterns like "such as", and so on) which have been determined empirically to be good predictors of such information.

For example, here are the top four grammatical relations which Pantel and Ravichandran found:

Apposition (N:appo:N), e.g., ...*Oracle,* a *company* known for its progressive employment policies...

---

[4]Grammatical collocates represent terms which appear together in a sentence and are related by a grammatical relation such as, e.g., subject, object or noun modifier.

Nominal subject (-N:subj:N),[5] e.g., …*Apple* was a hot young *company*, with Steve Jobs in charge…

Such as (-N:such as:N), e.g., …*companies* such as *IBM* must be weary…

Like (-N:like:N), e.g., …*companies* like *Sun Microsystems* do not shy away from such challenges…

After determining the name of the class, *is-a* relations are added between each element of the class and the class name.

It is also possible to extract instances of *is-a* relations without clustering. Kozareva et al. [2008] proposed an algorithm which learns hyponyms/hypernyms for a target hyponym/hypernym. The algorithm instantiates, as an exact-phrase query, a doubly-anchored pattern (DAP) of the following general form:

$$\text{``\textit{sem-class} such as \textit{term}}_1 \text{ and \textit{term}}_2\text{''}$$

sem-class is a semantic class, and *term*$_1$ and *term*$_2$ are members of this class.

This DAP is related to one of Hearst's [1992] widely used lexico-syntactic patterns, presented in Section 4.3:

$$\text{NP}_0 \text{ such as NP}_1, …, \text{NP}_{n-1}, \text{(or | and) NP}_n$$

Unlike that general pattern, this DAP posits exactly two arguments after such as, and makes the coordinating conjunction and obligatory.

A DAP can take other forms. For example,

$$\text{``\textit{sem-class} such as \textit{term}}_1 \text{ and *''}$$

can extract from the position of the asterisk the semantic class members semantically related to *term*$_1$, potential co-hyponyms of *term*$_1$. Similarly, the form

$$\text{``* such as \textit{term}}_1 \text{ and \textit{term}}_2\text{''}$$

enables the extraction of semantic classes common to the two terms, i.e., common hypernyms of *term*$_1$ and *term*$_2$. Finally, the two-placeholder form

$$\text{``* such as \textit{term}}_1 \text{ and *''}$$

allows for the simultaneous acquisition of pairs of hypernyms and co-hyponyms of *term*$_1$.

The power of DAPs comes from the two anchoring points, which act as disambiguators, and so yield more accurate hyponym-hypernym pairs. For example, given the term *jaguar*, the Hearst-style singly-anchored pattern

$$\text{``* such as \textit{jaguar}''}$$

would yield hypernyms such as *cars* and *animals*, which mix two senses of *jaguar*. In contrast, the doubly-anchored pattern

$$\text{``* such as \textit{jaguar} and *''}$$

could prevent such sense-mixing by learning hypernym-hyponym-hyponym triples:

$$\textit{cats–jaguar–puma}$$
$$\textit{predators–jaguar–leopard}$$
$$\textit{cars–jaguar–ferrari}$$

---

[5]The dash indicates that the right-hand side of the relation is the head.

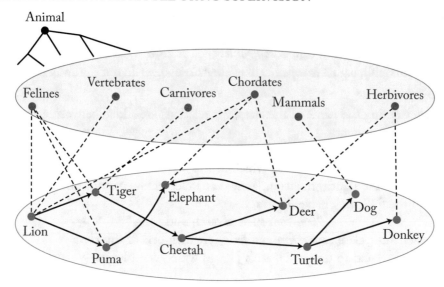

Figure 4.3: DAPs in taxonomy construction [Kozareva and Hovy, 2010].

Kozareva and Hovy [2010] extend the method. They make it capable of building entire taxonomies in a bootstrapping fashion, starting with a root concept and a basic-level concept or an instance. Figure 4.3 shows an example of how the process starts, given the root concept *animal* and the instance *lion*. First, other basic-level concepts—such as *tiger*, *puma*, *deer* and *donkey*—are learned using the DAP "*animals* such as *lion* and *". Next, hypernyms for these basic-level concepts are learned by applying a DAP with a placeholder for the superclass, e.g., "* such as *lion* and *tiger*"; this yields other basic-level categories like *vertebrate*, *chordate*, *feline*, and *mammal*. The goal is to tackle semantic drift and to focus on the most reliable instances, and so to minimize the number of Web queries. To that end, a graph algorithm ranks the unexplored nodes at every iteration, based on their *popularity* (the ability of a class to be discovered by other class instances; *in-degree* in graph terms) and *productivity* (the ability of an instance to discover new instances; *out-degree* in graph terms).

Finally, special patterns—"*X* are *Y* that", "*X* such as *Y*", "*X* including *Y*", "*X* like *Y*", "such *X* as *Y*", and so on—help determine the mutual position of the harvested hypernyms with respect to one another (this is not shown in Figure 4.3). For example, the first pattern can be used to determine whether *vertebrate* is a more general or a more specific term than *chordate*: check which of the two queries yields more Web page hits: "*vertebrates* are *chordates* that" or "*chordates* are *vertebrates* that". If the former query returns more hits, *chordates* will be assumed to be the more general term. Applied to all pairs of intermediate nodes, this yields a graph in which the longest path is to be found so that unnecessary transitive links can be removed. There

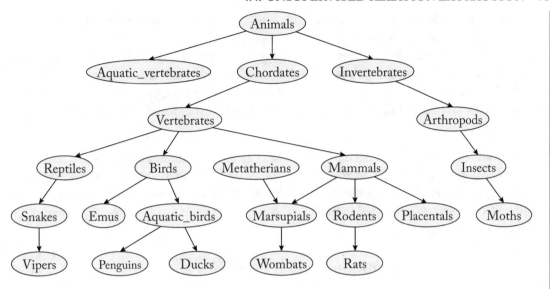

Figure 4.4: Part of the taxonomy for *animal*, made using DAPs [Kozareva and Hovy, 2010].

arise chains such as *animal → chordate → vertebrate → mammal → feline → lion*, which are eventually merged into a taxonomy shown in Figure 4.4.

4.4.2 EMERGENT RELATIONS IN OPEN RELATION EXTRACTION

Suppose a Web-scale information extraction system receives an *a priori* set of relations. This precludes the discovery of any relations which exist in texts but have not been supplied in advance. The system must be able to identify instances of previously unseen relation types, so telling it what relations to extract is not good enough. For unrestricted detection of relations, the system needs to know how they "look like". It also requires a mechanism which recognizes when different phrases represent the same relation, and when they refer to different relations.

It is difficult to describe how a relation "looks like". That is because there are many ways of phrasing the same relation. For example, the expressions a shot against the flu and a shot to prevent the flu arguably convey the same relation between shot and flu. The same relation can also be expressed implicitly by the noun compound flu shot, where there is no lexical material to connect the relation arguments. It is intuitive to treat verbs and prepositions as relation holders. Different verbs, however, may signal the same relation (e.g., create and produce) and the same verb may signal different relations in different contexts (chocolate made in Belgium vs. breakfast made in the morning); some do not even communicate any relations (e.g., "It rains", "I do"). A noun can be part of the expression of a relation, too (consider president / *be president of*). Still, part-of-speech (POS) information and partly lexicalized patterns offer a good starting point [Wu and Weld, 2010]. These can be strengthened with syntactically informed constraints [Fader et al., 2011], and can incorporate additional context as conditions which modify a potential relation instance [Mausam et al., 2012].

Recognizing when different phrases signal the same relation is often treated as a clustering problem: aim for one relation per cluster and one cluster per relation. There is a variety of methods of determining if two phrases express the same relation, e.g., string similarity between the lexical forms (the edit distance), similarity of their contexts, shared contexts or shared latent semantic factors.

String similarity model   To decide if two phrases s_1 and s_2 communicate the same relation R, one may compare them as character strings, and then define a suitable score or probability based on string similarity. This gives rise to the *string similarity model*, one of the two information sources for phrase similarity used in the RESOLVER system [Yates and Etzioni, 2009], part of the Machine Reading project:

$$\Pr(R|sim(s_1,s_2)) = \frac{\alpha * sim(s_1,s_2) + 1}{\alpha + \beta} \tag{4.9}$$

α and β help smooth the probability, giving more or less weight to the similarity measure. Overall, the probability ranges from $1/\beta$ for $\alpha = 0$ to $sim(s_1,s_2)$ for very large values of α. Yates and Etzioni note that the RESOLVER system is not sensitive to different values for α and β. The similarity score $sim(s_1,s_2)$ is calculated by an appropriate string similarity function. The Levenshtein string edit distance has been found apt for this task [Cohen et al., 2003].

Distributional similarity model   Suppose two phrases connect argument pairs similar to each other. The phrases may convey the same relation. Consider `solves` and `finds a solution to`, which may appear as binary relations (*solves, the student, the problem*) and (*finds a solution to, the government, the issue*). Now, *the problem* is similar to *the issue*, and *the student* is somehow similar to *the government*. The similarity between these elements of the triples can help establish the degree of similarity between the relation-carrying phrases.

Lin and Pantel [2001] implement such a system, called *Discovery of Inference Rules from Text* (DIRT), which learns paraphrases over paths in dependency parse trees. Relation candidates are extracted as triples (r, w_1, w_2) based on dependency relations/paths $argument_1 \xrightarrow{\text{dependency relation/path}} argument_2$. Arguments are nominals, and the dependency path contains a verb. The similarity measure between two relation expressions r_1 and r_2 adopted in DIRT combines the similarity between the first and second arguments, respectively, in the corresponding relation triples.

Latent factor models   The similarity between different expressions which convey the same relation type can also be based on hidden variables in probabilistic generative models. The hidden variables model latent factors, in this case relation types. A relation type will be described by the probability distribution over the various expressions. Yao et al. [2011] developed such a model, and used it to construct phrase clusters which correspond to relation types; the number of relation types is a parameter in the model. A relation tuple—two named entities connected by a dependency path in a sentence—is an observed random variable, and is described by a set of features. The features include the source and target entities, the dependency path connecting them, and maybe other information: the type of the entities, the POS sequence corresponding to the dependency path, dependency relations on the path, and so on.

A document is a mixture of relation type probabilities, that is to say, topic probabilities. This probability mixture for the documents in the corpus is modelled as a Dirichlet distribution with hyperparameter α ($Dirichlet(\alpha)$), and for each document it is drawn from this distribution ($\theta_{doc} \sim Dirichlet(\alpha)$). To generate a relation tuple in a document, the system draws a relation r according to the document's relation mixture ($p(r|doc) \sim Multinomial(\theta_{doc})$). The values of each feature for this tuple are then independently generated from a feature-and-relation-specific multinomial distribution ($p(f|r) \sim Multinomial(\phi_{f,r})$; $\phi_{f,r} \sim Dirichlet(\beta_f)$).

Yao et al. exploit information about the selectional preferences of relations to their arguments. They model entity types as hidden variables connected to the relation type; the argument types T_1 and T_2 are generated from r. The features for the source entity are generated from T_1, and for the destination entity from T_2. Entity type information leads to better (on average) relation extraction results on the dataset used, a corpus of New York Times articles. Whether entity type information is useful will depend on the nature of the text collection, and on the expected relations being typed—when their arguments have a specific type, like *person*, or *location* as is the case for the *born-in* relation—or not typed. Modelling entity types can also have useful side-effects, for example the clustering of a relation's arguments. Such clustering can be viewed as defining specific forms of the main relation. As an example, for the more general relation *worksFor*, this model discovers subrelations which can be described as *leaderOf* and *editorOf*.

Extracted shared property model   The decision if two relation expressions s_1 and s_2 represent the same relation R can be based on the similarity of the properties with which s_1 and s_2 appear in a corpus. For example, if both (*lacks, Mars, ozone layer*) and (*lacks, Red Planet, ozone layer*) are observed, then *Mars* and *Red Planet* share a context consisting of *lacks* and *ozone layer*. In the Extracted Shared Property (ESP) model [Yates and Etzioni, 2007], such a shared context is called a *property*. ESP models the extraction of relation expressions such as (*lacks, Mars, ozone layer*) as a generative process (inspired by Downey et al.'s [2005] URNS model) which associates a number of properties, P_i, with each string s_i. The properties are written on balls placed in an urn. ESP calculates the probability that two relation strings s_i and s_j corefer by estimating in how many ways the numbers n_i and n_j of balls (i.e., properties) can be sampled from an urn, so that strings s_i and s_j share k attributes.

4.4.3   EXTREME UNSUPERVISED RELATION EXTRACTION

The unsupervised learning of relation extraction without external clues relies on clustering two forms of data points: patterns which convey the same relation but connect different term pairs; and term pairs which express the same relation via various phrases.

Kemp et al. [2006] deploy a probabilistic generative model to build both entity and relation clusters. They assume that the set of entities—possibly partitioned into a set of types, e.g., people and locations—is given, and the Infinite Relational Model will discover entity clusters (within each type) and (potential) relations between these clusters. First, entities of each type are clustered by a form of the Chinese restaurant process [Pitman, 2006], where an entity is either assigned to an existing cluster or to a new one in proportion to

$$P(z_i = a|z_1,\ldots,z_{i-1}) = \begin{cases} \frac{n_a}{i-1+\gamma} & n_a > 0 \\ \frac{\gamma}{i-1+\gamma} & a \text{ is a new cluster} \end{cases} \tag{4.10}$$

n_a is the number of objects already assigned to cluster a. The prior provides the parameters γ which bias the cluster assignment. The next step produces relation types. The guiding assumption is that an entity's participation in relations is determined by its cluster assignment. The parameter $\eta^i(a,b)$ models the probability that there is a relation R^i between objects in cluster a and objects in cluster b. If z is the vector of cluster assignments for the arguments of an n-ary relation $R(i_1,\ldots,i_n)$, then

$$P(R|z) = \int P(R|\eta,z)P(\eta)d\eta \tag{4.11}$$

η and R are assumed to be drawn from conjugate distributions for binary or n-ary relations ($\eta \sim Beta(\beta)$ or $Multinomial(\beta)$ and $R_n(i_1,\ldots,i_n) \sim Bernoulli(\eta_{R_2})$ or $Dirichlet(\eta_{R_n})$). Kemp et al. have shown that with this type of modelling one can learn a biomedical ontology (given data from the Unified Medical Language System),[6] or entity clusters and relations (given entity descriptions and generic relation information).

The Infinite Relational Model assumes that an entity may belong to only one cluster. Kok and Domingos's [2007] model, based on Markov logic, allows multiple relational clusterings (MRC), to reflect better the complexities in relational data, e.g., clustering people as co-workers or as friends. As part of the process of clustering objects and relations, MRC invents predicates which capture discovered regularities over relations.

The Infinite Relational Model can find additional structure in an unsupervised manner but it has to rely on already (even if weakly) structured data. When working with unstructured text collections, both relation arguments and relations need to be found. Davidov and Rappoport [2008a] find relation arguments and relation expressions by mapping onto texts the following very generic pattern:

---

[6]www.nlm.nih.gov/research/umls/

```
Prefix CW₁ Infix CW₂ Postfix
```

CW_i represent a relation's arguments, and are conveyed by content words, those with a frequency within given bounds. The Prefix, Infix and Postfix comprise only high-frequency words: actual words or punctuation with a frequency above a given lower bound. The three make up the context of the relation between the content words. Pairs of CWs in similar relational contexts should be clustered, and so should relational contexts which signal the same relation. The process starts with the set of contexts for each pair of CWs. These sets are filtered, and then combined with each other by considering their degree of overlap. These initial clusters are filtered and then gradually merged. The final clustering represents the various relations and their possible expressions in texts. Examples of clusters show patterns which should look familiar:

label	patterns
(pets, dogs)	{ such X as Y, X such as Y, Y and other X }
(phone, charger)	{ buy Y accessory for X, shipping Y for X, Y is available for X, Y are available for X, Y are available for X systems, Y for X }

The clusters are labelled with the five highest-ranking instances according to a HITS score (Equation 3.1 in Section 3.3.2). HITS quantifies the affinity of a word pair (w_1, w_2) to a cluster C. It considers how many of the patterns from which one obtains (w_1, w_2) can be used to extract multiple word pairs (P_{core}), or just the current pair (P_{unconf}).

Several parameters control the performance of this algorithm: the frequency boundary for determining high-frequency words and CWs; the window size in which the pattern is applied (narrower means more precision but lower recall, wider means more specific and possibly incorrect relations); the minimal overlap for cluster merging; α which can penalize very specialized patterns to a desired degree.

Language independence is an advantage of this method. Davidov and Rappoport [2008a] apply it to English and to Russian. They demonstrate a further benefit: the clusters can be used as background relational features (in the sense discussed in Section 3.3.2) for supervised relation classification.

Such extreme relation extraction from open texts relies on the assumption that when two entities co-occur, they always interact or are connected in the same manner. The assumption is relatively safe for ontological relations, but context matters. A person, for example, may be connected to a location by such varied relations as *born-in*, *work-in* or *travel-to*.

Davidov and Rappoport's application was the solving of SAT-analogy questions, collected by Turney and Littman [2005], with performance higher than the average obtained by human subjects. In the verbal analogy questions at SAT exams, one must estimate relational similarity in order to choose, from a set of several given word pairs, the pair which resembles the test pair the most. Table 4.1 shows two examples; the subject must decide if, e.g., the relation between

Table 4.1: SAT verbal analogy, example questions. The correct answer is in *italics*, and the distractors are in plain text.

ostrich:bird	palatable:toothsome
(a) *lion:cat*	(a) rancid:fragrant
(b) goose:flock	(b) chewy:textured
(c) ewe:sheep	(c) *coarse:rough*
(d) cub:bear	(d) solitude:company
(e) primate:monkey	(e) no choice

ostrich and *bird* is more similar to the relation between *lion* and *cat*, or rather between *primate* and *monkey*.

4.5   SELF-SUPERVISED RELATION EXTRACTION

Suppose there are heuristics which help produce training instances automatically. That would obviate the need to provide seed examples or patterns for bootstrapping, or to perform unsupervised relation extraction. The heuristics can be informed by particular overt characteristics of relation instances discovered via supervised learning, or by correlations between data points. The verb which connects the arguments in a sentence is one such kind of overt indicator for certain semantic relations; it can support the learning of specific relation extractors. While deeper processing (e.g., syntactic parsing) is not yet feasible on a Web scale, it is possible on a smaller text collection. This information can then be used to annotate automatically instances of semantic relations, based on which relation extractors are learned and then deployed on Web-scale data.

In the *Machine Reading* project at the University of Washington [Poon et al., 2010], the relation extraction process begins with the parsing of a small corpus. The parsing results are then used to extract and annotate relation instances; this is informed by heuristics related to the connecting path between entity mentions. The automatically annotated examples are applied to the training of *generic* relation extractors which extract relation instances not guided by or assigned to any particular relation type. The features are shallow: lexical and part-of-speech information from the immediate context and the connecting path between the two entities, similar to those in bootstrapping. Such features are easily obtained and applied to Web-scale text collections.

The extraction of entity-linking phrases as relations does not ensure good quality. The resulting relations may be

- not coherent (lacking a meaningful interpretation, e.g., *The Mark 14 was central to the torpedo scandal of the fleet.* → was central torpedo),
- not informative (e.g., …*is the author of* … → is),
- not general enough (e.g., is offering only modest greenhouse gas reductions targets at).

Such unwanted effects can be partly remedied by imposing syntactic, positional and argument frequency constraints on the extracted relations [Fader et al., 2011].

An adverse effect can also be avoided if the target relations have specific properties. Lin et al. [2010] work with *functional relations*, in which exactly one value of the second argument is possible for a given value of the first argument. Consider, for example, the relation birthplace between persons and locations: everyone has precisely one birthplace. This seems to simplify the problem considerably. The same argument, however, can be expressed in many different ways. For example, Barack Obama was born in Hawaii/Honolulu/the United States/USA. It may also be too difficult to check all pairs of arguments, even if one manages to circumvent argument ambiguity and other likely restrictions on relation instances.

Downey et al. [2005, 2010] rely on the redundancy of information and the "KnowItAll hypothesis": extractions drawn more frequently from distinct sentences in a corpus are more likely to be correct. When working on the Web scale, however, it is difficult to test if a particular example satisfies this hypothesis, because it is not easy to estimate frequency. The same relation can manifest itself in various ways, and frequency is (possibly) not absolute but rather relative. For example, in October 2012 a search for `Elvis killed JFK` yielded 19,300 hits, which is high and could be considered correct, but for the comparison with the 39,200 hits for `Oswald killed JFK`. Extracting the correct information, then, depends not only on redundancy but on corroborating the outcome of different extraction heuristics. The scoring depends on measures similar to those in the extracted shared property model, as described in Section 4.4.2.

There are now many more domains, some narrowly specialized, in which relation extraction or classification can be applied. Crowd-sourcing platforms do not ensure high-quality annotations in such domains, because the process requires deep understanding of the terminology and the targeted phenomena. To help circumvent large-scale, expensive manual annotation, Ratner et al. [2017] proposed Snorkel, a platform which applies weak supervision to the automated annotation of training data. Snorkel's user writes labelling functions which encode heuristics for the recognition of relations based on patterns, external knowledge sources, weak classifiers, crowd-sourced labels, and so on. For example, a labelling function can check if the word `cause` appears between the mentions of a chemical substance and a disease.

Labelling functions work on unlabelled data. Snorkel considers agreement and disagreement between the labels those functions produce, and learns a generative model which is a re-weighted combination of the labelling functions. The output is a set of probabilistic training labels for the input data. The generative model can also account for dependencies between the labelling functions. There have been experiments on annotating semantic relations in several domains: chemical relations from PubMed abstracts, relations in electronic health records, and family relations (such as *parent* or *sibling*) from news articles. The experiments have shown that the elicitation of labelling functions can lead to annotated data of a quality on a par with, or better than, traditional data labelling.

4.6   DISTANT SUPERVISION

Distant supervision for task T relies on data annotated for a related task to automatically produce training data for T. The difference between distant supervision and self-supervision is the fact that in self-supervision a system uses heuristics to generate its own training data. Craven and Kumlien [1999] first proposed this type of learning, and called it "weakly supervised". Instances of relation *subcellular-localization* from the Yeast Protein Database were mapped onto abstracts from PubMed. Craven and Kumlien found 336 relation instances in 633 sentences. They assumed that a particular instance of a relation appears in a sentence if that sentence contains a match for both arguments of the relation. They compared Naïve Bayes classifiers built on the automatically annotated sentences, and separately on manually annotated sentences, and observed a comparable performance.

Craven and Kumlien's corpus and KB of facts were quite small. There are now very large and convenient sources of distant supervision for relation extraction. The most common are WordNet, Cyc and Freebase, as well as Wikipedia infoboxes which cover a variety of relations (see Section 3.2.5). More knowledge repositories in both general and specific domains are now available, many of them part of the Linked Open Data cloud.[7] The relation triples from these knowledge repositories are mapped onto large text corpora in order to find (potential) instances of those relations in free-form texts. The contexts so discovered next serve as training data in the learning of models for relation extraction. This automatic process of generating annotated data for relation extraction suffers from noise and bias.

Noise. Even if two entities appear together, there is no guarantee that they are in any relation; if they *are* related, it need not be the targeted relation. Consider these matched instances for the relation triple ⟨GERMANY, *part-of*, EUROPE⟩.

> Germany set to lift travel warnings for Europe.
> Europe took a step toward post-virus normality on Friday when restaurants in Germany and Austria reopened for the first time in two months.
> Germany, country of North-central Europe, ...

Only the last of these instances is relevant.

Bias. The training data will only contain potential relation instances whose arguments are entities present in the source of distant supervision, in the lexical form in which they appear there. This may introduce unwanted biases into the model.

Distant supervision has been applied both to relations in a sentence and to those which cross sentence boundaries. Section 5.5.2 takes up this topic in the context of deep learning: it reviews new ways of filtering out the noise.

---

[7]lod-cloud.net/

4.6.1 RELATIONS IN A SENTENCE

Snow et al.'s [2005] variant of bootstrapping based the learning of instances of hypernymy (the *is-a* relation) on WordNet. They start with a very large WordNet-sourced seed set, and enlarge this set iteratively. They first discover dependency path features which connect known hyponym-hypernym pairs in text, and then use them to discover more hyponym-hypernym pairs.

Bunescu and Mooney [2007] start with a small seed of entity pairs, and extract large bags of potential instances by querying the Web with each entity pair. After extraction, the entities are replaced by generic placeholders. From the returned results, sentences containing the pair are kept, and the bags which contain these sentences are considered positive. Negative bags are built in a similar fashion for unconnected entity pairs. An SVM with subsequence kernel learns relation models from these data. To mitigate the effect of words closely associated with the (obfuscated) entities, Bunescu and Mooney introduce weights which lower the effect of words in context derived from their co-occurrence probability.

Wikipedia provides a unique environment for learning extraction patterns. As discussed briefly in Section 3.2.5, a Wikipedia article's infobox contains a summary of information, in the form of attribute-value pairs. The attribute is in fact a relation; its implicit first argument is the concept denoted by the encompassing Wikipedia article. The information summarized in the infobox also appears in the associated article. Matching the information in the infobox with sentences in the article gives examples of relation occurrence in text, from which patterns can be learned. Figure 4.5 shows an example.

Access to Wikipedia allows one to build a corpus of sentences which contain instances of specific relations. Other sentences from the articles can provide negative examples (sentences with no instances of the target relation). Wu and Weld [2007] were the first to combine Wikipedia infoboxes and the text of the Wikipedia pages. They restricted the mapping of relations to the corresponding Wikipedia pages. Mintz et al. [2009] expanded Wu and Weld's work. They mapped 102 Freebase relations—many of them coming from Wikipedia infoboxes—with 17,000 seed instances onto (any of the) Wikipedia article texts, of which in 2009 there were 1.2 million; the system extracted 1.8 million instances connecting 940,000 entities.

Having such a corpus facilitates a two-step learning procedure: first, learn to identify sentences which contain a relation instance; next, learn relation extractors from sentences which contain relation instances. In principle, any of the supervised learning methods described in Chapter 3 could be used in tandem with an argument identification stage. Conditional Random Fields (see Section 3.4.2) are particularly appropriate for this problem [Banko and Etzioni, 2008, Wu and Weld, 2007], because they combine the strength of sequence modelling with the advantages of supervised learning, to find in the given sentence the arguments (of varying length) of a targeted relation [Lafferty et al., 2001]. Consider the relations in the infobox and the associated article in Figure 4.5. A system would need to learn to recognize that the sentence Jones is most famously played by Harrison Ford and has also been portrayed by River Phoenix [...] contains (at least) an instance of the *portrayed by* relation,

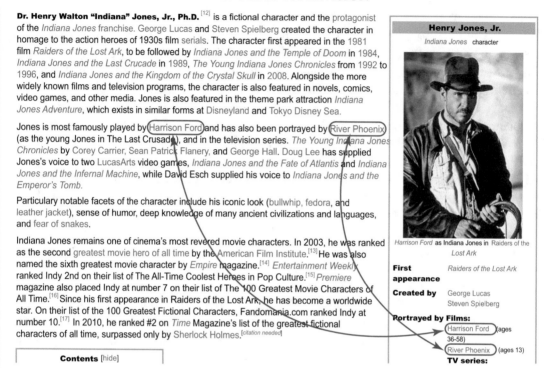

Figure 4.5: Example of a Wikipedia article, showing that the information in the infobox can be found in the article's text.

and then to extract the instances (Jones, *portrayed by*, Harrison Ford) and (Jones, *portrayed by*, River Phoenix).

Mintz et al. [2009] have analyzed the textual Wikipedia data extracted to match relations in Freebase, and noted that approximately 70% of those contain a correct relation. Riedel et al. [2010] use Freebase relations to extract textual instances from Wikipedia and the New York Times Corpus.[8] A manual inspection of a sample of the extracted sentences reveals that the distant supervision assumption fails on 13% of the data extracted from Wikipedia, but on 31% of the NYTC. This is not surprising. Freebase contains "background" relations—place of birth, nationality, profession, and so on—whereas the articles in the NYTC concern mostly current events; background information about the mentioned entities (e.g., the profession) is mentioned in passing if it is relevant to the topic of the article.

Another way of modelling distantly supervised data is to focus on the pattern of a relation, defined as the types of entities and the sequence of words (dependency path) which connect them [Takamatsu et al., 2012]. A probabilistic generative model can then predict if a pattern

---

[8]catalog.ldc.upenn.edu/LDC2008T19

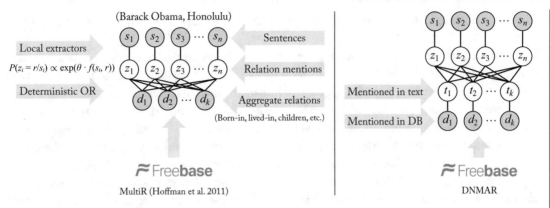

Figure 4.6: The MultiR model [Hoffmann et al., 2011] and its extension with the missing data model [Ritter et al., 2013] (image from Ritter et al.).

communicates a relation. This is done by means of hidden variables which model the relationship between entity pairs and the observed pattern, and the noise in the KB which supplies the entity pairs.

Probabilistic generative models have various applications in relation learning. Hidden variables can be used to model not only (potentially multiple) relations communicated by a sentence but sentence-level decisions: does the sentence contain a targeted relation? Hoffmann et al.'s [2011] MultiR model uses sentence-level latent variables to help filter out sentences which do not contain targeted relations, and to model predictions about specific relations holding for given entity pairs in the sentence. MultiR can handle overlapping relations, and deal with sentences which may contain a specific entity pair but no targeted relation between them. Surdeanu et al. [2012] model multiple instances (by modelling the latent labels assigned to instances) and multiple labels (by recognizing dependencies between labels). The overlap in relations and relation instances in Freebase helps learn a relation extraction model which combines evidence from the sentence level with aggregated information from a corpus.

Distant supervision relies on two assumptions: (i) if a sentence contains a pair of entities which have a relation in the KB, it contains an instance of this relation; (ii) if a sentence does not contain a pair of entities which have a relation in the KB, it does not contain an instance of a relation from the KB. To counter the effect of these assumption, Ritter et al. [2013] expand Hoffmann et al.'s MultiR to model missing data, as illustrated in Figure 4.6. They split MultiR's variable which models if a sentence contains a relation from the KB into two variables, to represent separately two possibilities: if a Freebase fact is mentioned in the text (in at least one sentence), and if a potential fact in a sentence appears in the KB. Two relation-specific parameters penalize missing information in the text and the KB respectively. Relations with few instances in the KB get a lower penalty for missing from texts; relations with many occurrences in texts get a higher penalty for missing from the KB. The system explicitly models the possibility of missing data, so it can use relation instances in text absent from the KB, and vice versa.

Distant supervision can generate large amounts of automatically annotated data but such data are noisy. Not all sentences containing a pair of entities signal the same relation between these entities. Mintz et al.'s system aggregates information from all sentences containing a given entity pair, and produces a feature vector for relation classification. This reduces to some degree the effect of noisy annotations at the level of single sentences. Systems which consider each (automatically) annotated sentence as a relation instance must find ways to filter out the noise.

Riedel et al. [2010] dispense with the assumption that a pair of terms has the same relation regardless of the context in which this pair appears. Instead, they assume that at least one of all available contexts conveys the target relation. They use a factor graph [Kschischang et al., 2001] to model the decision: are two entities identified in a context related, and is the relation between them indeed the target? S and D are the observed variables which model the source and the destination of a relation. A hidden variable Y models the relation between a source and a destination, and another hidden variable Z_i takes the value *true* if the relation present in instance i (between source S_i and destination D_i) matches relation Y. The model computes the joint probability $p(Z = z, Y = y \mid \mathbf{x})$, where $\mathbf{x}$ is the sequence of observations (the text containing relation instances). The parameters of the model are optimized to ensure that the predictions satisfy the "expressed-at-least-once" constraint.

Various knowledge facets can help decide whether a sentence contains an instance of a target relation: type restrictions on relation arguments (a CEO is a business person); relations between the targeted relations (e.g., entailment: *capital_city_of* ⊨ *located_in*, or co-occurrence: *CEO_of* ≈ *founder_of*); and label consistency between neighbours (similar instances tend to carry the same kind of relation). Han and Sun [2016] aggregate all this information in a Markov Logic Network model. They compensate for the lack of direct supervision from the KB with indirect supervision knowledge (e.g., argument types), and they overcome the uncertainty in distant supervision by relying on the inter-dependencies between relations types. They aim, ultimately, to produce cleaner automatically annotated data.

Distant supervision can also be viewed as label propagation in a graph. A node can be a labelled or an unlabelled sentence. Nodes are connected by edges weighted using distance/similarity information [Chen et al., 2006, Zhou et al., 2009]. A label propagation algorithm tries to obtain a labelling function which satisfies two constraints: it is fixed on the labelled nodes, and it is smooth on the whole graph.

The purpose of distant supervision is to reduce sharply the manual effort in providing annotated training data for relation extraction/classification. The automatically annotated data are useful but noisy. A minimal amount of manual intervention can improve relation models. Angeli et al. [2014] propose such a solution. A committee of classifiers selects instances based on their uncertainty and representativeness scores. The selected instances are to be manually annotated and added to the automatically annotated data. This augmentation of the training data, used with Surdeanu et al.'s [2012] multi-instance multi-label relation extraction model, improves the performance.

4.6.2   RELATIONS ACROSS SENTENCE BOUNDARIES

The work discussed in Section 4.6.1 produces automatically annotated relation instances based on the co-occurrence of the relation arguments in one sentence. The relation arguments must occur in the same sentence, and possibly be connected by a constrained syntactic path, if this is to be considered a relation instance candidate. This assumption is clearly a limitation. An example from a biomedical text (quoted from [Quirk and Poon, 2017]) shows a relation which crosses sentence boundaries:

> *The p56Lck inhibitor **Dasatinib** was shown to enhance apoptosis induction by dexam-ethasone in otherwise GC-resistant CLL cells. This finding concurs with the observation by Sade showing that **Notch**-mediated resistance of a mouse lymphoma cell line could be overcome by inhibiting p56Lck.*

There is a relation here which spans the two sentences: the drug Dasatinib could overcome resistance conferred by mutations to the Notch gene. Such instances indicate that recall improves if one considers relations above the sentence level. Quirk and Poon show how to obtain relation instance candidates by combining intra-sentential dependencies, discourse relations and sentence adjacency information. Their source is a curated KB of 162 biomedical facts, which are then matched with texts from a million articles from PubMed.[9]

4.7   WEB-SCALE RELATION EXTRACTION

Two large-scale knowledge acquisition projects aim to harvest relations from the Web. They are both based on some form of bootstrapping, which they constrain and enhance in different ways. The following sections paint the bigger picture, in particular the learning philosophy behind these systems' long-term view of relation extraction.

4.7.1   NEVER-ENDING LANGUAGE LEARNER

Never-Ending Language Learner (NELL)[10] is an ongoing knowledge acquisition project at Carnegie Mellon University. Its starting point was a seed ontology. It comprised approximately 600 categories and relations, each seeded with a small set of 10-20 examples. NELL aims to enrich this ontology with new concepts, new concept instances, new instances of the existing relations and new relations.[11]

---

[9]pubmed.ncbi.nlm.nih.gov/
[10]rtw.ml.cmu.edu/rtw/
[11]The project's home page, accessed in August 2020, says: "So far, NELL has accumulated over 50 million candidate beliefs by reading the web, and it is considering these at different levels of confidence. NELL has high confidence in 2,810,379 of these beliefs [...]"

NELL's philosophy is that learning multiple relations simultaneously—doing it in context—and using models based on different types of evidence from various sources is easier and less error-prone than learning isolated relations using only one model. This is illustrated in Figure 4.2 in Section 4.3.1. Carlson et al. [2010b] call this form of learning multiple models at once *coupled learning*. They combine three techniques—mutual exclusion, argument type checking and a form of co-training[12]—using structured and semi-structured text features, e.g., HTML tags. The system then takes these subcomponents (which make uncorrelated errors) to learn multiple types of inter-related knowledge. It learns predicates from texts, and it learns to infer new relations from the learned ones. To learn predicates, it has the three coupled semi-supervised methods, which leverage constraints between the predicates to be learned.

NELL effectively implements a form of bootstrapping which relies on coupled learning to avoid semantic drift (see Section 4.3.2). The additional constraints—which come from learning multiple functions in a coupled manner—help keep the system focused. The system runs on a corpus of hundreds of millions of Web pages, which is queried and analyzed daily. Minimal manual intervention, a few minutes a day, removes some of the erroneous facts retrieved by the system.

To add new relations to the existing ontology, NELL employs clustering. It first finds in its ontology pairs of known category instances which co-occur in texts. It then co-clusters them together with phrases (also known as candidate relation expressions) which connect these pairs where encountered. A September 2012 version contained 15 million extractions, 2.8 million of which had high confidence scores, estimated at 85% precision [Mohamed et al., 2011].

Mitchell et al. [2018] report that NELL's KB expanded to approximately 120 million confidence-scored relations (beliefs). The system's achievement is not only the ever-expanding KB but its learning of interrelated functions, which allow it to improve its reading competence over time. It has also been endowed with the capacity to reason over its KB, to infer new relations from those it has already acquired [Gardner and Mitchell, 2015, Gardner et al., 2014], taking advantage of the development of deep-learning methods—we discuss such methods in Chapter 5.

4.7.2   MACHINE READING AT THE UNIVERSITY OF WASHINGTON

The AI group at the University of Washington have developed a machine reading system with an open information extraction component [Poon et al., 2010].[13] The goal of the project was to develop a system that would essentially teach itself to gradually extract more and better knowledge. It would start with a simple bootstrapping process to find easily extractable knowledge by

---

[12]Co-training is a semi-supervised learning algorithm. Two models are trained separately on the same initial dataset represented by two sets of conditionally independent features. The models are used to enlarge iteratively each other's training set: they add instances with high confidence predictions produced by one model to the other model's training data [Blum and Mitchell, 1998].

[13]www.cs.washington.edu/research/machine-reading

exploiting redundancy and high-precision patterns, and use these to build more complex and comprehensive models via self-supervision.

The continuous work on this large-scale project shows an interesting evolution of relation extraction.

The initial open IE system, KnowItAll [Etzioni et al., 2005], implemented a form of bootstrapping using Hearst patterns. It evolved into TextRunner [Banko et al., 2007], a self-supervised system; TextRunner built models for specific relations from a small corpus, which were then applied to candidate extractions from a larger corpus. Bootstrapping returned in the Kylin system [Wu and Weld, 2007] and the WPE system [Hoffmann et al., 2010], this time using much larger seed sets—relations in Wikipedia infoboxes—combined with their associated articles; the purpose was to learn extractors for those relations.

There followed a step toward open information extraction: rely on part-of-speech information or dependency patterns to define how a relation "looks like". WOE [Wu and Weld, 2010], an extension of Kylin, used such patterns to define the possible expression of a relation as a phrase which consists of at least one verb or preposition. ReVerb [Fader et al., 2011] introduced lexical and syntactic constraints on potential relation expressions. The constraints allow the system to get cleaner extractions, with fewer uninformative or incoherent expressions. OLLIE [Mausam et al., 2012] improved on WOE by allowing more flexible patterns; they include nominals such as *Bill Gates, co-founder of Microsoft...*, which WOE would have missed. Patterns are gathered and generalized (e.g., from words to parts of speech), and that boosts recall.

Previous work in the project has noted the fact that some relations have dependencies: they are only true for some time, or are contingent on external conditions. That work, however, does not represent such additional information. OLLIE confronts these issues. Suppose a sentence was found to contain a dependent clause modifying the main assertion from which the relation was extracted. OLLIE adds a ClausalModifier field to the relation tuple.

This evolving line of research, embedded in a large-scale system, shows the robustness and endurance of bootstrapping, as well as interesting methods which address its weaknesses. The latest version of the OpenIE system built within this evolving framework is available on GitHub.[14]

4.8   SUMMARY

This chapter has reviewed methods which require little or no supervision, and aim for relation extraction from large text collections or from the Web. Bootstrapping is still a popular method. Its basic iterative match-and-extract process has been enhanced with measures which enable the filtering of candidate patterns and instances to avoid noise and semantic drift. Another trend is the development of large-scale KBs or structured knowledge repositories by collaborative endeavour over the Web. It has facilitated the development of distant and semi-supervised methods, which combine the strength of supervised and bootstrapping methods to process more

---

[14]knowitall.github.io/openie/

relations with better results. These methods are part of more traditional information extraction, where the relations to be learned are given to the system as seed pairs of patterns.

Open relation extraction aims for comprehensive relation extraction, often in combination with entity identification. Extreme methods model relations as hidden variables or consider very generic patterns based on word frequencies, which are iteratively clustered to counter the variation in the lexicalization of relation expressions. The adoption of variants of bootstrapping in large-scale knowledge acquisition systems like NELL and Machine Reading at the University of Washington shows the endurance of this research direction. Both projects have developed interesting methods of tackling the weaknesses of the basic bootstrapping algorithm. NELL employs coupled learning, and so takes advantage of the mutual constraints which argument-sharing relations impose on each other in order to get cleaner extractions. In Machine Reading, we find familiar patterns, evolved from automatically discovered sequences to patterns over parts of speech with a variety of restrictions.

The chapter has shown how the ever-increasing amount of available data can be both a boon and a challenge. The ample redundancy of Web-scale data can help make knowledge extraction systems more robust. On the other hand, it introduces a great deal of inaccurate information. The partly-supervised and unsupervised methods reviewed here can identify relations in texts while harnessing redundancy to deal with noise.

CHAPTER 5

Semantic Relations and Deep Learning

5.1 THE NEW PARADIGM

The theoretical foundations of artificial neural networks, inspired by biological processes, were laid in the 1940s [McCulloch and Pitts, 1943]. The firing of a neuron would represent a proposition, simulating logical calculus in a (neural) network by the activation or inhibition of connections. The perceptron, the algorithm behind the functioning of a single artificial neuron, was invented in the late 1950s [Rosenblatt, 1958]. There followed the layered structure of the networks familiar to us now, and the back-propagation mechanism, the core of the learning process in this paradigm. Rumelhart et al. [1986] showed how the back-propagation mechanism can lead to a useful representation on intermediate hidden layers, when they encoded people and family relationships.

The term *deep learning* is rather new, and the "take-over" of NLP is quite recent, driven mostly by the advances in hardware that have made the theoretical models computationally feasible and efficient on NLP's large-scale corpora, including the induction of semantic representations of words [Mikolov et al., 2013c]. Neural networks were fully formed by the time NLP adopted them. They came with many architectures and with mathematical models which the machine learning community developed over the intervening decades. The interplay goes both ways: the particular requirements of NLP tasks have spurred further developments and innovations.

The adoption of deep learning in work on semantic relations has led to methods and modelling assumptions unlike those explored in the previous chapters. There are differences at several levels.

Modelling. In the work described in the preceding chapters, the process of building representations for relation instances is separate from the model which learns to predict relations. First, relation instances are represented by a specially designed set of features; next, a machine-learning algorithm works on the training data represented by the chosen formalism. This two-step process is not necessary in the neural framework. Semantic relations and their arguments can be, and often are, encoded (that is to say, modelled) together. The encoding of entities depends on the

The penultimate version of this chapter is available at arxiv.org/abs/2009.05426.

semantic relations in which they participate, while the encoding of semantic relations depends on the arguments they connect.

Assumptions about relations.   Disjointness was one of the desiderata for a "good" list of semantic relations; see Section 2.1. The set of semantic relations would in effect partition the space of relation instances. This constraint was useful in traditional learning, where one seldom allowed an instance to belong to multiple classes. When relations which express world knowledge were added to the mix (e.g., *bornIn*, *diedIn*), it became common to have two entities connected by more than one semantic relation. In deep learning, the loss of this constraint is not troublesome. Neural networks can deal quite easily with multi-class learning. This means that one can use richer inventories of semantic relations, such as those coming from knowledge graphs (KGs), which are often multi-graphs: two vertices can be connected by edges of more than one type.

Data sources.   Traditional machine learning usually acts on a collection of instances, represented in a systematic manner. Information from different sources can be combined in one feature vector, but the production of feature values for pre-specified features may lead to loss of valuable structural or contextual information. In deep learning, hybrid models easily combine different sources of information such as free-form text and structured KGs. The use of data as a KG—a set of interconnected relation triples—affects the modelling of the arguments and of the relations.

We begin the chapter with a very high-level overview of deep learning in Section 5.2. We then revisit the research problems relevant to semantic relations, introduced in Section 3.3 and elaborated on in Chapters 3 and 4. Deep learning for semantic relations often combines in one architecture the processing of an entire sentence which contains a candidate relation. The matter of representing the meaning of the arguments will be intertwined with the representation of the context and the relational clues—the expression which connects the relation arguments, and the surrounding text. To make things clearer, and to allow for untried combinations, word representations (attributional features, Section 5.3) are presented separately from relation clues and context (relational features, Section 5.4). Section 5.5 discusses concerns around datasets, notably deep-learning solutions to distant supervision: how to get automatically, and handle, large amounts of noisy training data. Section 5.6 deals with the learning and modelling of semantic relations, either as particular structures or as neural models; it shows how argument representations and contextual clues are interwoven in various learning models.

The new possibilities in the learning of semantic relations have led to a wide variety of solutions; we survey them here. But new methods crop up even as we write, so this chapter is doomed to remain incomplete. The goal is to give the reader a solid overview of the current topics in relation learning, to elaborate on some of the solutions in the literature, and to point her, whenever possible, toward a reference which presents some of these matters in more detail.

5.2   A HIGH-LEVEL VIEW OF DEEP LEARNING FOR SEMANTIC RELATIONS

Our presentation relies on the reader's exposure to the theory and methods of deep learning. For the uninitiated, there are tutorials and books online. For example, Goodfellow et al. [2016] give an excellent account of deep learning paradigms and methods.[1] This section is a brief overview of the main concepts relevant to the task at hand.

A deep-learning algorithm accepts an input, usually represented as a real-valued vector, and applies to it a function which maps it onto some output values; those values determine the classification decision. In the case of semantic relations, the input represents a relation's arguments, its sentential context, additional relational information from a corpus, or a combination thereof. The output represents the prediction: does the posited relation hold between these arguments? The function and its parameters are the relation model, and it depends on the modelling assumptions and the underlying architecture. This sounds like traditional machine learning but there is an essential difference. In deep learning, model derivation (i.e., learning the parameter values) takes multiple steps of back-and-forth processing through the layers of the neural network. As a result, even the input state can be transformed according to the neural architecture, the parameters and the discrepancy between the expected and the computed output.

Consider an example. We can choose to give our neural network information only about a relation's arguments, as a concatenation of the representations of these arguments as real-valued vectors. If there is little training data, the representation can consist of vectors which were pretrained on very large corpora—now commonly known as *word embeddings* (see Section 5.3). They can be adjusted during training, or kept fixed. If a large amount of training data is available, the vectors can be seeded with random values which are then adjusted during training, so that in combination with the mapping function, i.e., the model, they produce a good approximation of the output, i.e., relation labels.

The mapping function can be a scoring function. Such a function combines the input vector $\mathbf{i}$ with the parameters $\mathbf{r}$ which model a target relation r,[2] with the output as a real value between 0 and 1:

$$f(\mathbf{i}, \mathbf{r}) \in [0, 1] \qquad (5.1)$$

To continue with our example, let us make the following assumptions:

- the input $\mathbf{i}$ consists of the embeddings for the relation's two arguments $\mathbf{v}_1$ and $\mathbf{v}_2$, which are real-valued vectors of size d: $\mathbf{v}_1, \mathbf{v}_2 \in \mathbb{R}^d$;
- the relation r is modelled as a $d \times d$ matrix $\mathbf{r}$: $\mathbf{r} \in \mathbb{R}^{d \times d}$;
- multiplication is chosen to model the interaction between the arguments and the relation.

---

[1]www.deeplearningbook.org.

[2]Throughout this chapter, representations—e.g., embeddings of entities and relations—are written in **bold**, and entities and relations in *italics*.

In this case, the mapping function will look as follows ($\top$ is matrix transposition):

$$f : \mathbb{R}^d \times \mathbb{R}^d \times \mathbb{R}^{d \times d} \to [0, 1] \tag{5.2}$$

$$f(\mathbf{v}_1, \mathbf{v}_2, \mathbf{r}) = \mathbf{v}_1^\top \mathbf{r} \, \mathbf{v}_2 \tag{5.3}$$

This is actually a model called RESCAL [Nickel et al., 2011]. f should return 1 if relation r holds between these arguments, 0 otherwise. In practice, the function will return a real value in [0,1].[3] During training, the parameters will be adjusted in order to bring the value as close to the actual expected value as possible. During testing, a preset threshold usually helps determine if a new combination ($\mathbf{v}_i, \mathbf{r}, \mathbf{v}_j$) represents the instance of a relation r which holds between arguments i and j represented by their corresponding vectors.

A mapping function can be almost arbitrarily complex, and can be implemented by various neural network architectures. Let us engage for a while in name-dropping—and acronym-dropping. At our disposal, there are recurrent neural networks (RNN), convolutional neural networks (CNN) or stacks of different types of neural networks, so as to model different types of interactions between the various parts of the input. Each architecture has its own implementation choices, e.g., long short-term memory units (LSTM), rectified linear activation units (ReLU) or gated recurrent units (GRU), each with its own specific properties which make them more suitable for some applications than for others. Long sequences are often encoded with, e.g., a bidirectional RNN using LSTM (BiLSTM). The latest advance is the Transformer architecture, starting with the Bidirectional Encoder Representations from Transformers (BERT) [Devlin et al., 2018, 2019][4] and Generative Pretrained Transformer (GPT).[5] The input vector itself can be the output of a neural network.

The parameters of the model are learned during training. The output of a computational unit is a function over the input combined with the unit's weights—its internal parameters. The algorithm uses a *loss function* to compare the predicted output of the entire network to the expected output (referred to as the gold standard). The difference between the expected output and the one actually produced, together with a learning rate, determines the amount by which the internal parameters should change so that the error will be reduced. To avoid overfitting the training data, the loss function can include a *regularization* factor. This factor biases the model toward a simpler one which obeys specific constraints on the parameters: representations close in the Euclidean space, fewer non-zero weights, and so on.

Dropout [Srivastava et al., 2014] can also help avoid overfitting. The idea of dropout is that nodes in the network (both their inputs and outputs) are randomly ignored during training. This, in effect, resembles training in parallel a large number of configurations for a neural network.

---

[3] A softmax function may be necessary to map the actual value into the [0,1] interval.

[4] Devlin et al.'s [2018] truly seminal paper on BERT has started a veritable cottage industry. There are versions named SpanBERT, StructBERT, DistilBERT, BERTje, CamemBERT, FlauBERT, RobBERT, KnowBERT, MobilBERT, BERTweet, RuBERT—with certainly **much** more to come.

[5] openai.com/blog/language-unsupervised/

Such a random configuration of nodes makes the training process noisy, and that forces each of the nodes in a layer to contribute more to the final output, to compensate for the inactive ones. It also simulates sparse activation from a given layer, and that encourages the network to actually learn a sparse representation as a side-effect.

When people look at a sentence with an instance of a semantic relation, they see which parts of the sentence are relevant in deciding if the relation holds. The *attention mechanism*—an important enhancement to the neural machinery—allows us to model this insight. An implementation of attention filters the representation of the relation instance through a set of weights, and so boosts the contribution of certain parts of a layer in the network (e.g., specific words in the context on the input layer) while limiting the effect of others. These weights, as everything in the model, are learned during training.

This chapter will present several options for each of these aspects of deep learning in the task of semantic relation classification. Sections 5.3 and 5.4 describe types of input. Section 5.3 shows how to represent a relation's arguments given only an unstructured text collection, only a KG or a wordnet, or both. Section 5.4 shows how to represent the relational features when taking into account individual words, word sequences, or phrases with grammatical information. Section 5.6 describes architectures which combine the input with internal parameters in a variety of models useful in detecting and classifying semantic relations.

In this chapter, we often write that a representation of words or relations obtained by deep learning is *induced*. We want to clarify the term here, because it helps distinguish between what is deliberately learned, and what is a felicitous side-effect. As noted in the foregoing, learning in neural networks means determining iteratively the best values of internal parameters which lead to a good mapping of the input onto the expected output. The process has "side-effects", such as the adjustment of the starting input representations, the representation computed by a hidden layer which summarizes the larger-sized input in a useful and compressed manner, and so on. Such side-effects are not the target of the learning process, and their emergence (as it comes about in working with the data provided) can be seen as not deliberate. When a deep-learning formalism discovers semantic relations, the aim is to map an input instance (e.g., a sentence) onto a relation type. The representations of arguments, relations or even sentences are a useful by-product.

5.3 ATTRIBUTIONAL FEATURES: WORD EMBEDDINGS

The identification of the semantic relation for a given pair of arguments relies heavily on a good representation of the meaning of the arguments, and of the context in which they appear—if such context is available. Section 3.3.1 reviewed a few methods of representing lexical semantics. Word embeddings in continuous vector spaces are another type of distributional representation. The vectors are no longer indexed by specific words but by more abstract dimensions, assumed to model some underlying latent semantic characteristics of words or entities. Such a representation projects words/entities/morphemes into a multi-dimensional space, in which distance is a proxy for relatedness or similarity. Depending on the data to be modelled or the task at hand, the source of word embeddings can be distributional information (Section 5.3.1), graphs which capture a relational model of meaning (Section 5.3.2), or a combination thereof (Section 5.3.3).

5.3.1   WORD EMBEDDINGS FROM TEXTS

When a large corpus is available, word meaning can be encoded in a very informative way by distributional representations based on co-occurrences in a window or on grammatical relations. The beauty of such representations is that they are easy to interpret given that the dimensions are themselves words. There are, however, considerable drawbacks.

- The vectors are very large: the vocabulary is often on the order of at least 10^5.
- The dimensions are words, so they are ambiguous, e.g., *run* can refer to exercising, standing for office or executing a program.
- Multiple dimensions can refer to the same thing or perhaps to closely related things, e.g., *buy* and *purchase*.
- Words as dimensions do not solve the sparseness problem because only the same shared dimension indicates an overlap in meaning between words.

A number of methods have been proposed to induce a representation for words in a space with fewer dimensions, much lower than the dimensions in a distributional representation. The number d of dimensions is a preset parameter. A high value of d will lead to a larger but more precise representation, while a lower value will yield a more abstract representation. Finding the best balance between these options often depends on the task; commonly chosen values for d are in the hundreds.

Furnas et al. [1988] applied Singular Value Decomposition (SVD) to the approximation of a word-document co-occurrence matrix. In the process, they uncovered the latent semantic structure of words and documents as low-dimensional vectors in a new space with orthogonal dimensions.[6] SVD is presented schematically in Figure 5.1. This was a step toward projecting words (and documents) into a continuous low-dimensional vector space.

In follow-up work, Jolliffe [2002] showed that Principal Component Analysis (PCA), a variation of SVD, can project the word-document vectors into a lower-dimensional space, and that can help reveal the hidden structure of the data.

SVD and PCA rely on a mathematical theory of decomposing a matrix into a product of matrices, each taken to correspond to some part of the input. These methods are applied to fully specified matrices, i.e., matrices whose every cell has a defined value.[7] To induce word or document representations using SVD and PCA, one most commonly works with word-document or word-word co-occurrence matrices. The values in such matrices can be either binary (record-

---

[6]The dimensions were low in comparison with the size of the vocabulary, which was the base for standard distributional bag-of-words representations.

[7]This contrasts with adjacency matrices for KGs—presented later in the chapter—which have mostly unspecified values.

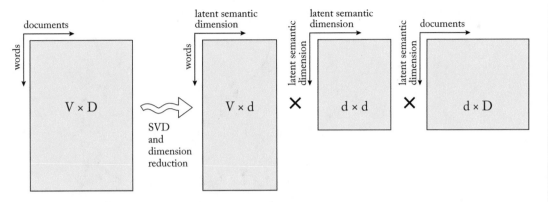

Figure 5.1: A schematic representation of approximating a word-document matrix by means of Singular Value Decomposition. V is the size of the vocabulary, D is the number of documents in the corpus, and d is the chosen reduced number of dimensions.

ing simple co-occurrence), or real-valued (getting frequency, perhaps normalized, tf-idf or PMI scores).

Topic modelling seldom has the express purpose of deriving vector representations for words. Even so, topics can be viewed as high-level, abstract, semantic dimensions, and they can be used to produce a representation of words in terms of the probability of their appearance under each of the posited topics [Blei et al., 2003, Steyvers and Griffiths, 2006].

Bengio et al. [2003] developed a probabilistic framework for predicting a word from the previously seen words. Every word is encoded as a vector, and a window-based context surrounds a target word. After random initialization, the word representations are adjusted to maximize the probability of the seen text. Bengio et al.'s innovation was that they used a neural network to encode the probability function of word sequences in terms of the feature vectors of the words in the sequence. This allowed the system to learn together the vector representations of the words and the parameters of the function. Collobert and Weston [2008] expanded this framework to multi-task learning.

Real-valued vectors which represent word meanings have been more widely adopted since deep-learning methods became widespread in NLP, and renamed as *word embeddings*; see Figure 5.2. Mikolov et al. [2013b,c] developed two complementary techniques of inducing word embeddings, i.e., d-dimensional real-valued vector representations of words. The *skip-gram model* induces the "true" vector for each word by learning to predict the context (the surrounding words) given a word. The *continuous bag-of-words (BOW) model* induces word representations while learning to predict a word given its context.

It has also been noted that the word embeddings induced by this method acquire several types of syntactic and semantic information about words. Such information is reflected as regularities in the relative position of words in the low-dimensional vector space: plurals, derivations,

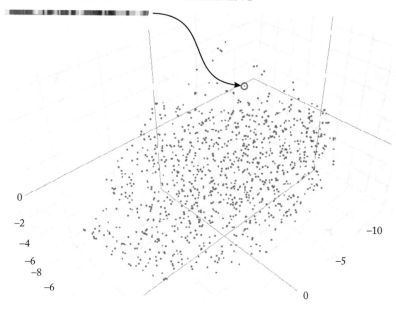

Figure 5.2: Example of a word embedding as a real-valued vector, projected into a 3D-space for visualization.

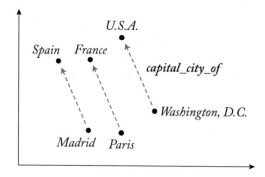

Figure 5.3: Semantic relations as relative positions of their arguments.

analogies, and so on [Ethayarajh et al., 2019]. That allows one to use vector arithmetics on word embeddings as proxies for syntactic and semantic operations on words.

These operations can also be useful in establishing that different argument pairs are in the same semantic relation. For example, it can be verified that the relative positions of the first and the second arguments are consistent, e.g., that the vectors connecting capital cities to their respective countries tend to be parallel; see Figure 5.3. Most of the time, there is a more complicated connection between the arguments' position in this space and the relation between them. Nonetheless, even a complex model of relations relies on there being a degree of similarity (maybe only along certain dimensions) between a relation's arguments across numerous instances.

There are many methods of inducing word embeddings. Each method leverages slightly differently the information in a word's context, emphasizes different aspects of a word's meaning, or produces a context-specific embedding. The earliest methods produced "stand-alone" embeddings. Mikolov et al. [2013c] worked with a context window, Pennington et al. [2014] with grammatical collocations. Iacobacci et al. [2015], Neelakantan et al. [2014] and Pilehvar and Collier [2016] derive word-sense embeddings.

Sennrich et al. [2016] produce embeddings below the word level. To segment words, they use character n-gram models and a byte-pair encoding compression algorithm. The motivation comes from the problem of out-of-vocabulary words in machine translation.

Word embeddings are, in effect, projections of words into a multi-dimensional space; the words' coordinates in the new space preserve their specific properties. For example, semantically or functionally similar words should be close in such a space. Most models project words onto a Euclidean space, and take various distance metrics as proxies for word similarity.

Other types of spaces may be even more appropriate for meaning representation. Nickel and Kiela [2017] embed words into a hyperbolic space, or more precisely into a Poincaré ball; that is a topologically open space bounded by a d-dimensional sphere with unit radius, $B^d = \{x \in \mathbb{R}^d \mid \|x\| < 1\}$.

Distances in this space are measured along its equivalent of straight lines: arcs orthogonal to the space's surface boundary. Nickel and Kiela show that the properties of hyperbolic spaces make this kind of representation particularly suited to the modelling of hierarchical data. Distances between words in the hyperbolic space mirror distances between nodes in a tree: distances between words closer to the root (situated somewhere close to the center of the ball) will be larger than distances between words closer to the leaves. Figure 5.4 shows the projection in two dimensions of the embeddings in the Poincaré space for words in WordNet. Nickel and Kiela [2018] further optimize this by embedding the taxonomy in the Lorentz model of hyperbolic space.

Contextualized word embeddings are the most recent development. Embeddings from Language Models (ELMo) [Peters et al., 2018] employ a neural architecture based on BiLSTMs. ELMo captures different characteristics of the input words at different levels of the neural architecture, corresponding roughly to characters, syntax and semantics; the representation of a word is a combination of the representations at these levels. Bidirectional Encoder Representations from Transformers (BERT) [Devlin et al., 2018, 2019] dynamically produce word representations informed by the surrounding words. BERT's architecture—the transformer architecture—is based on attention. Improvements on these models keep coming, for example A Lite BERT (ALBERT) [Lan et al., 2020] (it separates a "general" and lower-dimensional word embeddings from a higher-dimension contextualized representation on the upper levels of the network), Ro-

Figure 5.4: Two-dimensional Poincaré embeddings of transitive closure of WordNet's mammal subtree [Nickel and Kiela, 2017].

bustly Optimized BERT Pretraining (ROBERTa) [Liu et al., 2019c], and Text-To-Text Transfer Transformer (T5) [Raffel et al., 2019].

Many of the embedding methods supply pretrained word embeddings in a number of languages, or even cross-lingual data such as XLM [Conneau et al., 2019]. These representations, built from very large corpora, can be used as-is, or they can be fine-tuned (or retrofitted) during the relation-learning process. If the relation dataset is large enough—as are some KGs—the representation of the arguments can be fine-tuned or even learned together with the relation models.

5.3.2   WORD/ENTITY EMBEDDINGS FROM KNOWLEDGE GRAPHS

The word embeddings discussed thus far came from distributional representations of words in unstructured texts. Words/entities can also be represented by relational models: their meaning is identified by their relations with other words (as in a wordnet) or other entities (as in a KG). Wordnets and KGs are symbolic structures but they can be cast into continuous low-dimensional vector spaces. Representations for nodes (words/entities) and edges (relations) can be derived jointly, and these representations encode the relational (graph) structure. Such representations arise from matrix factorization or can be learned by various types of neural networks.

Matrix factorization works on the adjacency matrix or matrices, representing the graph. The factorization operation has a parallel scoring function which combines the representation of entities and relations, and mirrors the factorization split. For example, the bilinear model RESCAL [Nickel et al., 2011] described briefly in Section 5.2 is a matrix factorization model. The adjacency matrix A_k for relation r_k is factorized as $A_k = E^\top M_k E$; every column of matrix E corresponds to an entity embedding, and M_k is the representation of relation r_k. The scoring function parallels this expression; each entry in matrix A_k corresponding to a triple (e_i, r_k, e_j) is computed as

$$f_{ijk} = \mathbf{v}_i^\top M_k \mathbf{v}_j \tag{5.4}$$

This function has a clear mathematical expression in terms of the representations of the entities and the relation. The scoring function can also be learned by a neural network, and then it is modelled by the chosen architecture and its learned parameters.

Formally, a graph $G = \{\mathcal{V}, \mathcal{R}, \mathcal{E}\}$ is a triple: vertices, relation types and edges.[8]

$$
\begin{aligned}
\mathcal{V} &= \{x_i \mid i = 1, n\} \\
\mathcal{R} &= \{r_k \mid k = 1, m\} \\
\mathcal{E} &= \{(x_i, r_k, x_j) \mid x_i, x_j \in \mathcal{V},\ r_k \in \mathcal{R}\}
\end{aligned}
\tag{5.5}
$$

To embed a graph is to find a representation $\mathbf{v}_x$ for each vertex $x \in \mathcal{V}$, and a representation $\mathbf{r}_k$ for each relation $r_k \in \mathcal{R}$. This is based on information about edges—the relation instances (x_i, r_k, x_j). The usual assumption is that each $\mathbf{v}_x \in \mathbb{R}^d$ is a d-dimensional real-valued vector, with d chosen *a priori*. The relation can be a vector, a matrix, a higher-order tensor (for n-ary relations, $n > 2$), and so on.

Other representations are possible. For example, in a KG built from grammatical relations—so that an edge represents a (*subject, verb, object*) triple—it could make sense to represent these as pairs with composite arguments: (*subject–verb, object*) or (*subject, verb–object*), and so constrain the representation of the arguments with the given relation. Consider an example. If the subject and the verb in (*man, climb, mountain*) are combined, the pair to be represented will be (*man–climb, mountain*). That will constrain the (composite) first argument *man–climb* only to objects which a man can climb, as opposed to the more general and separate representations of *man* and *climb*. Figure 5.5 shows the different types of graph representations as adjacency matrices obtained when following these various representations of a relation triple.

---

[8]There are various terms in graph theory. A *vertex* can also be called a *node*, and an *edge* referred to as an *arc*. We will not try to standardize the terminology because the context is quite unambiguous.

Adjacency tensor	Adjacency matrix (entity pair)	Adjacency matrix (relation–entity pair)

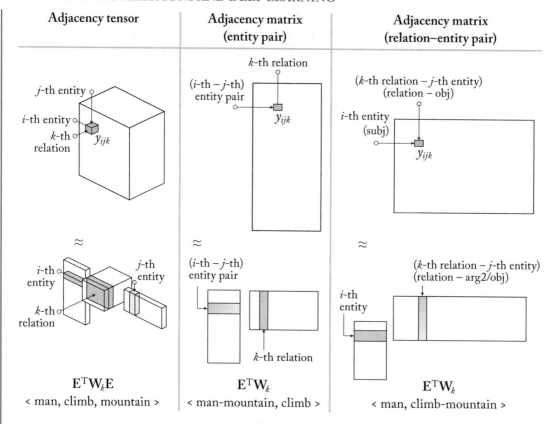

Figure 5.5: Representations of vertices and relations in a graph for different views of relation tuples. The adjacency tensor illustration comes from Nickel et al. [2016a].

The adjacency matrix or tensor of a graph, A, contains information about the connectivity structure. For a graph containing relation types r_k, A's elements are:

$$a_{ijk} = \begin{cases} 1 & \text{if } (i, r_k, j) \in \mathcal{E} \\ NaN & \text{if } (i, r_k, j) \notin \mathcal{E} \end{cases} \tag{5.6}$$

1 is the only defined value in A (Not-a-Number is the other). That is because KGs represent only positive instances, i.e., only known relation instances. To learn a non-trivial model, some negative instances are required. Section 5.6.1 will explain the assumptions needed to produce negative relation instances, as a set $\mathcal{E}'$ of "negative edges". The corresponding *scoring function* $f_{i,j,k}$ parallels the information in the adjacency matrix, and uses the negative edges to learn

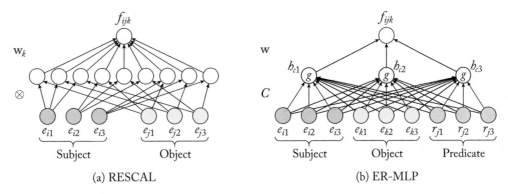

(a) RESCAL   (b) ER-MLP

Figure 5.6: Embedding graphs with neural networks, two examples from Nickel et al. [2016a]. In essence, they learn/implement the scoring function f_{ijk}. (a) A neural network implements the RESCAL matrix factorization model; the representation of the relation is given by the parameters of the hidden layer. (b) A neural network implementation takes a (*subject, predicate, object*) triple as an input; the embedding of the relation (i.e., the *predicate*) is learned in parallel with the representation of the *subject* and the *object*.

non-trivial models:

$$f_{ijk} = f(\mathbf{v}_i, \mathbf{r}_k, \mathbf{v}_j) = \begin{cases} 1 & \text{if } (i, r_k, j) \in \mathcal{E} \\ 0 & \text{if } (i, r_k, j) \in \mathcal{E}' \end{cases} \qquad (5.7)$$

The function can combine the representation of the entities and relations in various ways. Table 5.2 in Section 5.6.1 shows examples.

Depending on the assumptions about the mathematical form of the representations of entities and relations, and the function f, these representations can be induced by matrix factorization, as illustrated in Figure 5.5, or by deep-learning methods, as shown on two concrete examples in Figure 5.6. Levy and Goldberg [2014a] very nicely explain the equivalences among some of these methods. Comprehensive overviews of such methods appear in Nickel et al. [2016b], Wang et al. [2017] and Ji et al. [2020]. Section 5.6.1 discusses the effect of these representation on relation learning.

The structure of the KG directly affects the representations of entities and relations in it. More frequent relations have more informative representations because their adjacency matrices are denser. Low-frequency relations, particularly when they connect low-frequency entities, have less informative representations. An analysis of the profile of some of the most frequently used KGs shows that this is a real concern. Figure 5.7 illustrates it for Freebase and NELL: most of the nodes appear in very few relations, numerous relations have very few instances. This imbalance can be partially countered by the use of entity type information and relation schemata. Such information can be included as an additional factor in the scoring function and in the

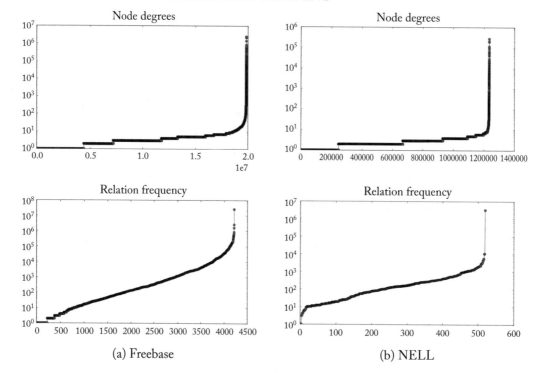

Figure 5.7: KG statistics on a logarithmic scale: relation and node frequencies for frequently used subsets of Freebase and NELL (data from Gardner et al. [2014]). Every data point is the degree of a node (top plots), or the frequency of a relation (bottom plots). The data points are ordered monotonically. The x axis is just an index.

loss function [Kotnis and Nastase, 2017, Ren et al., 2017], or can help organize and optimize adjacency matrix factorization [Chang et al., 2014].

The origins of graph embedding go back a few decades. Rumelhart et al. [1986] used a neural network with several hidden layers to learn and predict family relationships. They noted that the network weights and the hidden layers capture representations for the entities (people) and their relationships; that allowed them to predict the second argument of a relation given the first argument and the relation. The weights and node values in the network were not used outside the specific experiment.

Paccanaro and Hinton [2002] deliberately set out to induce concept representations from binary relations between concepts in a process they call *linear relational embedding*. They aim for n-dimensional vector representations of concepts, and $n \times n$ matrix representations of relations. When a relation is R^c applied to a concept a^c—multiplying the corresponding matrix $\mathbf{R}^c$ by the vector $\mathbf{a}^c$—the result is expected to be a related concept b^c with representation $\mathbf{b}^c$. Paccanaro and

Hinton obtain the concept and relation representations by maximizing a *discriminative goodness function G*. It rewards all concepts which can fill the same $(a^c, R^c, *)$ spot, while maximizing each concept's distance to other concepts nearby (to avoid collapsing all representations to zero).

$$G = \sum_{c=1}^{C} \frac{1}{K_c} \log \frac{e^{-\|\mathbf{R}^c \mathbf{a}^c - \mathbf{b}^c\|_2}}{\sum_{\mathbf{v}_i \in \mathbf{V}} e^{-\|\mathbf{R}^c \mathbf{a}^c - \mathbf{v}_i\|_2}} \tag{5.8}$$

$K_c = |\{(a^c, R^c, *)\}|$ and $\mathbf{V}$ is the set of all vector representations. This discriminative goodness function is approximated using gradient ascent.

Matrix factorization for the representation of entities in interconnected data was initially motivated by the goal of clustering multi-type interrelated data objects, for example papers, keywords, authors and venues in the domain of scientific publications, or movies, actors and genres in the movie domain [Long et al., 2006]. Clustering was achieved by collective factorization of matrices which represent each relation type (e.g., *movie_genre*, *movie_rating*). Two matrices are related if their row or column indices (i.e., their first or second arguments) refer to the same set of objects. Long et al.'s focus was on clustering, reflected in the matrix factorization as a product of cluster and cluster association information. The representation of concepts—their association with the induced clusters—is a side-effect not explicitly applied outside these experiments.

Singh and Gordon [2008] address directly the task of relation learning for similar multi-type interrelated data. Unlike Long et al., they use matrix factorization to derive entity and relation representations, and focus on predicting new relation instances in a dataset which covers information about movies (genres, rating, and so on). Each matrix to be factorized represents instances of one relation type. Like in Long et al.'s work, Singh and Gordon's collective matrix factorization relies on shared arguments among relations to connect the factors of the different matrices.

The left and right arguments of a relation can have different roles. It may be useful for an entity a to have two different representations, a_L and a_R, depending on the role it plays. Sutskever and Hinton [2009] induce such a representation by combining topic modelling with matrix factorization. The latent variables in the topic model represent entity and relation clusters. A cluster is represented by its mean and diagonal covariance, and the dual representations for an entity are sampled as vectors from the corresponding cluster. The score of a triple (a_L, r, b_R) is determined by the product of their representations $\mathbf{a}_L{}^\top \mathbf{R} \mathbf{b}_R$, and that is determined by the clusters to which a, R and b belong.

Bordes et al. [2011] use a neural network to induce entity and relation representations. Entities are represented as d-dimensional vectors, and each relation as two $d \times d$ matrices $R_k \approx (\mathbf{R}_k^{lhs}, \mathbf{R}_k^{rhs})$. Bordes et al. hypothesize that if a transformation is applied to each of the two relation arguments e_i, e_j, then they should become similar. The scoring function, then, is this:

$$f(e_i, r_k, e_j) = \left\| \mathbf{R}_k^{lhs} \mathbf{v}_i - \mathbf{R}_k^{rhs} \mathbf{v}_j \right\| \tag{5.9}$$

KGs can also be embedded in non-Euclidean spaces. Balazevic et al. [2019] introduce a method of embedding a multi-relational graph in a Poincaré space. Their Multi-Relation Poincaré (MuRP) model learns relation-specific parameters which transform the embeddings of source/target entities. If a relation holds between a source and a target entity, their transformed embeddings are close in the Poincaré space.

Weber and Nickel [2018] discuss and compare the types of embedding spaces with respect to their sectional curvature κ: Euclidean ($\kappa = 0$), spherical ($\kappa = 1$), and hyperboloid ($\kappa = -1$). They note that none of these spaces is optimal for all relational structures. There arises the question of identifying the most suitable embedding space for a given KG. Weber and Nickel analyze the characteristics of local graph neighbourhoods, which they call "motifs". A matching space is the space in which the graph motifs can be embedded with the least distortion (or with none). Here are the spaces particularly suited to certain embeddings: hyperbolic spaces (such as the Poincaré space) for tree structures, spherical spaces for n-cycles, and Euclidean spaces for grid structures. The match is apt because the growth rate of these structures matches the growth rate and curvature of the space with respect to its parameters (e.g., radius). Weber and Nickel compute a heuristic which estimates the growth rate of a graph from its motifs, and map it onto a curvature value. This determines the best space for embedding the graph.

Nodes in a graph, as well as relations, can also be encoded by methods similar to language models. Perozzi et al. [2014] transform a (social) network into a set of "sentences": sequences of nodes obtained by random walks started on different nodes of the network. Every such sentence represents part of a node's neighbourhood information. They are processed by a method similar to the SkipGram model; the obtained node embeddings maximize the probability that the nodes appear in the observed sequences. Wang et al.'s [2020] method is similar; it combines "sentences"—random walks over the graph—with a multi-layered BiLSTM which encodes contextual information. The entity and relation embeddings are weighted linear combinations of the model's internal states from each layer of the model.

A graph contains various types of structural information which should be reflected in a node's representation. The neighbourhood of a node can help describe its structural role (e.g., as hubs), while dense paths among nodes define node communities. Grover and Leskovec [2016] aim to develop a graph embedding method in which the node representations reflect all these structural characteristics. Nodes in a closely connected community should be close in the embedding space. Nodes with the same structural roles should have similar representations, too. The proposed node2vec model finds node representations which maximize the probability of their neighbourhoods. The local neighbourhood of a node is best described by paths found using breadth-first search (BFS), whereas more distant connections and community structure are best captured by depth-first search (DFS). Random walks can produce paths which combine characteristics of BFS and DFS to various degrees. Grover and Leskovec experiment with two parameters which can bias a random walker toward BFS or DFS. The node representations based on the random walks so obtained lead to state-of-the-art results on a variety of applications, including link prediction on Facebook and a protein-protein interaction network.

5.3.3 WORD/ENTITY EMBEDDINGS FROM TEXTS AND KNOWLEDGE GRAPHS

The distributional model and the relational model of language complement each other. Their combination could create a richer and more informative representation of meaning: it would identify both the syntagmatic and the paradigmatic information about words.

There are differences between the unstructured language of texts and the consistent—normalized/canonical—representation of nodes and relations in structured KGs. The differences must be reconciled to take advantage of the information from both these sources. It would be good to be able to "recognize", or leverage somehow, concepts from KGs which surface in texts with different lexicalizations; the same goes for relations.

One can add text co-occurrence information—(*subject, verb, object*) triples extracted by an open information extraction system (Open IE)[9]—to the adjacency matrix, and factorize this enhanced matrix to learn shared embeddings of entities and relations in KGs and in text [Riedel et al., 2013]. Each argument pair, whether from the graph or from the text, has a corresponding row in the matrix; each relation and predicate has a column. The scoring function for modelling the adjacency information in this matrix combines a few kinds of data: latent feature compatibility between an argument tuple and a relation, neighbourhood information which benefits from relation similarity, and selectional preferences of relations expressed by the entity models of their arguments.

Riedel et al. take the atomic view of nodes and relations from the graph, and of arguments and predicates from texts. This means that the procedure relies on (exact) overlaps between arguments and relations in the KG and triples extracted by Open IE. The lexical expressions of predicates and arguments from texts, as well as the forms of relations and nodes from structured knowledge repositories, can be leveraged to find deeper similarities. For example, the knowledge base (KB) relation *person/organizations_founded* between a person and the organization which they founded can occur in texts as `founder of`, `co-founded`, `one of the founders of`, `helped establish`, and so on. Toutanova et al. [2015] use a convolutional neural network to get a vector representation for all textual and KB relations based on their expressions. From these representations, they compute the similarity between predicates and relations, and between nodes and arguments from texts. This similarity is further exploited in the loss function which finds an approximation of the adjacency matrix combining KB information and textual relations.

Alsuhaibani et al. [2019] learn hierarchical word embeddings from a corpus and a taxonomy. The taxonomy supplies data about all the ancestors of a word in the taxonomy, and the corpus provides information on the co-occurrence of a word and those ancestors. The signal for tuning the embeddings comes from both sources. The objective function on the taxonomy tries

---

[9]e.g., stanfordnlp.github.io/CoreNLP/openie.html

to push the embedding of a word in the taxonomy toward a distance-weighted average of the embeddings of its ancestors. The objective function on the corpus tries to push the embeddings of co-occurring words toward more similarity.

Section 5.6.3 gives a deeper overview of the combination of KGs and unstructured texts which aims to derive entity and relation representations for learning semantic relations.

5.4 RELATIONAL FEATURES: MODELLING THE CONTEXT

Section 3.3.2 introduced the relational features which characterize the relation either directly (e.g., via an expression or a dependency path between the two relation arguments in a given context), or by background relational features, i.e., a collection of patterns from a large corpus. The length and the syntactic complexity of such expressions vary, so it is problematic to model them formally in order to provide a learning system with a consistent form. Convolution and tree kernels are frequent solutions in traditional machine learning methods. One can also project background relational features into a fixed-size low-dimensional space. There are solutions particularly suitable to deep learning: learning a composition function which produces a representation of fixed dimensions—usually a vector, a matrix, or both—for any input string (Section 5.4.1 discusses compositionality), or representing and using directly a complex tree or graph structure (Section 5.4.2 discusses graph neural networks).

5.4.1 COMPOSITIONALITY

The context—and even the relation arguments—can have variable length. The relevant clues for relation learning can be spread across one or more words, which can appear in different positions and in different grammatical roles. Various methods have been developed to represent such information as a fixed-size data structure and to use it efficiently for relation classification. They assemble the representation of a text fragment, taking into account different types of information, e.g., the word sequence, the grammatical information, direct dependency paths, or the entire dependency structure. One can also make assumptions about what the final representation will be (a vector, a matrix, or both), and so design an architecture which models an appropriate composition function. This section presents several ways of assembling the textual clues and the context of a relation instance. It focuses on compositionality not as a general concept and set of techniques but as specific techniques already tried in the context of relation extraction or classification. That is why it will not discuss configurations of recurrent and recursive neural networks, convolutional neural networks or transformers not yet applied in relation learning. In theory, at least, one can use any technique which builds a semantic representation for a text fragment of variable length to represent this kind of contextual information.

Averaged Representation

The representation of a phrase as the average of the (distributional) representations of its words is a good approximation of the meaning of a phrase, despite the simplicity and the obvious disregard for word order [Mitchell and Lapata, 2010]. A phrase x of n words $x = w_1, w_2, \ldots, w_n$, would be represented as

$$\mathbf{v}_x = \frac{\sum_{i=1}^{n} \mathbf{v}_{w_i}}{n} \tag{5.10}$$

where $\mathbf{v}_{w_i}$ is the embedding of word w_i. It is trivial to get such a representation for word embeddings, which are real-valued vectors.

Part-of-speech (POS) information and the grammatical role which a word plays in a sentence can add knowledge useful for representing the meaning of a word in context. So, word embeddings can be combined with additional features, e.g., syntactic roles or a word's POS, to represent sentence substructures. Gormley et al. [2015] compute *substructure embeddings* $h_{w_i} = f_{w_i} \otimes v_{w_i}$, where f_{w_i} is a vector of hand-crafted features, and $\otimes$ is the outer product. The *annotated phrase embedding* sums over the substructure embeddings:

$$\mathbf{v}_x = \sum_{i=1}^{n} h_{w_i} = \sum_{i=1}^{n} f_{w_i} \otimes \mathbf{v}_{w_i} \tag{5.11}$$

Such a model can integrate in the low-dimensional continuous representation of words either additional information from those words' (local or global) context, or general information such as types or categories.

Recurrent Neural Networks

Taking into account the word order, a phrase can be encoded as a sequence of words. The representation of a phrase can be derived by an RNN which combines at each (time) step t the representation of words $w_1, w_2, \ldots, w_{t-1}$ with the current word w_t [Mikolov et al., 2010]. An RNN has an input layer connected to one or more hidden layers, and an output layer. The activation on the hidden layer at the last step is customarily taken as the sequence encoding. The output layer depends on the task (e.g., at each step t it is a word in a target language, or the type or topic of the sentence in a classification task), and feedback trains or fine-tunes the input word representations and the weights of the hidden layers. The hidden state is updated at each step t with the representation $\mathbf{v}_{w_t}$ of the current word w_t:

$$h_t = f(h_{t-1}, \mathbf{v}_{w_t}) \tag{5.12}$$

f is a nonlinear activation function, e.g., an element-wise logistic sigmoid function or an LSTM/GRU/ReLU unit.

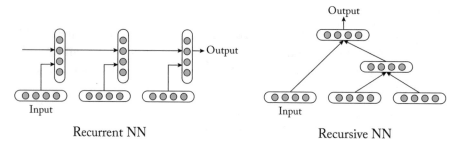

Figure 5.8: Recurrent and recursive neural networks [Socher et al., 2011b].

A bi-directional RNN can also be used. At each time step t, the hidden layer combines two representations: one for the forward sequence (as for the regular RNN), the other for the backward sequence (the input phrase in reverse order, to allow the model to see the "future", i.e., the upcoming words).

An RNN helps ensure that word order is accounted for, and that a word sequence of arbitrary length can be encoded as a fixed-length vector which then serves as an input to a relation classifier, typically another neural network. In practice, RNN units such as LSTMs [Hochreiter and Schmidhuber, 1997] or GRUs [Cho et al., 2014] are used to address such matters as vanishing (or exploding) gradients during back-propagation.[10]

Recursive Neural Networks

While RNNs model word order, word relations beyond linear order, e.g., grammatical structure, might also be worth modelling. The next level of complexity are recursive neural networks, which can create a bottom-up representation for a tree-structured context by recursively combining representations of sibling nodes—see Figure 5.8.

Given a phrase x of n words, $x = w_1, \ldots, w_n$, and a tree which represents its syntactic structure in some formalism, a recursive neural network assembles the representation of the phrase bottom-up:

$$\mathbf{a}_{i,j} = f(\mathbf{a}_i, \mathbf{a}_j) \qquad (5.13)$$

$\mathbf{a}_{i,j}$ is the representation of the node $a_{i,j}$ in the hierarchical structure of the phrase, with children a_i and a_j. A child can be an internal node in this structure, assembled from the representation on *its* children, or a leaf node. For the latter, the representation will be the embedding of the corresponding word: $\mathbf{a}_i = \mathbf{v}_{w_i}$. The function f can take different forms, just as it does for RNNs.

---

[10]www.cs.toronto.edu/~rgrosse/courses/csc321_2017/readings/L15%20Exploding%20and%20Vanishing%20Gradients.pdf

Incorporating Dependency Paths

The methods noted before—the averaged representation and the composition via RNNs and recursive neural networks—have slowly incorporated more and more of the available contextual information, including grammatical structural information. The next step is to include information about the type of grammatical relations which connect the nodes in the tree or graph representation of the context of a relation instance.

Section 3.3.2 explained how relational features pick out evidence about two entities' interaction in a given context. One of the successfully applied types of relational features is the dependency path which connects the potential relation arguments.

When it comes to the dependency structure, several levels of information can describe the connection between two words in a sentence. The first level is the dependency path, a linear chain or a tree with two linear branches. The nodes on this basic path can have more dependencies, which lie outside the path of interest but may add information relevant to their meaning or role in the path. Such "side" dependencies makes it an *augmented dependency path* [Liu et al., 2015], with a more complex tree structure which can be encoded with string/tree/graph kernels—see Section 3.4.2. In deep learning, it can also be encoded with various types of neural networks which gradually assemble the context into a fixed-size input, and in effect implement a compositionality function.

The dependency path can be viewed as two branches which join the relation arguments with a common ancestor [Xu et al., 2016]. Either branch can be encoded separately, and with various types of information: words, parts of speech, grammatical relations, WordNet hypernyms, and so on. The dependency relations depicted in Figure 5.9 are encoded by means of deep RNNs, as shown in Figure 5.10. Relation prediction is based on a vector representation which combines the outputs of the encoding of this multi-layered information of the dependency paths.

Each word in a dependency path may have additional relations which clarify its semantics and its role in the phrase. Some of this information may help recognize the semantic relation between the target arguments. Can et al. [2019] use the richer-but-smarter shortest dependency path—augmented with dependent nodes selected by various attention mechanisms with kernel filters. This smartly augmented path is then processed by a CNN.

Compositionality Models

The methods just discussed approach compositionality gradually, by combining semantic representations of words. This ranges from simple averaging to the use of grammatical structure in assembling the meaning of a phrase. Grammatical relations, while also used, are not modelled explicitly. This next step models the grammatical relations themselves, either as part of word semantics or separately.

A word's embedding is induced from the contexts in which it appears. This represents a variety of aspects related to the word's form and meaning, as properties of its position in the embedding space relative to the position of its morphologically inflected forms, or other words [Etha-

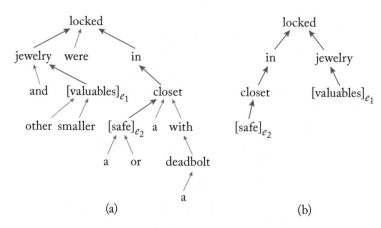

Figure 5.9: The dependency path (red) between entities *e*1 and *e*2 in the sentence "Jewelry and other small [valuables]*e1* were locked in a [safe]*e2* or a closet with a deadbolt." [Xu et al., 2016].

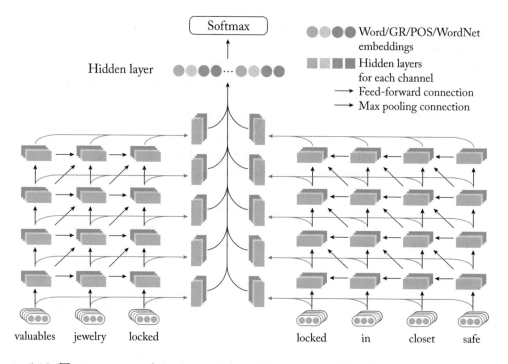

Figure 5.10: The two parts of the dependency path—separated by the common ancestor—are encoded by RNNs over four information channels: words, part-of-speech tags, grammatical relations, and WordNet hypernyms [Xu et al., 2016]. Relation prediction is based on a final hidden layer, in which these representations are combined.

Recursive Matrix-Vector Model

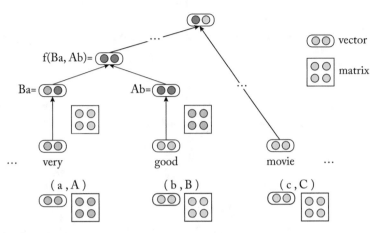

Figure 5.11: A recursive neural network which learns semantic vector representations of phrases in a tree structure. Each word and each phrase is represented by a vector and a matrix, e.g., *very = (a, A)*. The construction of the representation of a phrase, e.g., *very good*, is based on the representations of its words [Socher et al., 2012].

yarajh et al., 2019, Finley et al., 2017, Levy and Goldberg, 2014b, Mikolov et al., 2013c]. It may be desirable to build word representations which address specific aspects relevant to assembling the representation of a phrase. In particular, they can have separate components to model the meaning of a word and its "composition function", essentially an operator which encodes how the word modifies the meaning of another word it combines with. The meaning vector and the composition function of a phrase can be recursively assembled from their constituents in *recursive matrix-vector spaces* [Socher et al., 2012]. The word's meaning is modelled as a vector, and its composition function as a matrix, as shown in Figure 5.11.

These representations are induced during training. Words whose semantic component is stronger (e.g., content words such as nouns or verbs) will have a more informative semantic component. Words with a more structural role (e.g., function words such as prepositions or conjunctions) will have a more informative compositional component. Both components would probably be equally strong for any content-altering modifier (such as *fake*) or for a verb which functions as a hub for the event it signals.

Dependency relations can also be encoded explicitly. This keeps the composition information outside a word's representation, and allows different combinations to take syntactic information into account. Liu et al. [2015] encode augmented dependency paths. They use vector encodings of dependency relations and dual representations for words: a word's semantics, and the subtree it dominates. The (shortest) dependency path between two entities is augmented with the subtrees dominated by each head word along the path. The network recursively assembles

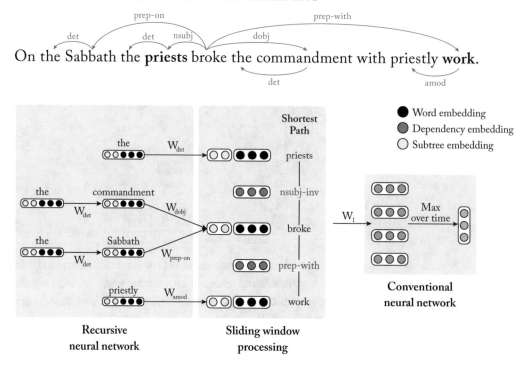

Figure 5.12: Recursive representation of a phrase based on the augmented dependency path and on the dependency relations [Liu et al., 2015].

the representation of a phrase which connects two entities, using the augmented dependency path and the dependency relation representations. Figure 5.12 illustrates.

Transformer-Based Sentence Embeddings

The methods we have reviewed thus far assemble the representation of a text fragment gradually from pre-trained or learned word representations. The representation of a word is fixed, regardless of the context in which the word appears. Transformer-based methods tackle the problem differently: a text fragment (often a sentence) is directly encoded, and a word may have different representations for different contexts. An adaptation of transformers for relation learning poses the problem of providing information on the relation's arguments. Such information enables the system to learn the targeted relation, and to assemble the fixed-length relation representation from the various layers of information in the transformer.

Soares et al. [2019] change a transformer into such a relation encoder. They experiment with various ways of supplying information about the location of the arguments in the input text, and with different learning set-ups. The first set-up was relation classification from manually annotated data. The results were the best when entity markers (special tokens [E1$_{start}$], [E1$_{end}$], [E2$_{start}$], [E2$_{end}$]) signaled the start and end positions of the two relation arguments in the text fragment, and when the concatenation of the final hidden states corresponding to [E1$_{start}$] and [E2$_{start}$] was taken as a relation instance representation. This mirrors the use of the output state which corresponds to the special [CLS] token as the sentence representation [Devlin et al., 2018, 2019].[11]

In the second set-up, distant supervision, Soares et al. take the transformer configuration developed for the classification task, and aim to produce and then compare the relation representations for pairs of entities in context. The loss function in this case is adjusted to lead to similar representations for relations which link the same pairs of entities. To encourage the system to incorporate contextual information and avoid excessive reliance on the entities in a pair, a special [BLANK] token replaces one or both of them in the automatically annotated corpus. For each positive instance, Soares et al. sample negative examples which do not contain the same entity pair, and use contrastive estimation to learn to rank positive instances higher than those presumed negative.

5.4.2   GRAPH NEURAL NETWORKS FOR ENCODING SYNTACTIC GRAPHS

The foregoing was a survey of the mapping of a phrase relevant to relation classification onto a fixed-sized representation, which can be used as input to a neural network for relation classification. The success of such mappings depends on the method of composing the meaning of the larger phrase from its atomic components and from structural information. The encoding of a phrase can also be based on its constituency or dependency graph structure. Previous neural architectures which expect a sequence as input require preprocessing to linearize the graph. This is troublesome: a graph does not have one natural order, unless it is a linear chain. The output of a model which encodes a graph should not depend on the input order of the nodes. Since the patterns possibly relevant to relation learning may in fact be structural patterns in the graph, it is advantageous to encode the graph structure rather than one of its linear projections.

The recursive neural networks discussed in the preceding section do encode a nonlinear structure: the directed acyclic graph (DAG). They still require preprocessing of the input to decide how this information is to be presented to the neural network. They also can only process certain types of graph structures.

Scarselli et al. [2009] introduced a connectionist model, graph neural networks (GNNs), which subsumes recursive neural networks. A GNN models the structure of a graph via functions which aggregate a node's local or even wider neighbourhood, and it iteratively updates an initial graph representation. To learn the representation of the graph, the GNN minimizes a loss function which captures the difference between the task-dependent predicted output and the gold standard. Scarselli et al.'s GNN model works on homogeneous undirected graphs. Fur-

---

[11]The first token of every sequence in BERT is a special classification token [CLS].

ther work has produced models for directed, heterogeneous, dynamic and other types of graphs; there is an overview in Zhou et al. [2018].

Our discussion here focuses on a few models which have been applied to encoding the structured textual context for relation instances, in particular on dependency graphs. (Section 5.6.1, in the segment of the book devoted to relation learning, will look at the encoding of large KGs using GNNs.) From the point of view of structured textual context, of particular interest are the aggregation functions which encode a node's neighbourhood, and the update steps. The aggregation functions, apart from capturing the neighbourhood structure of the nodes, can incorporate additional information, such as attributes of the nodes and of the edges, e.g., bags of words, geolocation, timestamps, images.

The dependency path between the arguments of a relation can be regarded as a tree rooted in a common ancestor. From the standpoint of deep learning, such a structure can be encoded as a bidirectional (top-down and bottom-up) tree-structured LSTM-RNN [Miwa and Bansal, 2016]. The bidirectional model ensures that the information from the root of the path and from the leaves is propagated to each node. Weight matrices for same-type children are shared, and they allow for a variable number of children. This model can encode either the full dependency tree, or the shortest path between the relation arguments and the sub-tree, i.e., the tree below the lowest common ancestor of the target nodes.

As noted earlier, the augmented dependency path includes dependency information on the words on the path. Too much of such information can distract from the relevant portions. One way to control the path is to prune the augmented dependency path: the syntactic tree is pruned below the lowest common ancestor by removing tokens further than k steps away from the dependency path between the target words. This ensures that negation and relevant modifiers are kept, while the size of the tree is reduced [Zhang et al., 2018].

GNNs can also help tackle cross-sentence relations. Links beyond the sentence level can be established by sequential or discourse relations. Figure 5.13 shows a document representation which incorporates intra- and inter-sentential dependencies, such as sequential, syntactic and discourse relations.

This structure can be encoded with graph LSTMs by partitioning the document graph into two directed acyclic graphs (DAGs). One DAG contains the left-to-right linear chain and other forward-pointing dependencies. The other DAG covers the right-to-left linear chain and the backward-pointing dependencies. The effect is a mapping of the graph structure into a BiLSTM formalism [Peng et al., 2017]. This representation is used to learn a contextual representation for each word. Such representations give the input to a relation classifier either by simple concatenation, if the arguments are single words, or by first building an averaged representation for multi-word terms.

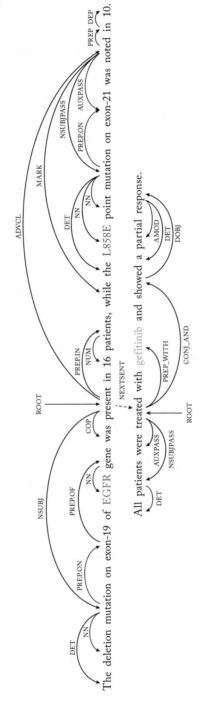

Figure 5.13: Example of a document relation graph, obtained using sequential and syntactic relations; discourse relations are omitted for clarity [Peng et al., 2017].

5.5   DATA

Neural networks are powerful but they require copious training data because they must learn many parameters. Some of the datasets described in Section 3.2 have been used in deep learning, although mostly as test data because of their small size. Section 5.5.1 reviews additional datasets created and applied in this framework. Just as in traditional learning, distant supervision methods have been developed, taking advantage of particular characteristics of deep learning to deal with automatically annotated noisy data. Section 5.5.2 describes a few of the deep-learning methods of coping with noisy data, such as adversarial networks and reinforcement learning.

5.5.1   DATASETS

Wikipedia infoboxes (see Section 3.2.5) were one of the sources of clean relation instances needed in relation extraction. This was the starting point of Freebase, a collaboratively built database, currently available from Wikidata.[12] Various subsets of these data have been in use, frequently for link prediction methods, e.g., Gardner and Mitchell [2015], Socher et al. [2011a], Trouillon et al. [2017], or for distant supervision based on KGs. Other KGs, taken from such resources such as NELL (Section 4.7.1) and WordNet, have also played a role in link prediction and as sources for distant supervision. Table 5.1 shows the statistics of some of the datasets most commonly used in relation learning.

Sun et al. [2013] discuss the Google Relation Extraction (RE) corpus.[13] It consists of instances of five binary relations: *perGraduatedFromInstitution*, *perHasDegree*, *perPlaceOfBirth*, *perPlaceOfDeath*, and *NA* (none of the above). The corresponding sentences come from Wikipedia. Annotation was manual but the instances do contain noise, also in the test partition. Jat et al. [2018] introduced a variation of this dataset, the Google Distant Supervision dataset. It starts with the Google RE relation triples, and adds sentences which contain the relation's arguments in the triple, found by searching the Web.

Zhang et al. [2017] present TACRED.[14] This dataset consists of sentences extracted from data created for the TAC Knowledge Base Population tasks. Sentences containing one of 100 target entities were extracted. The annotators were asked to mark subject and object entity spans, and the relation between them. The dataset, split into training, development and test subsets, contains both positive and negative instances.

Yao et al.'s [2019] dataset, DocRED,[15] represents both intra-sentence and cross-sentence relations. There are instances of 96 relation types from Wikidata. The dataset has several types of annotations apart from relations: mentions, coreference links, and text fragments marked as supporting evidence for the annotated relations.

---

[12] www.wikidata.org/
[13] code.google.com/p/relation-extraction-corpus/
[14] nlp.stanford.edu/projects/tacred/
[15] github.com/thunlp/DocRED

Table 5.1: KG datasets used for link prediction or as sources for distant supervision. (The question marks signal the absence of published statistics. 79.5% of TACRED instances are "no relation".)

Data Set	# Entities	# Relation Instances	# Relation Types
FB	20M	67M	4,215
FB15K	14,951	600k	1,345
FB [Mintz et al., 2009]	940k	1.8M	102
FB [Riedel et al., 2010]	?	743k	53
NELL	1.2M	3.4M	520
WN18	40,943	150k	18
Google RE	?	54k	5
GDS	?	18,824	5
FewRel	?	70,000	100
FewRel 2.0	?	72,500	125
TACRED	?	106,264	42
DocRED	132,375	63,427	96
DocRED (DS)	2,558,350	1,508,320	96

Several datasets are available for n-ary relations. There are Wiki-90k and WF-20k,[16] built from binary relation instances in Wikidata and Freebase. Akimoto et al. [2019] defined ternary relations by combining binary relations. Instances of these relations were mapped onto paragraphs consisting of at most three sentences from the English Wikipedia, processed with Stanford CoreNLP for dependency parsing and coreference resolution, and with DBpedia Spotlight for entity detection.

Few-shot learning is a new direction of research in relation extraction/classification: learning from a small number of examples. Han et al.'s [2018] dataset FewRel serves this specific purpose.[17] It consists of 70,000 instances, 700 instances for each of 100 relation types. The relations are derived from Wikidata and matched with Wikipedia articles, and then crowd-sourced for annotation. FewRel 2.0,[18] developed by Gao et al. [2019], adds a test set from the biomedical domain for exploring few-shot domain adaptation. It also provides a few-shot none-of-the-above detection setting.

---

[16]github.com/aurtg/n-ary-dataset
[17]zhuhao.me/fewrel
[18]thunlp.github.io/fewrel.html

A catalogue of annotated datasets for relation extraction—reference papers and links—appears in a very useful GitHub repository.[19] Please refer back to Section 3.2.7 for a discussion on the quality of datasets used in relation extraction/classification.

5.5.2   DISTANT SUPERVISION

Distant supervision is a popular method of acquiring additional (large amounts of) training data starting with (a small set of) annotated data from some related tasks. For relation extraction in particular, large amounts of automatically annotated data—in the form of sentences with source and relation targets marked—can be obtained using out-of-context (*source, relation, target*) relation triples in knowledge repositories. The sources and targets in these triples are mapped onto unstructured texts. The assumption is that all or most of the newly found sentences will carry the target relation. This naturally produces noisy data. Dealing with noise—or reducing it during the data generation process—is a thorny problem. Section 4.3.2 presented several methods of countering it. The switch to deep learning has led to new solutions of this problem; we survey them in this section.

Structured Learning

Evidence that a sentence contains an instance of a targeted relation can come from the sentence itself or from a larger corpus. One can filter out false positives by establishing similarity between the phrase which connects potential relation arguments in a corpus and the name of the relation in the KB [Ru et al., 2018]. The evidence from the sentence and from the corpus can be further aggregated to induce latent variables helpful in predicting if a relation has an instance in the given sentence [Hoffmann et al., 2011]. Such latent variables which model relational information can be induced from a low-dimensional representation of a sentence produced by a convolutional neural network [Bai and Ritter, 2019].

An entity pair from a KG can be connected by relations of several types. Relation learning in such cases is therefore often treated as a multi-instance multi-label learning problem [Hoffmann et al., 2011, Surdeanu et al., 2012]. The labels themselves, i.e., the relations, can also have semantic connections. For example, the Freebase relation */location/location/capital* connecting a capital city with its country is subsumed by */location/location/contains*. Information of this kind can be harnessed to learn the filtering of the automatically annotated sentences.

An efficient way of filtering automatically generated data is to filter sets—usually bags—of instances rather than individual instances. Automatically annotated sentences can be grouped in bags in various ways. For example, a bag may contain all sentences extracted for a given relation triple. Zeng et al. [2015] learn such a filter; their objective function applied at the bag level incorporates the uncertainty of the instance labels. The function assigns each bag a positive label (the bag has at least one positive instance) or a negative label (the bag has no positive instances).

---

[19] github.com/davidsbatista/Annotated-Semantic-Relationships-Datasets

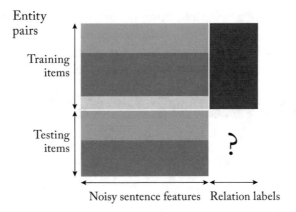

Figure 5.14: Entity-pair × sentence matrix in distant supervision [Fan et al., 2014].

Su et al. [2018] build an encoder-decoder model for each bag to predict a sequence of relations—starting with the most specific one—instantiated in the bag. The encoder produces a semantic representation of the whole bag of instances; to do that, it considers a representation of the source and target entities, and a semantic representation of the sentences assembled using a CNN. The decoder is a neural model which learns dependencies between the semantic relations in the entire set from the representation of the bags. For each input bag representation, it produces a sequence of relation predictions, starting with the most specific relation which can be instantiated in the sentences in the bag.

Distant supervision can be seen as the filling of entries in the label section of an entity-pair×sentence co-occurrence matrix—see Figure 5.14. The matrix combines gold-standard training instances and automatically labelled instances: rows represent entity pairs, columns represent (noisy) textual features from the corresponding sentences and (incomplete) relation labels. To fill in the incomplete relation labels, the matrix is factorized into two low-rank matrices: item×feature and item×label. The assumption is that the noisy features and the incomplete labels are semantically correlated [Fan et al., 2014]. The resulting low-dimensional feature and label representations can help compute the relation labels for the test data.

A KG—the usual source in distant supervision—provides much more information than just individual relation triples. Wang et al. [2018] do not use the labels associated with automatically extracted sentences. Instead, they devise a relation-learning process which relies on the fact that multiple entity pairs from a KG communicate the same relations, and that some pairs may appear in only one kind of relation (e.g., the relation between Toronto and Canada can be */location/location/contains* but not */location/location/capital*); there also is information about the type of entities connected by a given relation and an encoding of the KG relation. From the relation triples in the KG, the system induces entity and relation representations using the TransE model. The model approximates each relation type as a translation vector in a low-dimensional

Table 5.2: A small sample of graph embedding methods. There is a comprehensive overview in Wang et al. [2017] and Ji et al. [2020]. References for the methods: TransE [Bordes et al., 2013], DistMult [Yang et al., 2015], Rescal [Nickel et al., 2011], ComplEx [Trouillon et al., 2017], TransG [Xiao et al., 2016], ConvE [Dettmers et al., 2018], MuRP [Balazevic et al., 2019].

Method	Entity Emb.	Relation Emb.	Scoring Function
TransE	$\mathbf{v}_s, \mathbf{v}_t \in \mathbb{R}^d$	$\mathbf{r} \in \mathbb{R}^d$	$\|\mathbf{v}_s + \mathbf{r} - \mathbf{v}_t\|$
DistMult	$\mathbf{v}_s, \mathbf{v}_t \in \mathbb{R}^d$	$\mathbf{r} \in \mathbb{R}^d$	$\mathbf{v}_s^\top diag(\mathbf{r})\mathbf{v}_t$
Rescal	$\mathbf{v}_s, \mathbf{v}_t \in \mathbb{R}^d$	$\mathbf{M_r} \in \mathbb{R}^{d \times d}$	$\mathbf{v}_s^\top \mathbf{M_r}\mathbf{v}_t$
ComplEx	$\mathbf{v}_s, \mathbf{v}_t \in \mathbb{C}^d$	$\mathbf{r} \in \mathbb{C}^d$	$Re(\mathbf{v}_s^\top diag(\mathbf{r})\overline{\mathbf{v}}_t)$
TransG	$\mathbf{v}_s \sim \mathcal{N}(\mu_s, \sigma_s^2 I)$ $\mathbf{v}_t \sim \mathcal{N}(\mu_t, \sigma_t^2 I)$ $\mu_s, \mu_t \in \mathbb{R}^d$ $\Sigma_s, \Sigma_t \in \mathbb{R}^{d \times d}$	$\mu_r^i \sim \mathcal{N}(\mu_t - \mu_s, (\sigma_s^2 + \sigma_t^2)I)$ $\mathbf{r} = \Sigma_i \pi_r^i \mu_r^i \in \mathbb{R}^d$ (μ_r^i are weights)	$\Sigma_i \pi_r^i exp\left(-\dfrac{\|\mu_s + \mu_r^i - \mu_t\|_2^2}{\sigma_s^2 + \sigma_t^2}\right)$
ConvE	$\mathbf{v}_s \in \mathbb{R}^{d_h \times d_w}$ ($d_h, d_w = d$) $\mathbf{v}_t \in \mathbb{R}^d$	$\mathbf{r} \in \mathbb{R}^{d_h \times d_w}$	$f(vec(f([\mathbf{v}_s; \mathbf{r}] * w))W)\mathbf{v}_t$ (* is the convolution operator, w is a CNN filter, W is a weight matrix)
MuRP	$\mathbf{h}_s, \mathbf{h}_t \in \mathbb{B}_c^d$ $\mathbb{B}_c^d = \{x \in \mathbb{R}^d : c\|x\|^2 < 1\}$	$\mathbf{r} \in \mathbb{B}_c^d$ $\mathbf{R} \in \mathbb{R}^{d \times d}$	$-d_\mathbb{B}(\mathbf{h}_s^{(r)}, \mathbf{h}_t^{(r)})^2 + b_s + b_t$

space: *source + relation ≈ target* (this will be shown in Table 5.2 in Section 5.6.1). In the extracted sentences, source and target entities are replaced with their types as supplied by the KG. A neural network with attention learns sentence embeddings such that the embedding of a sentence is close to the target-source pair, so ultimately close to the representation of a relation. At test time, a sentence is assigned a relation label dictated by its embedding and its closest relation induced with TransE.

Vashishth et al. [2018] also take advantage of entity type information from Freebase and relation alias information—different relation names in (*subject, verb, object*) triples extracted from texts—to impose soft constraints on relation prediction. A graph convolution network formalism is used to encode syntactic information from candidate sentences and to produce sentence embeddings. From these representations, the system induces representations of bags of instances, which are then combined with relation embeddings and entity type embeddings, and a softmax classifier predicts the relation.

Adversarial Networks

Generative adversarial networks (GANs) have had much success in dealing with the lack of training data, because they automatically generate new data to match a small set of gold-standard annotated data. In this formalism, a generator is pitted against a discriminator. The generator tries to generate data according to an underlying (unknown) distribution, and the discriminator tries to distinguish automatically generated data from the (relatively little) gold standard data with the desired distribution. The generator works best when the discriminator fails; this shows that it can generate data from the desired distribution. While this idea is not new [Schmidhuber, 1999], and has been implemented for traditional learning paradigms [Dalvi et al., 2004, Zhou et al., 2012], it has proven particularly fruitful in deep learning [Goodfellow et al., 2014].

The training of a generator and a discriminator has been applied in filtering instances for the distance supervision of relation classification. Here, the generator need not actually generate new instances; it can just sample from the set of sentences automatically annotated for relations. The problem is to sample the true positives from the automatically generated noisy data. The discriminator is tested on a small amount of gold-standard annotated data. According to Goodfellow et al., the process "wins" when the discriminator cannot distinguish between its gold-standard true positives and the sentences selected from the automatically annotated data.

The sampling of true positives can be based on a computed probability that a given sentence contains an instance of the target relation [Qin et al., 2018a]; the sentences with the highest probability are passed on to the discriminator. Normally, a GAN's discriminator would pitch the automatically selected instances against a gold-standard annotated set. Qin et al. forgo supervision. They assume a rough split of the automatically annotated data, based on the overlap with the source of distant supervision. A set P of "true positive" data comprises sentences with both arguments of an existing relation in Freebase. In the sets N^G and N^D (negative data for the generator and the discriminator, respectively), the entities in the sentence do not appear in a relation instance in Freebase.

Qin et al. use P and N^G to pretrain a generator model; the model is updated until a stopping criterion has been met, as in typical GANs. Unlike a typical GAN, the discriminator is also pretrained, and this configuration is restored at the beginning of each epoch. The generator assigns a probability score to every instance in P. The set of instances is split into T (instances with a high probability) and $F = P \setminus T$. The parameters of the discriminator are adjusted in such a way that T plays the role of negative data, F of the positive data. The loss function of the discriminator computes a signal which is only used to determine the reward function for adjusting the parameters of the generator. The performance of the discriminator is evaluated on N^D, the set of negative examples. The intuition seems to be as follows: if the discriminator learns to assign lower probability to instances of T (which it treats as negative), then it will become

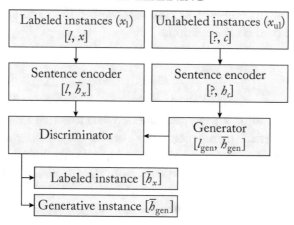

Figure 5.15: Li et al.'s [2019a] GAN architecture: the same encoder for gold-standard and automatically annotated sentences.

worse at distinguishing positive and negative instances, so it will perform poorly at scoring the negative data N^D.

Information in a sentence often ends up compressed into a single probability value. Such compression obscures the various facets of the sentence. There is an alternative: construct a vector representation of the sentence, perhaps using a CNN; next, use it to build and train the generator and the discriminator [Li et al., 2019a]. This procedure, illustrated in Figure 5.15, can be combined with additional methods of filtering the automatically annotated data. Li et al. produce a cleaner training set from entity descriptions collected from Wikipedia. As positives instances, they take the sentences with entity mentions which appear not only in a relation in the source of distant supervision, but in each other's description. If they do not, the sentence is considered a negative instance.

Neural Networks with Attention

Automatically generated true positive and false positive sentences may share features which can be exploited to filter the distantly supervised dataset. To find such features, the meaning of the sentences should be represented in a systematic manner, by a mechanism which reveals shared patterns.

CNNs are good at finding patterns. The induced sentence representations can be used directly with a sentence-level attention model which reduces the weights of noisy (false positive) sentences [Lin et al., 2016]. They can also lead to aggregate representations of groups of sentences, in particular bags of sentences extracted for each relation r and (*source, target*) pair.

Ye and Ling [2019] apply a bag-level attention mechanism to relation-aware representations built for each bag as (attention-)weighted sums of sentence representations matched against each relation. Sentence representations are built by CNNs over word embeddings, taking into account positional information about the source and the target. This weighted sum of sentence representations is matched against every possible relation, not just the target relation: the same entity pair can have different relations in different contexts (e.g., *Barack Obama was born in the United States* and *Barack Obama was the 44th President of the United States*). Bags which share a relation label are assembled into a bag group. An attention mechanism helps weight sentences for the construction of the bag representation. The mechanism is expected to give smaller weight— pay less attention—to noisy sentences. A similar attention mechanism should give lower weight to noisy bags in a bag group. The attention model is trained to weight more highly sentences more likely to express the desired relations.

Beltagy et al. [2019] combine adversarial training with attention; that improves the automatic selection of positive instances from automatically selected—therefore noisy—sentences which contain the target relations. Beltagy et al.'s work improves the model's ability to assign lower weights to noisy sentences, those which do not contain the target relation.

Another trouble with distant supervision is that sentences contain more information than just the target relation, and such additional phrases may conceal the target relation. Filtering out some of the noise can make it easier for an attention model to find, and properly weight, relevant features. Liu et al. [2018] implement such a filter. In word-level distant supervision for relation extraction, where filtering is based on syntactic information, a robust entity-wise attention model will give more weight to semantic features of relational words in a sentence.

Attention models are usually implemented as weight vectors. This one-dimensional view may insufficiently account for complex interactions in textual contexts. Du et al. [2018] propose a multi-level multi-dimensional attention model in a multi-instance learning framework. A 2D attention matrix identifies aspects of the interaction of two entities in a sentential context, while another 2D attention matrix picks up relevant sentence-level features.

The attention mechanism relies on the neural model for the encoding of relevant and noteworthy features. With respect to relation extraction, some such features should capture semantic aspects of the entities involved. The sentential context may not contain enough information for this, so one could give the model additional information in the form of entity descriptions. Ji et al. [2017] extract entity descriptions from Freebase and Wikipedia pages, and give those to a model which includes sentence-level attention.

Reinforcement Learning

The decision which instance is useful—is a true positive—can be treated as a game. In a game, generally speaking, an agent starts in an initial state, chooses a series of actions which lead to a final state, and is rewarded or penalized depending on whether the final state is good or bad. This reward/penalty controls the adjustment of the agent's model, which dictates what actions to take in a given state.

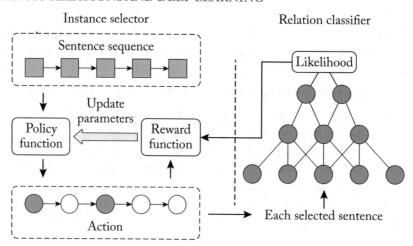

Figure 5.16: Example of a reinforcement-learning architecture in which a relation classifier selects instances [Feng et al., 2018].

In relation extraction, the purpose of the game is to find true positive sentences among those automatically extracted and annotated. At each step, the agent chooses an instance from this automatically generated set. When it reaches the final state, the set of instances gathered is considered to be a training set of properly labelled instances. A model is built from this training set, and evaluated on a small set of gold-standard data. A good training set yields a good model for learning to predict relations, and a noisy training set leads to poor performance on the task. The result of this evaluation determines the agent's reward or penalty; based on that, the agent adjusts its method of choosing instances and assigning each of them a positive or negative label.

Formally, *state* s_t corresponds to the training data selected until time t, the target relation r_i, and the relation arguments—*source* and *target*—in the currently considered instance. Three *actions* are possible: accept it as true positive and include it in the training data; include it as a negative instance; or reject it. The *reward* is computed after the instances in the automatically generated dataset (or in a bag corresponding to a given *source-target* pair) have been processed, and the final relation classification model built and evaluated.

Feng et al. [2018] and Qin et al. [2018b] apply this form of reinforcement learning in the selection of training data for relation learning. When the agent decides on the action, it relies on a relation classification model, implemented as a CNN. The reward/penalty feedback guides the adjustment of the parameters of this CNN. Figure 5.16 illustrates.

The process can be improved if the focus is not only on false positives but on false negatives. (A false positive is an automatically generated sentence which does not actually have one of the target relations, despite containing both arguments of a relation. A false negative is a sentence discarded because it did not contain an exact expression of the arguments of a relation.) Yang et al. [2019] focus on identifying both false positives and false negatives. They treat this as a reinforcement problem, in which an agent should decide if an instance is mislabelled. The task is split between two agents: one of them detects false positives, the other false negatives.

The adjustment of action selection as a result of feedback is a critical step in reinforcement learning. Earlier work relied on a relation classifier to take an action, and the reward/penalty indicated how to adjust the parameters of the model. The action can also be the result of more complex processing. Liu et al. [2019b] developed a reinforcement learning process in which a GAN-like method performs a *policy* improvement step. A policy is a probability distribution which maps states to actions. The improvement of a policy was modelled as a form of imitation learning.[20] It takes the current policy as the prior knowledge, and generates improved policies. The reward is implicit in the policy improvement operator. In the policy evaluation step, the current policy network is rated by a measure of the difference between the probability distribution under the current policy and under the improved policy.

5.6   LEARNING SEMANTIC RELATIONS

There are many ways of representing the semantics of words/entities, relational clues from the context, and even the relations themselves. Various architectures can combine this information, and in fact it is often derived jointly. This section presents several ways in which such representations can be integrated in a deep-learning method. The methods are grouped by the sources and information support for the relation learned: learning relations in KGs (Section 5.6.1), learning relations from texts (Section 5.6.2), learning relations from texts and KGs (Section 5.6.3), n-ary and cross-sentence relations (Section 5.6.4), unsupervised relation extraction (Section 5.6.5), and finally lifelong learning (Section 5.6.6).

5.6.1   LEARNING RELATIONS IN KNOWLEDGE GRAPHS

A KG $G = (\mathcal{V}, \mathcal{E}, \mathcal{R})$ contains knowledge in the form of relation triples $(s, r, t) \in \mathcal{E}$, where the vertices $s, t \in \mathcal{V}$ are entities and $r \in \mathcal{R}$ is a relation type. KGs are not complete. Additional links (facts) can be inferred because similar nodes participate in similar relations, e.g., every country has a capital city. This is, in effect, *link prediction*. To do this, a KG may be encoded by a learning model which approximates its connectivity information; or one can apply a GNN to encode its structure via node neighbourhoods.

Encoding Graph Connectivity Information

Graph embedding methods rely on the idea that the graph's connectivity structure informs the representations of entities and relations. The representation of an entity takes into account the relations it is part of; the representation of a relation takes into account the entities it connects.

---

[20]Imitation learning aims to mimic human behaviour in a given task. An agent is trained to perform the task from demonstrations by learning a mapping between observations and actions.

A few essential design decisions must be made: the type of structure to represent entities and relations (e.g., vectors or matrices); the scoring function to calculate a score for a pair of entities and a relation type based on these representations (the score should be 1 if the edge in question exists); and the loss function to compare the automatic predictions with the gold standard. Nickel et al. [2016a] present a survey of statistical relational learning methods for KGs, including graph embeddings, path-based algorithms and Markov logic networks. Wang et al. [2017] and Ji et al. [2020] focus on KG embedding methods, and present a comprehensive overview. This section summarizes some of those methods; the surveys offer the reader a deeper look.

KGs contain only positive instances, i.e., relation instances known to exist. The link prediction task precludes the closed-world assumption, otherwise, every missing link would be a legitimate *not_related* relation. To produce non-trivial models, "negative" edges are needed. There is variety of methods which sample a number of missing edges for each positive instance [Kotnis and Nastase, 2018]. A scoring function applied to such apparently negative instances should return a score close to 0. Alternatively, since these instances are only presumed to be negative, the scoring and the loss functions can implement *contrastive estimation* [Gutmann and Hyvarinen, 2012]: the score for a positive instance should be higher that the score for all the negative instances sampled for it.

Graph embedding methods learn representations $\mathbf{v}_x$ for entity x and $\mathbf{r}$ for relation r. The fact that relation r holds between the source and target nodes s and t is modelled by a scoring function f (discussed briefly in Section 5.3.2). The entity embeddings $\mathbf{v}_x$ are usually d-dimensional vectors, where d is a parameter. The representation of the relation has taken various forms, e.g., a d-dimensional vector (Trans* [Bordes et al., 2013, Lin et al., 2015, Wang et al., 2014]), a diagonal matrix (DistMult [Yang et al., 2015]), or a $d \times d$ matrix (RESCAL and its variations [Nickel et al., 2011]).

The entity and the relation embeddings can be considered to belong to different embedding spaces, and projections can map entity embeddings onto the relation space [Ji et al., 2015, 2016, Lin et al., 2015]. Entities and relations are most commonly modelled as deterministic points or vectors in continuous vector spaces. In contrast, He et al. [2015] and Xiao et al. [2016] propose models which represent both entities and relations as vectors drawn from Gaussian distributions. Such representations allow variations in the meaning of a semantic relation for different (*source, target*) pairs, and for sources and targets in different contexts.

Table 5.2 shows examples of graph embedding models. The column *Entity emb.* contains the implementation choice for the entity embeddings: a real- or complex-valued d-dimensional vector, or a d-dimensional vector drawn from a normal distribution.[21] The column *Relation emb.* lists the chosen representation structure for the relation: a real- or complex-valued d-dimensional vector, a real-valued $d \times d$-matrix, or a d-dimensional real-valued vector drawn from a normal distribution. The *Scoring function* column presents the calculation of the score for a relation triple, given the representation choices.

---

[21] $\mathcal{N}(\mu, \sigma^2 I)$ represents the normal distribution with mean μ and covariance matrix $\sigma^2 I$.

Methods such as RESCAL [Nickel et al., 2011] and Neural Tensor Networks [Socher et al., 2013] learn millions of parameters. That makes them more flexible—they can model a variety of relations well—but there are costs: increased computational complexity and a chance of over-fitting. Methods such as TransE [Bordes et al., 2013] and DistMult [Yang et al., 2015] learn simpler models, with far fewer parameters, and are easier to train, but they cannot model certain types of relations, such as many-to-many relations (TransE) and asymmetric relations (Dist-Mult). Nickel et al. [2016b]'s holographic embeddings (HolE) achieve the modelling power of RESCAL with fewer parameters by compressing the tensor product. Complex-valued embeddings (ComplEx) [Trouillon et al., 2017] extend DistMult to model antisymmetric relations.

Nickel and Kiela [2017] first proposed embedding (part of) WordNet's *is-a* hierarchy in a Poincaré space; their hyperbolic embeddings (of very low dimension: $d = 5$) predicted unseen *is-a* instances. Balazevic et al.'s [2019] model embeds and predicts links in a multi-relational KG. Their MuRP model, illustrated in Table 5.2, represents entities as points in a Poincaré ball. A scoring function determines if two entities are in a relation r. The function relies on relation-specific parameters $\mathbf{r}$ (a hyperbolic translation vector) and $\mathbf{R}$ (a diagonal relation matrix). The parameters transform the source and target hyperbolic embeddings $\mathbf{h}_s$ and $\mathbf{h}_t$ into $\mathbf{h}_s^{(r)}, \mathbf{h}_t^{(r)}$. Two biases, b_s and b_t (which are among the model's parameters), define a "sphere of influence" around each of the transformed vectors. If r connects the source and target entities, then their spheres of influence should overlap.

A graph-structure encoding approximates, in effect, the adjacency matrix of a graph. The matrix captures the view of a graph as a collection of triples. A graph can also be represented as a collection of paths. Paths in graphs can result from graph traversal (breadth-first, depth-first, and so on) or random walks.

Paths can assist relation learning in various ways. When regarded as a sequences of nodes and relations, a path can serve as a "sentence" for the purpose of deriving node and relation representations. Paths are the input, in lieu of a regular corpus, to word2vec [Mikolov et al., 2013a], and representations of the nodes and relations are produced just as one would do it for words in a sentence [Perozzi et al., 2014].

A path can be treated as a description of the source and target nodes (it contains information about their neighbourhoods) or the relation between them (it shows alternative chains of links from the source to the target). Paths, then, can contribute directly as features to the prediction of new links in a KG. Lao et al. [2011] show how to obtain and apply bounded-length path types, or meta-paths (sequences of relations): they generalize alternative paths found between the source and the target in the graph connected by the same relation r. The meta-paths work as features in predicting if relation r holds between node pairs previously not connected by r.

Gardner and Mitchell [2015] use paths to describe the source and target nodes, and the relation between them. They extract features from the local subgraphs around each node in a potential pair. The local information around node n is the set of (*path type, end node*) pairs collected by random walks which originate in n. The representation for a (*source, target*) pair combines the two nodes' subgraphs by merging the paths based on shared end nodes on those paths. This representation is used to learn a corresponding relation for the entity pair.

Guu et al. [2015] show that most latent factor models, notably matrix factorization models, can be modified to learn from paths rather than from individual triples. RNNs which learn path representations have also been used for link prediction [Das et al., 2016, Neelakantan et al., 2015].

Relations can also share information. For example, the relation *currency_of_film_budget* can be viewed as a composition of the relations *currency_of_country* and *country_of_film*. This kind of information may promote better relation representations. Takahashi et al. [2018] use an autoencoder which further processes the relation matrices obtained by matrix factorization with the RESCAL model. The autoencoder compresses the relation matrix into a smaller vector representation, from which the matrix is regenerated. This encoding-decoding process encourages the induction of relation matrices which incorporate similarities and dependencies between the relations.

The previously described graph embeddings took into account the structure of the graph, and encoded entities and relations in various types of structures. The entity and relation representations determine the scoring function used to approximate the graph structure and then to predict new edges.

Information in a KG can be encoded in other ways, for example when relation triples are taken into account as separate instances. The focus in such a case would be on modelling the interaction between arguments and relations to boost latent patterns, such as shared or interacting dimensions. Dettmers et al. [2018] use a multi-layer CNN, whose input is a 2D encoding of the source entity and relation in a (*source*, *relation*, *target*) triple. The filters applied to this source-relation "image" are common to all instances in the training data, and so to all relation types. The application of the filters over the 2D representation produces feature maps; a fully connected layer projects the maps onto a hidden layer which represents an entity embedding. The predicted embedding vector is multiplied with the entity matrix and then transformed by a sigmoid function; that, in effect, produces a similarity score between the predicted embedding and the embeddings of the entities in the graph. Dettmers et al.'s method makes it possible to perform a 1-to-N mapping, simultaneously testing all possible targets of a source-relation combination.

Jiang et al. [2019] take Dettmers et al.'s method further. They start from the premise that concatenating the 2D representations of the subject and the relation does not allow for enough interaction between the dimensions of the subject and relation. Jiang et al.'s system takes as input only a 2D representation of the source entity, and the representation of the relation is transformed into a set of filters. This enables a more diverse and comprehensive interaction between the representation of the subject and the relation. In contrast with Dettmers et al.'s work, each relation type has its own filters.

Graph Neural Networks

The graph encoding methods which we discussed in connection with link prediction do not take full advantage of the graph structure. For example, a node's neighbourhood should provide useful information. GNNs were designed to acquire such information down to any depth. GNNs, proposed first by Scarselli et al. [2009], aggregate this information into a fixed-sized representation. The aggregation function—message passing—must be invariant in the neighbourhood shape or size. Zhou et al. [2018] present a comprehensive view of GNNs; it is summarized here from the point of view of their connection to semantic relation learning.

GNNs were inspired by CNNs, which can find patterns at different levels and then compose them into expressive representations. There are three key aspects of CNNs which allow them to produce such representation: local information (in graphs, it is node neighbourhood); shared weights (this reduces the computing cost); and multi-layer structures which deal with hierarchical patterns and so capture features of various sizes (this maps naturally into the hierarchical structure of graphs). It is an important characteristic of a GNN that its output is invariant in the input order of nodes. The relation information, which represents the dependency between two nodes, can be explicitly integrated into the model, including the relation's potential attributes.

A node is defined by its features, the related nodes, and the type of relations which connect it with its neighbours. Learning a GNN implies learning a hidden state $\mathbf{h}_v \in \mathbb{R}^d$ which encodes the neighbourhood information for node v. This vector can be used to produce an output $\mathbf{o}_v$ which corresponds, for example, to v's label. The basis for inducing such representations is a *local transition function* f which combines the features of the node ($\mathbf{x}_v$), the features of its edges ($\mathbf{x}_{co[v]}$), the states of the nodes in its neighbourhood ($\mathbf{h}_{ne[v]}$), and the features of the nodes in its neighbourhood ($\mathbf{x}_{ne[v]}$). Formally, the hidden state is defined as

$$\mathbf{h}_v = f(\mathbf{x}_v, \mathbf{x}_{co[v]}, \mathbf{h}_{ne[v]}, \mathbf{x}_{ne[v]}) \tag{5.14}$$

The output depends on v's hidden state and feature vector. It is defined as

$$\mathbf{o}_v = g(\mathbf{h}_v, \mathbf{x}_v) \tag{5.15}$$

where g is a local output function. To learn g's and h's internal parameters, GNNs need a loss function. It compares the predicted output $\mathbf{o}_v$ for a node with the gold-standard $\mathbf{t}_v$ from a given training set $\mathcal{V}$:

$$loss = \sum_{v \in \mathcal{V}} (\mathbf{t}_v - \mathbf{o}_v) \tag{5.16}$$

Not only are KGs incomplete but they are incomplete in an imbalanced way. The node degrees and relation frequency plots for Freebase and NELL in Figure 5.7 (in Section 5.3.2) illustrate this difficulty. Because of the skewed structure, using GNNs to encode large-scale KGs can give low-quality encodings of nodes and relations. One way of dealing with this skewness is to limit the size of the considered neighbourhood by sampling. Niepert [2016] shows how to map discriminative Gaifman models (a new family of relational machine learning models) onto KGs by learning representations from local bounded-sized neighbourhoods. The model is built bottom up from these neighbourhoods, allowing for the efficient transfer of learned representations between connected objects.

A graph convolution network (GCN) aggregates the signal for each node in the network: it sums over the incoming signals from the node's predecessor nodes. The signal can be enriched with information about the type of relations between connected nodes, making them Relational Graph Convolution Networks (R-GCN). Schlichtkrull et al.'s [2018] transformation of the incoming signal from a connected node is based on the connecting relation. The transformation is encoded as matrix multiplication, where each relation is represented by its own matrix. The resulting representations can be used in a link prediction formalism, as discussed in the preceding subsection.

To assist in the task of relation classification/extraction, the GCN formalism can be applied not only to KGs but to graphs which identify connections between relation types. Freebase relations, for example, have specific names (such as */people/person/ethnicity* or */people/person/nationality*) which help organize the relations themselves into a graph structure. The adoption of such a relation graph as additional information in the KG encoding process encourages similar relations to have similar representations. Zhang et al. [2019b] initialize the representation of the leaf relations with representations induced by matrix factorization, and the representations of internal nodes with averages of the representations of their children. Zhang et al. then use GCN to update these representations, so that similar relations have similar representations. The purpose of this process is to bootstrap additional information from the KG to induce more informative representations for low-frequency relations, and ultimately help link prediction.

The GNN formalism is also particularly adept at including various types of information which express relevant features of the nodes and the edges. Schlichtkrull et al.'s R-GCN has shown how to integrate information about relation types in the model. García-Durán and Niepert [2017] focus on node information, and include a variety of attributes, including numeric and multi-media features.

Hyperbolic spaces have been shown to capture structural properties of graphs better than their Euclidean counterparts; see, e.g., Nickel and Kiela [2018]. That is why it is natural to consider an extension of GNNs, which exploit structural properties of graphs, to hyperbolic spaces [Chami et al., 2019, Liu et al., 2019a]. This requires tackling a few problems: map the input Euclidean node features to a hyperbolic space, perform set aggregation in hyperbolic space, and choose the hyperbolic spaces with the right curvature. Chami et al. [2019], building upon the GCN architecture, propose hyperbolic graph convolution networks (HGCN). This machinery combines the expressiveness of GCNs with hyperbolic geometry solutions of the issues of input representation and set aggregation for the problem of message-passing in GNNs. Chami et al. show that embeddings which their HGCN learns preserve hierarchical structure. That leads to improved performance, when compared to Euclidean counterparts, on link prediction on several sets of medical data.

5.6.2   LEARNING RELATIONS FROM TEXTS

Relation learning from texts takes two forms. One focuses on relation classification; it assumes that the relation arguments are given, and aims to predict the relation between them. The other is the joint learning of arguments and relations from unmarked texts.

Relation Classification

A successful model for relation classification relies on detecting shared patterns across a number of instances. CNNs do this particularly well. They were initially applied in image processing, and performed very well in noticing patterns distributed over various regions of an image [LeCun and Bengio, 1995]. The idea behind CNNs for relation classification is to find common patterns in the text which surrounds or connects instances of the same relation. The context, which has varying length and complexity, can be input to the CNN in diverse ways. Some systems [Can et al., 2019, Liu et al., 2015, Xu et al., 2016] rely on producing a fixed-length vector using one of the compositional methods (see Section 5.4.1). Another possibility is to have a fixed-size window centered on the relation arguments, or to slide it over the context and pool the representations to produce "summaries" of the context based on various input masks [Nguyen and Grishman, 2015, Zeng et al., 2014].

Once a fixed-sized vector for an input sentence has been acquired, this representation can help calculate a score for the sentence with respect to a semantic relation. The calculation is based on a vector representation for each relation type, which is also a learned parameter of the model [dos Santos et al., 2015].

The representation of a sentence can have multiple segments, to find separately information relevant to relation learning. For example, Zeng et al. [2014] produce a representation with two sections, one for the target words, another for sentence-level features. These global features are induced by a convolutional neural network on the words of the input sentence. A word has a two-pronged representation: its embeddings, and the position features which quantify its distance to the relation arguments. This is illustrated in Figure 5.17.

The arguments and their connecting patterns can be processed separately by a CNN. The arguments could be modelled by CNNs on representations of windows of several sizes centered on those arguments. The connecting phrase can be processed similarly, by applying a CNN to the sentence fragment between the relation arguments. This leads to fixed-sized vectors representing the arguments and the relation, to be used as input to a relation classification step [Zheng et al., 2016].

Dependency paths have been shown to be a useful relation indicator. Because of their varying length and structure, they require particular encoding methods. Section 3.3.2 has presented an

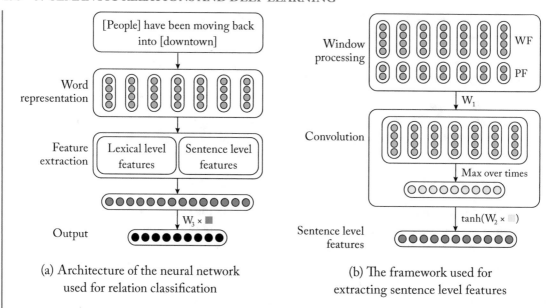

(a) Architecture of the neural network used for relation classification

(b) The framework used for extracting sentence level features

Figure 5.17: Learning relations using a CNN [Zeng et al., 2014].

overview of compositional and graph methods for encoding such features to produce fixed-sized vectors which can serve as input to other neural networks for relation classification.

Consider sentences which contain a pair of entities and are instances of the same semantic relation. The expressions of the relation in the different sentences (e.g., phrases which connect the two entities) are considered mutual paraphrases. In Rossiello et al.'s [2019] work, this assumption supports the fact that if two pairs of entities represent instances of the same relation, then they are analogous. Rossiello et al. compare pairs of entities using hierarchical Siamese networks. An entity pair is represented by all the sentential contexts found for it in a corpus. The Siamese network architecture is trained to minimize the difference between entity pairs with the same relation, even when they appear in (slightly) different contexts in the corpus. In that way, it learns the different paraphrases of the same relation.

Shwartz and Dagan [2018] apply deep learning to the prediction of paraphrases which explain noun-compound relations. They reformulate the paraphrase prediction task as three related subtasks: predict the head, the modifier, or the connecting pattern (found in a corpus). This causes a tuning of pre-computed word embeddings toward a state where modifier-head combinations which share similar patterns are closer in the embedding space, and so are patterns shared by similar modifier-head combinations.

In addition to the model architecture itself, what is essential is a good representation of the relation arguments and their contexts. When a Deep Bidirectional Transformer, or BERT, learns to predict targeted words in a sentence [Devlin et al., 2018, 2019], it builds a deep representation for the entire context by fusing the context on both sides of those words. Such a representation can help predict semantic relations; Shi and Lin [2019] study this hypothesis. BERT works with a masked language model: given a sentence, it masks certain words and then learns to predict them. For relation classification, the word/entity arguments are masked by their grammatical role and their entity type. Shi and Lin show that contextualized embeddings obtained in this manner predict very well the relation type between a given pair of words/entities in a sentence.

All these methods get and process only one path between a targeted pair of entities. In Christopoulou et al.'s [2018] system, the connection between a pair of entities is described by all possible paths between them (of length at most L) in a complete graph which connects all entity mentions in a sentence. Christopoulou et al. assume that entity mentions and their types are given. The directed edge connecting a pair of entities in this graph is initialized by a model which combines the representation of the entities and the context around them. An iterative algorithm then builds a representation of the connection between the entities by aggregating the graph walks between them of length at most L. This representation is used to predict the relation type.

The *is-a* relation is a frequent target of relation extraction. Distributional semantic models give good results, so it is natural to ask what the improved word embeddings and deep learning can bring to this task. According to the discussion in Section 3.3, the *is-a* relation can be detected from the meaning of the word themselves, or from their connective patterns.

For words projected into an embedding space, the *is-a* relation could ideally be a linear projection from the hyponym to the hypernym, or at least there can be several such projections, depending on the characteristics of the word pairs. Consider, for example, *(cat, animal)* vs. *(table, furniture)* vs. *(Germany, country)*. (Section 2.2.2 noted similar considerations related to subrelations of *is-a*.) Fu et al. [2014] propose word embeddings for the discovery of clusters in the set of arguments of the *is-a* relation. The training dataset's clustering into groups is based on the offset between the vectors of the word pair. The clustering step is expected to uncover hyponymy/hypernymy subrelations. For each cluster, a learned linear projection (in the form of a matrix) represents the hyponymy/hypernymy relation.

Textual patterns between terms in sentences, encoded by deep-learning methods, can also serve to detect *is-a* relations. Shwartz et al. [2016] investigate the effect of combining dependency paths encoded by means of RNNs with the embeddings of the relation's arguments. All paths between a pair of potential relation arguments participate in producing an averaged representation of the connection between the two arguments. This is assembled from a multi-layered representation of each word on the path. The representation includes the word's lemma and part-of-speech, the dependency label (for the dependency appearing on the considered path), and the direction of the dependency relation. The method outperforms those based on symbolic distributional models.

Le et al. [2019] learn the *is-a* relation from embeddings in a hyperbolic space and from Hearst patterns [Hearst, 1992], a reliable and resilient heuristic for *is-a* in many domains (the book discusses them in many places, notably in Chapter 4). Le et al. use Hearst patterns to get *is-a* candidates from a large corpus. From the potential *is-a* instances, they build a "Hearst graph", and embed it in a Poincaré ball. As Nickel and Kiela [2018] show, Poincaré balls are particularly apt for embedding tree structures, necessary in a taxonomy. Constraints on the hyperbolic space enable the detection of erroneous *is-a* instances and the insertion of new *is-a* links between existing nodes.

Joint Entity and Relation Extraction

Entities and relations can be acquired jointly if one uses their interaction to mutual advantage. Local decisions are made about the text spans which represent entity mentions, argument types and connections between them. Such decisions constrain named entities and relations, which can then be learned together [Roth and Yih, 2007]. Deep learning also makes it possible to get and combine such information. We will review methods which can be loosely grouped by how they deal with entity mention identification, and by the mention's varying length:

- use some form of span and entity type labelling: sequence labelling or table-filling with the same style of labels;
- explore all potential spans (or spans which can be quickly recognized as maybe representing entity mentions), link them in various ways, and predict together the correct spans and the relations between them;
- process a text fragment, and output relation instances which appear in the text.

Entity span and type labelling   Zheng et al. [2017] adopted a tagging scheme, similar to that in Li and Ji [2014], for joint argument identification and relation extraction. Inspired by named entity tagging, which also must identify sequences of various lengths, Zheng et al. combined a larger set of span indicators (BIESO: Begin, Inside, End, Single, Other) with the target relations and numerals which indicate the first or the second argument of the relation. Figure 5.18 depicts the model.

Miwa and Sasaki [2014] were the first to propose table-filling for relation classification; see Section 3.4.4. Gupta et al. [2016] reframe this method as a deep-learning problem. It is the same task: fill a word×word table which corresponds to sentence $s = <w_1, \ldots, w_n>$. The cells on the diagonal, (w_i, w_i), will be assigned the entity mention span and type labels. A "regular" cell $(w_i, w_j), i \neq j$, may be assigned a relation label if w_i and w_j correspond to the head of an entity mention. To perform this labelling, Gupta et al. choose an ordering of the cells in the table, and process them sequentially with a context-aware bidirectional RNN.

Miwa and Bansal [2016] propose a deep-learning architecture for relation extraction; bidirectional LSTM-RNNs encode the word sequence and the dependency tree. Miwa and Bansal pretrain the entity identification model and then the relation extraction model with scheduled

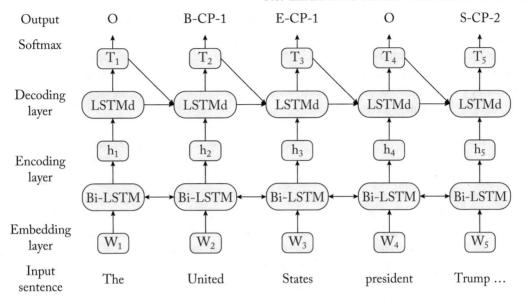

Figure 5.18: Zheng et al.'s [2017] joint entity and relation extraction model.

sampling. Such sampling replaces, with certain probability, predicted entity labels with gold-standard labels. The labels predicted for entity identification guide the selection of candidates for relation classification. The entities' heads are detected using the L and U tags, and the candidate pairs for relation classification are made from these head words. Compared to Li and Ji's [2014] joint model which gives the ACE04 and ACE05 data to a structured perceptron, Miwa and Bansal's model has better recall and F-score, while the structured perceptron gives higher precision. Compared to CNNs on the SemEval-2010 Task 8 data [dos Santos et al., 2015, Xu et al., 2015], there is a higher macro F1-score if bidirectional RNNs are used with long short-term memory units (BiLSTM-RNNs) to encode the word sequence and the dependency relations.

Dynamic spans   The basic concept here is also the span of an entity mention. Entity mentions are anchored in those spans, and relations connect two spans. The same entity can be mentioned in different places in a text. Linking different mentions of the same entity brings additional context and information to the detection of the correct span for each mention, and to the selection of the correct relation.

Luan et al. [2019] build upon the observation that entity identification, relation classification and coreference resolution share the common layer of entity mention spans. Luan et al. develop a multi-task learning framework to tackle the three tasks together. From unstructured input text, their system produces a set of candidate word spans. Each training step identifies the spans most likely to represent entity mentions; those spans serve as nodes in a graph structure. The system then constructs graph edges to represent coreference or semantic relation links, weighted by a confidence score. Span representation is refined by considering contextual information from the predicted relation and from coreference links. Luan et al. apply their system to four datasets from various domains. Wadden et al. [2019] build upon this method. They encode spans using contextual language models, and work with task-specific message updates passed over the graph of entity mention spans.

Direct relation extraction   Zeng et al.'s [2018] *end2end* neural model extracts potentially multiple relation instances directly from a sentence. There is an encoder and a decoder. The encoder transforms the input sentence into a fixed-length semantic vector. The decoder performs three steps to output relation instances based on this semantic vector. It first predicts a relation type. Taking into account the relation type, it determines the source entity, and then copies this entity from the input sentence. Now, given the relation type and the source entity, the decoder determines the target entity, and copies it from the input sentence. Zeng et al. designed the process in this manner in order to ensure that their system works well if a sentence contains multiple relation instances with overlapping arguments.

5.6.3   LEARNING RELATIONS FROM TEXTS AND KNOWLEDGE GRAPHS

Relation instances in large knowledge repositories often play a role in distant supervision (see Sections 4.6 and 5.5.2), in the learning of relation extraction or classification models. It is mutually beneficial to combine evidence from knowledge repositories and unstructured text, and either can help boost the other. This section shows a few examples of successfully combining evidence from unstructured data (either syntactic patterns, or phrases which connect entities/arguments in a text) with relation instances from knowledge repositories. Such methods have been used to enrich knowledge repositories with more triples for existing relations or with more relation types, or even to induce a complete relation schema from scratch.

Information from texts and KGs can be merged and then word and relation representations derived jointly, or the two sources of information can be processed separately, and then combined in a final classification step.

Merging Information from Texts and Knowledge Graphs

KGs contain structured information, while unprocessed texts have a linear form. To merge them, texts must also be cast into structures. This can be done in a variety of ways, for example using dependency parsing, or by extracting specific structured information such as (*subject, verb, object*) triples. The KGs and the structured textual information can then be merged by mapping nodes and relations, and this bigger structure is processed to produce word/entity and relation/predicate representations which drive relation learning in this hybrid graph. Nodes from KGs and dependency graphs/triples can be mapped using simple matching, similarity metrics, or more complex entity linking or word sense disambiguation techniques. Relations from the KG can also be mapped to predicates or phrases from texts, either before or after the encoding of the merged graph, depending on their induced representations.

Lao et al. [2012] build such a large graph by combining relation triples from Freebase with text processed by a dependency parser. Pronouns and anaphoric references are clustered with their antecedents, and entity mentions are linked to their corresponding nodes from the knowledge repository by an entity-linking system. To this hybrid graph, Lao et al. apply the Path Ranking Algorithm (PRA) [Lao et al., 2011] which predicts links from paths in KGs. In this case, PRA combines syntactic and semantic cues from the parsed text with relation information to build a model which can predict new relation triples for the knowledge repository.

In Lao et al.'s graph, the edges sourced from textual sources are dependency relations. Gardner et al. [2013] note that dependency relation names do not contribute semantic information, unlike relations from knowledge repositories. Instead of dependency graph representations of texts or text fragments, Gardner et al. propose to use (*subject, verb, object*) (SVO) triples extracted from texts which parallel (*source, relation, target*) triples in KGs; the link in an SVO triple—the predicate—is a lexicalized relation. For connected nodes in the graph built from the knowledge repository, Gardner et al. add new edges from SVO triples whose arguments match entities in the graph. There is a difficulty, naturally: adding such predicates directly from large-scale data (600 million SVO triples) would cause an explosion in the number of relation types in the graph, and would not catch equivalent expressions. That is why the lexicalized predicates are replaced with edge labels, which are latent features. These representations are learned by factorizing a *subject* × *object* frequency matrix, built from the SVO data.

The follow-up work gets deeper into the semantic territory, and explores a tighter merging of KGs and texts via the similarity among relations and predicates. Gardner et al. [2014] work with a graph which combines a KG with SVO triples from texts. They take advantage of the similarity between edge types to allow a random walk to follow edges semantically similar to a given edge type. Nodes obtained from texts and KGs are linked by an *alias* relation, which indicates that the two nodes *may* point to the same entity. Edges between subjects and objects extracted from texts are lexicalized predicates, whose vector representation is computed as in Gardner et al. [2013]. To compute the weight corresponding to a path—a sequence of relations $r_1, \dots, r_n$—for a given (*source, target*) node pair, at each step j the algorithm can follow either the exact relation type r_j in the path, or another relation type (i.e., predicate) close to it in vector space. This allows the score of a "canonical path" to combine the score of all (similar) path variations.

Many relation instances may go unnoticed if one restricts links between entities in text to predicates which connect subjects and objects. Toutanova et al. [2015] treat the lexicalized dependency paths, which they encode using CNNs, as relations. These semantic representations serve as relation embeddings; they are combined with evidence from the KG to predict either the target in a (*source, relation,* ?) query, or the source in (?, *relation, target*). The information from the two sources is combined in the model's loss function. One term accounts for the non-

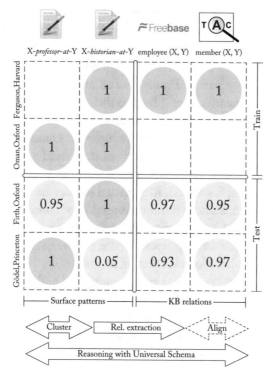

Figure 5.19: Induction of a universal schema from KBs and texts [Riedel et al., 2013].

negative log-likelihood of the correct entity filler with respect to the graph, computed from a combination of three graph embedding models. The other term accounts for the non-negative log-likelihood of the correct entity filler with respect to the text; here, the vector representation of the predicate learned by the CNN replaces the relation representation in the graph embedding models.

Toutanova et al. [2016] include all relation paths of bounded length which connect a source and a target node. The paths' contribution is computed as their weighted sum. The contribution of each path is a score which combines the matrix representation of each relation on the path with the weight of the node it connects to.

There is a quantitative and qualitative difference between the predicates obtained via Open IE, and the relations in knowledge repositories. Riedel et al. [2013] aim to bridge this gap by deriving a *universal schema* which combines surface-form predicates retrieved by Open IE with relations already present in KBs. A very large matrix represents jointly this heterogeneous information: columns correspond to relations from knowledge repositories and predicates found in texts; rows correspond to entity/word pairs. A cell is marked if the corresponding entity pair appears in the given relation or context—see Figure 5.19. Matrix factorization induces representations of the entity pairs and the relations/syntactic patterns, in the manner explained in Section 5.3.2. From such representations, one can determine associations between syntactic patterns and semantic relations, and map these lexical expressions onto the "canonical" relation form. The representations can also help cluster syntactic patterns to indicate new (unnamed) relations, not yet included in the knowledge repository.

Nimishakavi et al. [2016] derive a universal schema and a knowledge repository from unstructured text in a specific domain; they do it without the benefit of a "seed" knowledge repository. Instead of such prior knowledge, Nimishakavi et al. gather two types of "side information" to help structure, and make canonical, candidate (*subject, verb, object*) triples extracted by Open IE methods. The side information consist of hyponym/hypernym candidates extracted using Hearst patterns, and relation similarity (as similarities between verbs in the Open IE triples). The extracted triples are represented in a tensor, factorized together with the side information to induce the relation schema. Figure 5.20 illustrates the method.

Riedel et al. [2013] developed methods based on scoring functions for (*source, relation, target*) triples, which combine partial scores on various pairs of the three elements. This limits the applicability of the methods to already seen *source-target*, *source-relation* or *relation-target* pairs. Verga et al. [2017] address this limitation with a representation for a pair of entities based on the textual patterns in which they appear. Verga et al. [2016] extend the application of a universal schema to multilingual data: they leverage common representations for shared entities, and match the textual patterns in the representation with relations in the knowledge repository.

Zhang et al. [2019a] encode every entity; their model combines these representations with vector representations of the target (KB) relations, and with attention methods for relation prediction. The representation of a source or target entity is based on its neighbourhood in the KG, and on its co-occurrences in the triples extracted from texts. Zhang et al.'s method is applied to Freebase and to a subset of Freebase with film-related relations, as well as to triples extracted from IMDB [Lockard et al., 2019] and ReVerb extractions from ClueWeb whose subject is linked to Freebase [Lin et al., 2012].

Knowledge Graphs and Texts as Separate Information Sources

The merging of information from texts and KGs aims to build a larger graph which can be processed with methods similar to those developed for processing KGs: link prediction using paths, matrix factorization, and so on. Without casting texts in structured forms, they can provide additional information about the nodes or the relations in the graph, or an additional signal for relation learning in KGs.

Weston et al. [2013] encode information from the KG and the textual context separately, and use them together for relation extraction. The KG is encoded with Bordes et al.'s [2013] translation model, and TransE's scoring function provides one part of the information. Information from texts is encoded by a function which computes a similarity measure between a

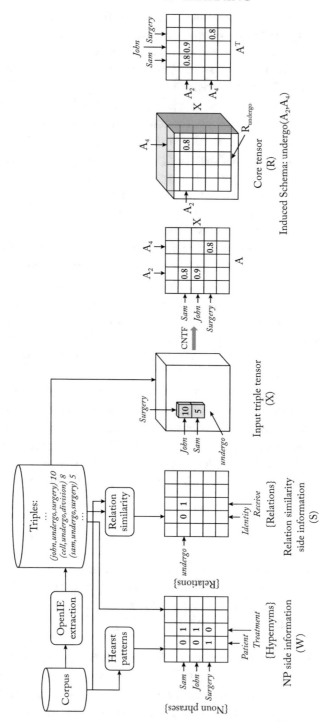

Figure 5.20: Relation schema induction from unstructured texts, using Hearst patterns and Open IE triples [Nimishakavi et al., 2016].

relation mention and a relation embedding. A (*source*, *target*) pair is assigned the relation *rel* with the highest score. This score combines the (*source*, *rel*, *target*) triple's KG score (TransE) and a text-based score; the latter is the cumulative score for the similarity of *rel*'s embedding to every mention of the arguments (i.e., every sentence which contains *source* and *target*).

Xie et al. [2016] combine textual evidence and KB relations by associating textual descriptions with entities in the KB. They encode relational triples with Bordes et al.'s TransE while inducing a representation of the entities which can be useful in predicting their textual descriptions. For the purpose of learning, these textual descriptions (included in Freebase) are encoded with two formalisms: continuous bag-of-words and CNNs. The method produces entity representations which capture both the relational information and their descriptions, and that affects the encoding of the TransE-derived relations. The representations give link prediction results better than any of the subsumed formalisms.

Fan et al. [2016] build on Xie et al.'s work. They reduce the number of parameters of the model, and cast it into a probability framework. The improved model measures the probability of each relational triple, and maximizes the log-likelihood of the observed knowledge to learn simultaneously the contextualized embeddings of entities, relations and words in descriptions. Zhang et al. [2019b] apply KGs (Freebase), texts and pretrained word embeddings to the problem of long-tail relations. The encoding of sentences which include specific relations helps supplement the information about low-frequency entity pairs. Hierarchical information for Freebase relations (as revealed by their names) goes into a GCN to induce similar representations for similar relations. This helps derive informative representations for low-frequency relations.

Natural language understanding—in particular reading comprehension—is one of the high-end tasks to which semantic relations can, or indeed should, contribute. Reading comprehension systems are commonly tested on question answering (QA) [Light et al., 2000]. Levy et al. [2017] show how to model the relation extraction/classification task as a QA task. They adopt a slot-filling framework—look for the entity to complete a triple (e_1, *rel*, ?)—where the relation ranges over all relation types plus *no relation*. To frame this as a QA problem, Levy et al. first *querify* the incomplete relation triple: transform it into a query/question using crowd-sourced templates. To extract a relation instance, a bi-directional attention flow network [Seo et al., 2017] is given as input a sentence with a potential relation instance, together with a query which pairs up a source entity with a relation type. The system outputs a span which corresponds to the target entity, or signals the absence of an answer.

It is an important characteristic of this method that it can generalize to relation types it was not trained on. That is because the model does not learn to associate specific relation types with a given context, but learns to focus on a sentence segment most relevant to the query. There are further developments in this line of research: incorporate relation extraction as a QA task in a multi-task setting [McCann et al., 2018]; and apply multi-turn QA [Li et al., 2019b] which allows sequential discovery of relations, potentially using previous results to answer the current question.

5.6.4   N-ARY AND CROSS-SENTENCE RELATIONS

Most research focuses on binary semantic relations. Even so, n-ary relations are often necessary to acquire sufficient knowledge, especially in specialized domains such as chemistry or medicine. Such relations may also be expressed over a number of sentences, and that makes their extraction even more difficult. Consider this fragment from the biomedical literature [Heuckmann et al., 2011].[22]

> *We next expressed ALK^{F1174L}, $ALK^{F1174L/L1198P}$, $ALK^{F1174L/G1123S}$, and $ALK^{F1174L/G1123D}$ in the original SH–SY5Y cell line.*
>
> [...15 sentences in 3 paragraphs...]
>
> *The 2 mutations that were only found in the neuroblastoma resistance screen (G1123S/D) are located in the glycine-rich loop, which is known to be crucial for ATP and ligand building and are the first mutations described that induce resistance to TAE684, but not to PF02341066.*

Interestingly, n-ary relations were a target at the first Message Understanding Conference.[23] The task was to determine the attributes of an event (who, where, when, and so on), but each of the n-ary relations was split into binary subrelations, and each of those was dealt with via binary relation extraction/classification.

Chen et al. [2019] similarly treat n-ary relation extraction as a collection of binary relation extraction subtasks. They also allow an explicit adjustment of the context window size up to two sentences. Working in a narrow domain (clinical corpus on breast cancer treatments) with limited data, Chen et al. find that the results improve when the text is modelled in terms of phrases and recognized concepts, and enriched with word embeddings and synonyms. A Support Vector Machine gives better results than a feed-forward neural network with two fully connected layers.

Akimoto et al.'s [2019] system for n-ary relation extraction combines universal schemas and the decomposition of n-ary relations into unary and binary relations. Representations for unary and binary relations found in a KB and in text are learned from the training data. The learning of the model for n-ary relations relies on optimizing a score which aggregates the lower-arity relation scores.

---

[22]The summary results in the paper include the following statement: "An independent resistance screen in *ALK*-mutant neuroblastoma cells yielded the same L1198P resistance mutation but defined two additional mutations conferring resistance to TAE684 but not to PF02341066." That is to say, the entities *ALK* and *PF02341066* are related.

[23]ir.nist.gov/muc

Quirk and Poon [2017], Peng et al. [2017] and Wang and Poon [2018] tackle the cross-sentence relation extraction task by taking into account a context larger than a sentence. They all combine inter-sentential relations (grammatical dependencies and word sequence information) with discourse relations and sentence-level sequence information. Peng et al. give this document-graph structure as input to a BiLSTM, as illustrated in Figure 5.13. The forward pass takes the word sequence information and forward-looking dependencies; the backward pass takes the reversed word sequence information and the backward-looking dependencies. The word representations derived by this formalism become the input to a relation classification step. Peng et al. [2017] classify every entity mention pair in their document graph.

This form of relation extraction does not scale well beyond one document because of the combinatorial explosion of entity mention combinations at such a high level. Jia et al.'s [2019] remedy is an entity-centric model: mentions are first mapped onto entities, and entity combinations are explored.

Christopoulou et al. [2019] build a document graph as well, but rely on different kinds of information. To obviate the need for grammatical properties, they use occurrence or co-occurrence to connect nodes which correspond to mentions, entities and sentences: mentions are connected to the sentences in which they occur, to the entities they correspond to, and to other mentions they cooccur with in a sentence; entities are connected to sentences which contain one of their mentions. Christopoulou et al. construct node descriptions from word descriptions. A mention and a sentence are represented by an average of the representations of their words, while an entity's representation averages the representations of its mentions. The aim is to build and represent edges between pairs of entities. The various paths between two entities are aggregated iteratively into edge representations. These representations are then used to classify every edge into a relation type.

Verga et al.'s [2018] model predicts mentions and relations at document level. Mention identification is simulated with an attention mechanism over tokens whose representation combines the actual token embedding and the positional embedding. This input is passed through several layers of multi-head attention—to attend to different types of relevant information—and through convolution components. From the output of this process, Verga et al. build two position-specific representations, for the head and the tail (the source and the target) of a relation. These representations yield a pair-wise relation affinity tensor, which drives the final relation prediction.

The work discussed thus far relies on document-level information—entity mentions, and intra- and inter-sentence relations—processed together. Singh and Bhatia [2019] predict single relations which may cross sentence boundaries. They rely on additional context tokens which mediate the targeted relation. The motivation is to deal with entity mention pairs distant in the text. Finding intermediary tokens in a relation with each of the targeted mentions can help address the distance problem, and give clues about the interaction of the original pair. Singh and Bhatia account for these *second-order relations* in a transformer-based model. The model initially scores the first-order relations to intermediary tokens. Next, it scores the second-order relations by aggregating the scores for all first-order relations which mediate the targeted second-order relations.

5.6.5 UNSUPERVISED RELATION EXTRACTION

Section 4.4 described several ways of tackling unsupervised relation extraction. They rely on semantic similarity to group extracted tuples. The similarity is calculated between the arguments of different relation instances or between the patterns which those instances display. Similarities can be used directly to find the closest relation instance match, or to cluster similar instances.

A good representation of a sentence with an instance of a relation r should be close to the representations of other sentences with other instances of r. This assumption can lead to "implicit" clusters; Marcheggiani and Titov [2016] rely on it for their variational autoencoder model. The encoder builds a semantic representation for a sentence based on a feature-rich representation. The expectation is that the representation so built will approximate the representation of a relation triple. The decoder can then reconstruct one of the arguments of the relation. The two components are trained together. In the encoding step, the argument to be reconstructed is obscured.

Information from a KB added to this model introduces similarity constraints between relation tuples. Liang et al. [2019] learn to discover instances of previously unseen relations. They expand Marcheggiani and Titov's model using the similarity between two entity pairs $x_1 = (x_{11}, x_{12})$ and $x_2 = (x_{21}, x_{22})$ as the cosine of the angle between the translation vectors connecting the entities in each pair:

$$sim(x_1, x_2) = \cos(\mathbf{v}_{11} - \mathbf{v}_{12}, \mathbf{v}_{21} - \mathbf{v}_{22}) \qquad (5.17)$$

$\mathbf{v}_{ij}$ is the KB embedding of entity x_{ij}.

Liang et al. compute two variations. One of them represents the *must-link* confidence score $s^+(x_1, x_2) = [sim(x_1, x_2)]_{\gamma+}^+$, the other the *must-not-link* confidence score $s^-(x_1, x_2) = [sim(x_1, x_2)]_{\gamma-}^-$, where the thresholds $\gamma^+, \gamma^- \in [0, 1]$ limit the two scores. ($[x]_{\gamma+}^+ =$ if $x > \gamma^+$ then x else 0; $[x]_{\gamma-}^- =$ if $x < -\gamma^-$ then x else 0.) These scores, together with the scores which compare the corresponding sentence representations, help determine if the two sentences containing these relation tuples should be in the same cluster, i.e., should represent the same relation. The sentence representations are derived by a system built upon Marcheggiani and Titov's variational autoencoder.

Papanikolaou et al.'s [2019] method generates its own training data for targeted relations on a pre-specified list. They first extract (*subject, verb, object*) triples, and use pre-trained embeddings to map the verbs onto the given set of target relations. The system drops verbs whose similarity to any given relation falls below a threshold. The triples with the accepted verbs are mapped onto texts, as in distant supervision. The sentences which contain the automatically annotated relation instances then help fine-tune a BERT model for relation classification.

5.6.6   LIFELONG LEARNING

Deep learning requires very large training data to build accurate models. The model consists of the network architecture and its parameters—weights in its various units—whose best values are determined during training. Training such a model costs a great deal of computing time and power. A deep-learning system which aims to continue learning faces a dilemma. It can keep retraining on ever-growing datasets, or be doomed to forget much of what it has learned if it gets none, or only a subset, of the old data together with newer instances for training a new model. That is because even a small change in the learned parameters (when the model is updated on new data) may cause unpredictable behaviour on the older data.

Wang et al. [2019] suggest a two-part solution. Inspired by previous research on handwriting and object recognition, they propose a new strategy: maintain a "training memory", and select instances from previously used data to add to a new training set, and so avoid forgetting the older data. They call their method *episodic memory replay* (EMR). The "memory" $\mathcal{M}$ consists of a number of training examples selected after each training session. When training on a new dataset, EMR adds a sample of instances from $\mathcal{M}$ to the current training data, so the model can retain the knowledge of previous data. The second part of the solution arises from the observation that a good model should not distort excessively the embedding space of the model's parameters when it gets additional training data. For the task of relation extraction in particular, Wang et al. use the sentence embeddings derived by the neural model in previous sessions as anchor points, and constrain the system to only minimally distort these anchor points with the processing of new data.

5.7   SUMMARY

This chapter has presented an overview of the recognition and classification of semantic relations in the deep-learning paradigm. The methods developed for the traditional learning of semantic relations—discussed in Chapters 3 and 4—can be directly mapped onto this new formalism but the power of deep learning is best unleashed when we can take advantage of its specific characteristics:

- low-dimensional representation of word meaning based on various types of knowledge;
- representation derived simultaneously for arguments and relations;
- the leveraging of multiple information sources;
- the availability of formalisms which encode variable-length sequences and find patterns in them;
- the encoding of graph structures (syntactic or semantic) together with a variety of additional attributes.

Deep learning requires, among other things, large amounts of training data. Some such data can be bootstrapped from existing knowledge repositories by distant supervision—see Chapter 4. The adoption of deep learning has led to innovative ways of cleaning the automatically annotated data. Many interesting methods have been developed to tackle noise in automatically generated data: people have applied adversarial learning, reinforcement learning and other fun formalisms. The new technology has opened a vast space of exploration. We have presented some of the main trends, but there are new directions to be found, and space in between.

CHAPTER 6

Conclusion

The book aims to disentangle two perspectives on semantic relations: as the connections which structure our knowledge of the world, linking concepts/entities/words in knowledge repositories; and as the connections between nominals which help understand what a text is about. Chapter 2 showed how these two perspectives have been evolving in parallel for about 2000 years until automatic understanding of language became a research topic. In AI and especially in NLP, these two views of semantic relations began to interact with each other, as well as with unstructured textual data, structured repositories of knowledge and computational methods. They all have been evolving in parallel, influencing each other, and substantive changes in any of them made researchers reevaluate and reinterpret what semantic relations are, how they describe meaning, how many there are, and how many are needed.

First, semantic relations were elicited from people, in an attempt to understand how they perceive the connections between words in a word pair, then words in a simple noun phrase, and then words in a text fragment. More insights came as semantic relations found application in the description of the meaning in general texts or in texts from specialized domains.

In knowledge repositories, the story has changed, too. Such repositories have evolved from taxonomies which structure specialized knowledge in scientific domains to collections of facts about lexical knowledge and world knowledge, employing a wide—eventually open-ended—variety of semantic relations to describe the connections. The concerns related to semantic relations, whether in texts or in knowledge repositories, include the level of granularity: *is-a* and *part-of*, for example, semantic relations usually considered atomic, can each have several sub-relations. Ultimately, semantic relations themselves can be organized into taxonomies, and connected by "meta" *is-a* relations.

The next step in the story of semantic relations was the gathering of data annotated with a set of relations which cover all necessary interaction types. The datasets have gradually grown both in size and in the number and type of relations included. After starting with a few specific relations which describe interactions between organizations, locations and people, the Web level has been reached, with repositories of collaboratively amassed knowledge over Web interfaces. The amount of available data had a direct effect on the attempts to detect relations. We have visited the entire spectrum, from supervised to unsupervised, crossing through self-supervised and semi-supervised methods, to distant supervision. All these methods share certain requirements. They need a good semantic representation of the words/phrases/entities which serve as arguments, and a good semantic representation of the relational clues: the connecting phrase and possibly the larger context. The semantic representation of words/phrases/entities has evolved in a nonlinear fashion. It began with symbolic methods based on distributional and relational models of meaning, moved into continuous representations, and finally combined them in a variety of ways, as the different types of knowledge they express have become appreciated for what that knowledge brings. It has been a challenge to represent contexts of varying length and structure in a manner digestible by computers. Simple bag-of-words models have been incorporated first; then syntactic information has been gradually added to the mix; finally, a variety of compositional models—which combine lexical semantics and syntactic information—have been explored, in conjunction with the machine-learning formalisms capable of putting them to use.

The available text has been a major element of change in this diachronic evolution of research in semantic relations. In the early 1990s, a large source of textual knowledge for acquiring *is-a* relations was a machine-readable version of a dictionary with a few million tokens. Currently, texts (even historical texts) are not a concern. There has been an expansion of textual data both as a source for relation instances and as support for inducing word meaning representations, relation patterns, paraphrases, and so on. It has pushed the community to reconsider semantic relations—having to ask ourselves again what they are, how many there are, where they are, how we can find them in this deluge of textual data—and to develop better learning methods. Techniques are required not only to cope with this amount of raw data but to take advantage of it by capitalizing on redundancies and noise detection.

The intercross between manually built, yet large, knowledge repositories and the colossal amount of free-form text has been most beneficial to the deep-learning methods. Their adoption for the learning of semantic relations has resulted in creative solutions at multiple levels of the process. At the representation level, the semantics of both the arguments and the relation can be encoded in a variety of forms, and they can interact in many ways. Many compositional methods can be used or learned to get the meaning of context with complex structure. At the level of the model, one need not separate the building of a representation of an instance from the learning of a model of a relation; they are interdependent, and they can be modelled as such. At the data level, while current deep-learning methods need copious amounts of data, they can also be relied upon to provide a plethora of ways for filtering noise for distant supervision; that includes methods inspired by games, such as reinforcement learning and adversarial training.

An abundant amount and variety of work on semantic relations has been accomplished in the past few years. It has proved impossible to cover all publications on the topic, specialized as it is, even if we included references to reference papers with an overview of some of the subtopics we touched upon. Yet there is so much more space for exploration, even if one only ponders established ideas, let alone ideas which may be just around the corner. Take the representation of meaning, for example. There is room to explore representations particularly suitable for capturing the dimensions along which words/entities/concepts interact. For models, one exciting direction for exploration is "few-shot learning", methods which can learn robust models from small amounts of data. Such new representations and new methods together could lead to more explainable models, capable of justifying the choice of one semantic relation over another to hold between a pair of words in a given context. The learning of n-ary and cross-sentence relations has grown in the past few years. It continues to grow, as it has become apparent that complex relations are necessary to make sense of the complex interaction between concepts, particularly in specialized scientific domains. Texts are available in a wide variety of domains and genres; each of them imposes different constraints on which relations are expressed, and how. It is now essentially important to study the application of relation extraction techniques in various domains, and their ultimate role in understanding language in its many published forms.

Bibliography

ACE. Automatic content extraction 2008 evaluation plan: Assessment of detection and recognition of entities and relations within and across documents, 2008. www.itl.nist.gov/iad/mig/tests/ace/2008/doc/ace08-evalplan.v1.2d.pdf 32

Eugene Agichtein and Luis Gravano. *Snowball*: Extracting relations from large plain-text collections. In *Proc. 5th ACM Conference on Digital Libraries*, pages 85–94, New York, 2000. DOI: 10.1145/336597.336644 80, 81, 83

Thomas Ahlswede and Martha Evens. Parsing vs. text processing in the analysis of dictionary definitions. In *Proc. 26th Annual Meeting of the Association for Computational Linguistics*, pages 217–224, Buffalo, NY, June 7–10, 1988. DOI: 10.3115/982023.982050 77, 79

Kosuke Akimoto, Takuya Hiraoka, Kunihiko Sadamasa, and Mathias Niepert. Cross-sentence N-ary relation extraction using lower-arity universal schemas. In *Proc. Conference on Empirical Methods in Natural Language Processing and the 9th International Joint Conference on Natural Language Processing (EMNLP-IJCNLP)*, pages 6225–6231, Association for Computational Linguistics, Hong Kong, China, 2019. www.aclweb.org/anthology/D19-1645 DOI: 10.18653/v1/d19-1645 135, 160

Hiyan Alshawi. Processing dictionary definitions with phrasal pattern hierarchies. *American Journal of Computational Linguistics*, 13(3):195–202, 1987. 77

Mohammed Alsuhaibani, Takanori Maehara, and Danushka Bollegala. Joint learning of hierarchical word embeddings from a corpus and a taxonomy. In *Automated Knowledge Base Construction (AKBC)*, 2019. openreview.net/forum?id=S1xf-W5paX DOI: 10.24432/C50591 123

Christoph Alt, Aleksandra Gabryszak, and Leonhard Hennig. TACRED revisited: A thorough evaluation of the TACRED relation extraction task. In *Proc. 58th Annual Meeting of the Association for Computational Linguistics*, pages 1558–1569, 2020. www.aclweb.org/anthology/2020.acl-main.142 DOI: 10.18653/v1/2020.acl-main.142 49

Robert Amsler. A taxonomy for English nouns and verbs. In *Proc. 19th Annual Meeting of the Association for Computational Linguistics*, pages 133–138, Stanford University, Stanford, CA, June 29–July 1, 1981. DOI: 10.3115/981923.981959 77, 78

Gabor Angeli, Julie Tibshirani, Jean Wu, and Christopher D. Manning. Combining distant and partial supervision for relation extraction. In *Proc. Conference on Empirical Methods in Natural Language Processing (EMNLP)*, pages 1556–1567, 2014. www.aclweb.org/anthology/D14-1164 DOI: 10.3115/v1/d14-1164 102

Ron Artstein and Massimo Poesio. Inter-coder agreement for computational linguistics. *Computational Linguistics*, 34(4):555–596, 2008. www.aclweb.org/anthology/J08-4004 DOI: 10.1162/coli.07-034-r2 49

Sören Auer, Christian Bizer, Jens Lehmann, Georgi Kobilarov, Richard Cyganiak, and Zachary Ives. DBpedia: A nucleus for a Web of open data. In *Proc. 6th International Semantic Web Conference and 2nd Asian Semantic Web Conference*, pages 722–735, Busan, Korea, November 11–15, 2007. DOI: 10.1007/978-3-540-76298-0_52 44

Mahmoud Azab, Stephane Dadian, Vivi Nastase, Larry An, and Rada Mihalcea. Towards extracting medical family history from natural language interactions: A new dataset and baselines. In *Proc. Conference on Empirical Methods in Natural Language Processing and the 9th International Joint Conference on Natural Language Processing (EMNLP-IJCNLP*, pages 1255–1260, Association for Computational Linguistics, 2019. www.aclweb.org/anthology/D19-1122 DOI: 10.18653/v1/d19-1122 48

Fan Bai and Alan Ritter. Structured minimally supervised learning for neural relation extraction. In *Proc. Conference of the North American Chapter of the Association for Computational Linguistics: Human Language Technologies, Volume 1 (Long and Short Papers)*, pages 3057–3069, Minneapolis, MN, 2019. www.aclweb.org/anthology/N19-1310 DOI: 10.18653/v1/N19-1310 136

Ivana Balazevic, Carl Allen, and Timothy Hospedales. Multi-relational poincaré graph embeddings. In *Advances in Neural Information Processing Systems*, pages 4463–4473, 2019. 122, 138, 145

Michele Banko and Oren Etzioni. The tradeoffs between open and traditional relation extraction. In *Proc. 46th Annual Meeting of the Association for Computational Linguistics: Human Language Technologies*, pages 28–36, Columbus, OH, June 15–20, 2008. 99

Michele Banko, Michael Cafarella, Stephen Sonderland, Matt Broadhead, and Oren Etzioni. Open information extraction from the Web. In *Proc. 22nd Conference on the Advancement of Artificial Intelligence*, pages 2670–2676, Vancouver, B.C., Canada, July 22–26, 2007. DOI: 10.21236/ada538482 105

Ken Barker and Stan Szpakowicz. Semi-automatic recognition of noun modifier relationships. In *Proc. 36th Annual Meeting of the Association for Computational Linguistics*, pages 96–102, Montréal, 1998. DOI: 10.3115/980451.980862 21, 22

Marco Baroni and Alessandro Lenci. How we BLESSed distributional semantic evaluation. In *Proc. GEMS Workshop on Geometrical Models of Natural Language Semantics*, pages 1–10, Association for Computational Linguistics, Edinburgh, UK, 2011. www.aclweb.org/anthology/ W11-2501 38, 87

Laurie Bauer. Compounding. In Martin Haspelmath, Ed., *Language Typology and Language Universals*. Mouton de Gruyter, The Hague, 2001. 16

Iz Beltagy, Kyle Lo, and Waleed Ammar. Combining distant and direct supervision for neural relation extraction. In *Proc. Conference of the North American Chapter of the Association for Computational Linguistics: Human Language Technologies, Volume 1 (Long and Short Papers)*, pages 1858–1867, 2019. DOI: 10.18653/v1/n19-1184 141

Yoshua Bengio, Réjean Ducharme, Pascal Vincent, and Christian Jauvin. A neural probabilistic language model. *Journal of the Machine Learning Research*, 3:1137–1155, 2003. 113

Giulia Benotto. Distributional models for semantic relations: A study on hyponymy and antonymy. Ph.D. thesis, University of Pisa, 2015. 38, 87

Matthew Berland and Eugene Charniak. Finding parts in very large corpora. In *Proc. 37th Annual Meeting of the Association for Computational Linguistics*, pages 57–64, College Park, MD, June 20–26, 1999. DOI: 10.3115/1034678.1034697 14, 80

Daniel M. Bikel, Richard Schwartz, and Ralph M. Weischedel. An algorithm that learns what's in a name. *Machine Learning*, 34(1–3):211–231, 1999. dx.doi.org/10.1023/A: 1007558221122 DOI: 10.1023/A:1007558221122 64

Christopher M. Bishop. *Pattern Recognition and Machine Learning*. Springer, 2006. 58

Christian Blaschke, Miguel A. Andrade, Christos Ouzounis, and Alfonso Valencia. Automatic extraction of biological information from scientific text: Protein-protein interactions. In *Proc. 7th International Conference on Intelligent Systems for Molecular Biology (ISMB)*, Heidelberg, Germany, 1999. 80

David M. Blei, Andrew Y. Ng, and Michael I. Jordan. Latent Dirichlet allocation. *Journal of Machine Learning Research*, 3:993–1022, 2003. dl.acm.org/citation.cfm?id=944919.944937 DOI: 10.1109/asru.2015.7404785 51, 113

Avrim Blum and Tom Mitchell. Combining labeled and unlabeled data with co-training. In *Proc. 11th Annual Conference on Computational Learning Theory*, pages 92–100, 1998. DOI: 10.1145/279943.279962 104

Antoine Bordes, Jason Weston, Ronan Collobert, and Yoshua Bengio. Learning structured embeddings of knowledge bases. In *Proc. 25th AAAI Conference on Artificial Intelligence, AAAI*, pages 301–306, 2011. 121

Antoine Bordes, Nicolas Usunier, Alberto Garcia-Duran, Jason Weston, and Oksana Yakhnenko. Translating embeddings for modeling multi-relational data. In C. J. C. Burges, L. Bottou, M. Welling, Z. Ghahramani, and K. Q. Weinberger, Eds., *Advances in Neural Information Processing Systems 26*, pages 2787–2795, Curran Associates, Inc., 2013. papers.nips.cc/paper/5071-translating-embeddings-for-modeling-multi-relational-data.pdf 138, 144, 145, 157, 159

Sergey Brin. Extracting patterns and relations from the World Wide Web. In *Selected Papers from the International Workshop on the World Wide Web and Databases, (WebDB)*, pages 172–183, Springer-Verlag, London, UK, 1998. 80, 81, 83
DOI: 10.1007/10704656_11

Ted Briscoe, John Carroll, and Rebecca Watson. The second release of the RASP system. In *Proc. 21st International Conference on Computational Linguistics and 44th Annual Meeting of the Association for Computational Linguistics*, Sydney, Australia, July 17–21, 2006. DOI: 10.3115/1225403.1225423 52

Michael L. Brodie and John Mylopoulos. Knowledge bases vs. databases. In Michael L. Brodie and John Mylopoulos, Eds., *On Knowledge Base Management Systems*, Topics in Information Systems, Springer, New York, 1986. DOI: 10.1007/978-1-4612-4980-1_9 7

Peter F. Brown, Peter V. deSouza, Robert L. Mercer, T. J. Watson, Vincent J. Della Pietra, and Jenifer C. Lai. Class-based n-gram models of natural language. *Computational Linguistics*, 18(4):467–479, 1992. 51

Markus Bundschus, Mathaeus Dejori, Martin Stetter, Volker Tresp, and Hans-Peter Kriegel. Extraction of semantic biomedical relations from text using conditional random fields. *BMC Bioinformatics*, 9(1):1–14, 2008. www.biomedcentral.com/1471-2105/9/207 DOI: 10.1186/1471-2105-9-207 65

Razvan Bunescu and Raymond J. Mooney. A shortest path dependency kernel for relation extraction. In *Human Language Technology Conference and Conference on Empirical Methods in Natural Language Processing (HLT-EMNLP)*, Vancouver, Canada, 2005. DOI: 10.3115/1220575.1220666 61

Razvan Bunescu and Raymond J. Mooney. Learning to extract relations from the Web using minimal supervision. In *Proc. 45th Annual Meeting of the Association of Computational Linguistics*, pages 576–583, 2007. www.aclweb.org/anthology/P07-1073 99

Cristina Butnariu and Tony Veale. A concept-centered approach to noun-compound interpretation. In *Proc. 22nd International Conference on Computational Linguistics*, pages 81–88, Manchester, UK, 2008. DOI: 10.3115/1599081.1599092 56

Cristina Butnariu, Su Nam Kim, Preslav Nakov, Diarmuid Ó Séaghdha, Stan Szpakowicz, and Tony Veale. SemEval-2 Task 9: The interpretation of noun compounds using paraphrasing verbs and prepositions. In *Proc. 5th International Workshop on Semantic Evaluation*, pages 39–44, Association for Computational Linguistics, Uppsala, Sweden, 2010. www.aclweb.org/anthology/S10-1007 DOI: 10.3115/1621969.1621987 23

Michael Cafarella, Michele Banko, and Oren Etzioni. Relational Web search. *Technical Report*, University of Washington, Department of Computer Science and Engineering, 2006. 3

Duy-Cat Can, Hoang-Quynh Le, Quang-Thuy Ha, and Nigel Collier. A richer-but-smarter shortest dependency path with attentive augmentation for relation extraction. In *Proc. Conference of the North American Chapter of the Association for Computational Linguistics: Human Language Technologies, Volume 1 (Long and Short Papers)*, pages 2902–2912, Minneapolis, MN, 2019. www.aclweb.org/anthology/N19-1298 DOI: 10.18653/v1/n19-1298 127, 149

Nicola Cancedda, Eric Gaussier, Cyril Goutte, and Jean-Michel Renders. Word-sequence kernels. *Journal of Machine Learning Research*, 3:1059–1082, 2003. jmlr.csail.mit.edu/papers/v3/cancedda03a.html 61

Andrew Carlson, Justin Betteridge, Bryan Kisiel, Burr Settles, Estevam R. Hruschka Jr., and Tom M. Mitchell. Toward an architecture for never-ending language learning. In *Proc. 24th Conference on Artificial Intelligence (AAAI)*, 2010a. 81

Andrew Carlson, Justin Betteridge, Richard C. Wang, Estevam R. Hruschka Jr., and Tom M. Mitchell. Coupled semi-supervised learning for information extraction. In *Proc. 3rd ACM International Conference on Web Search and Data Mining (WSDM)*, 2010b. DOI: 10.1145/1718487.1718501 84, 85, 104

Joseph B. Casagrande and Kenneth Hale. Semantic relationships in Papago folk-definition. In Dell H. Hymes and William E. Bittleolo, Eds., *Studies in Southwestern Ethnolinguistics*, pages 165–193, Mouton, The Hague and Paris, 1967. 15, 16

Roger Chaffin and Douglas J. Herrmann. The similarity and diversity of semantic relations. *Memory and Cognition*, 12(2):134–141, 1984. DOI: 10.3758/bf03198427 15, 16

Ines Chami, Zhitao Ying, Christopher Ré, and Jure Leskovec. Hyperbolic graph convolutional neural networks. In *Advances in Neural Information Processing Systems*, pages 4868–4879, 2019. 148

Yee Seng Chan and Dan Roth. Exploiting background knowledge for relation extraction. In *Proc. 23rd International Conference on Computational Linguistics (COLING)*, Beijing, China, 2010. 51

Kai-Wei Chang, Wen-tau Yih, Bishan Yang, and Christopher Meek. Typed tensor decomposition of knowledge bases for relation extraction. In *Proc. Conference on Empirical Methods in Natural Language Processing (EMNLP)*, pages 1568–1579, Association for Computational Linguistics, 2014. aclweb.org/anthology/D14-1165 DOI: 10.3115/v1/d14-1165 120

Eugene Charniak. Toward a model of children's story comprehension. *Technical Report AITR-266*, (hdl.handle.net/1721.1/6892), Massachusetts Institute of Technology, 1972. 13

Jinxiu Chen, Donghong Ji, Chew Lim Tan, and Zhengyu Niu. Relation extraction using label propagation based semi-supervised learning. In *Proc. 21st International Conference on Computational Linguistics and the 44th Annual Meeting of the Association for Computational Linguistics, ACL-44*, pages 129–136, 2006. DOI: 10.3115/1220175.1220192 102

Jiyu Chen, Karin Verspoor, and Zenan Zhai. A bag-of-concepts model improves relation extraction in a narrow knowledge domain with limited data. In *Proc. Conference of the North American Chapter of the Association for Computational Linguistics: Student Research Workshop*, pages 43–52, Minneapolis, MN, 2019. www.aclweb.org/anthology/N19-3007 DOI: 10.18653/v1/n19-3007 160

Kyunghyun Cho, Bart van Merriënboer, Caglar Gulcehre, Dzmitry Bahdanau, Fethi Bougares, Holger Schwenk, and Yoshua Bengio. Learning phrase representations using RNN encoder-decoder for statistical machine translation. In *Proc. Conference on Empirical Methods in Natural Language Processing, EMNLP*, pages 1724–1734, Doha, Qatar, 2014. www.aclweb.org/anthology/D14-1179 DOI: 10.3115/v1/d14-1179 126

Martin S. Chodorow, Roy Byrd, and George Heidorn. Extracting semantic hierarchies from a large on-line dictionary. In *Proc. 23th Annual Meeting of the Association for Computational Linguistics*, pages 299–304, Chicago, IL, July 8–12, 1985. DOI: 10.3115/981210.981247 77, 78

Fenia Christopoulou, Makoto Miwa, and Sophia Ananiadou. A walk-based model on entity graphs for relation extraction. In *Proc. 56th Annual Meeting of the Association for Computational Linguistics (Volume 2: Short Papers)*, pages 81–88, Melbourne, Australia, 2018. www.aclweb.org/anthology/P18-2014 DOI: 10.18653/v1/p18-2014 151

Fenia Christopoulou, Makoto Miwa, and Sophia Ananiadou. Connecting the dots: Document-level neural relation extraction with edge-oriented graphs. In *Proc. Conference on Empirical Methods in Natural Language Processing and the 9th International Joint Conference on Natural Language Processing (EMNLP-IJCNLP)*, pages 4925–4936, 2019. www.aclweb.org/anthology/D19-1498 DOI: 10.18653/v1/d19-1498 161

Massimiliano Ciaramita, Aldo Gangemi, Esther Ratsch, Jasmin Šarić, and Isabel Rojas. Unsupervised learning of semantic relations between concepts of a molecular miology ontology. In

Proc. 19th International Joint Conference on Artificial Intelligence, pages 659–664, Edinburgh, Scotland, July 30–August 5, 2005. 14

Kevin Cohen. *Handbook of Natural Language Processing, chapter 27. BioNLP: Biomedical Text Mining*, 2nd ed., CRC Press, Taylor and Francis Group, Boca Raton, FL, 2010. 45

William W. Cohen, Pradeep Ravikumar, and Stephen E. Fienberg. A comparison of string distance metrics for name-matching tasks. In *Proc. IJCAI Workshop on Information Integration on the Web*, pages 73–78, Acapulco, Mexico, August 9–10, 2003. 92

Ronald R. Coifman and Mauro Maggioni. Diffusion wavelets. *Applied and Computational Harmonic Analysis*, 21(1):53–94, 2006. DOI: 10.1016/j.acha.2006.04.004 57

Michael Collins and Nigel Duffy. Convolution kernels for natural language. In *Proc. 15th Conference on Neural Information Processing Systems (NIPS)*, Vancouver, Canada, 2001. books.nips.cc/papers/files/nips14/AA58.pdf 61, 62

Ronan Collobert and Jason Weston. A unified architecture for natural language processing: Deep neural networks with multitask learning. In *Proc. 25th International Conference on Machine Learning, (ICML)*, pages 160–167, ACM, New York, NY, 2008. DOI: 10.1145/1390156.1390177 113

Alexis Conneau, Kartikay Khandelwal, Naman Goyal, Vishrav Chaudhary, Guillaume Wenzek, Francisco Guzmán, Edouard Grave, Myle Ott, Luke Zettlemoyer, and Veselin Stoyanov. Unsupervised cross-lingual representation learning at scale. *ArXiv Preprint*, 2019. arxiv.org/abs/1911.02116 DOI: 10.18653/v1/2020.acl-main.747 116

Corinna Cortes and Vladimir Vapnik. Support vector networks. *Machine Learning*, 20(3):273–297, 1995. DOI: 10.1007/bf00994018 60

Seana Coulson. *Semantic Leaps: Frame-Shifting and Conceptual Blending in Meaning Construction*. Cambridge University Press, Cambridge, 2001. DOI: 10.1017/cbo9780511551352 18

Mark Craven and Johan Kumlien. Constructing biological knowledge bases by extracting information from text sources. In *Proc. 7th International Conference on Intelligent Systems for Molecular Biology*, pages 77–86, 1999. 98

Aron Culotta and Jeffrey Sorensen. Dependency tree kernels for relation extraction. In *Proc. 42nd Meeting of the Association for Computational Linguistics (ACL), Main Volume*, pages 423–429, Barcelona, Spain, 2004. www.aclweb.org/anthology/P04-1054 DOI: 10.3115/1218955.1219009 63

Aron Culotta, Andrew McCallum, and Jonathan Betz. Integrating probabilistic extraction models and data mining to discover relations and patterns in text. In *Proc. Conference on Human Language Technology Conference of the North-American Chapter of the Association of Computational Linguistics, (HLT-NAACL)*, pages 296–303, 2006. dx.doi.org/10.3115/1220835.1220873 DOI: 10.3115/1220835.1220873 65

James R. Curran, Tara Murphy, and Bernhard Scholz. Minimising semantic drift with mutual exclusion bootstrapping. In *Proc. Conference of the Pacific Association for Computational Linguistics*, pages 172–180, Melbourne, Australia, September 19–21, 2007. 82, 83

Nilesh Dalvi, Pedro Domingos, Mausam, Sumit Sanghai, and Deepak Verma. Adversarial classification. In *Proc. 10th ACM SIGKDD International Conference on Knowledge Discovery and Data Mining, (KDD)*, pages 99–108, ACM, New York, NY, 2004. DOI: 10.1145/1014052.1014066 139

Rajarshi Das, Arvind Neelakantan, David Belanger, and Andrew McCallum. Chains of reasoning over entities, relations, and text using recurrent neural networks. *ArXiv Preprint*, 2016. arxiv.org/abs/1607.01426 DOI: 10.18653/v1/e17-1013 146

Dmitry Davidov and Ari Rappoport. Unsupervised discovery of generic relationships using pattern clusters and its evaluation by automatically generated SAT analogy questions. In *Proc. 46th Annual Conference of the Association for Computational Linguistics: Human Language Technologies (ACL-08:HLT)*, pages 692–700, Columbus, OH, 2008a. 56, 94, 95

Dmitry Davidov and Ari Rappoport. Classification of semantic relationships between nominals using pattern clusters. In *Proc. 46th Annual Meeting of the Association for Computational Linguistics: Human Language Technologies*, pages 227–235, Columbus, OH, June 15–20, 2008b. 14, 34, 56

Ferdinand de Saussure. *Course in General Linguistics*. Philosophical Library, New York, 1959. Edited by Charles Bally and Albert Sechehaye. Translated from the French by Wade Baskin. 12, 26

Dina Demner-Fushman, Kin Wah Fung, Phong Do, Richard D. Boyce, and Travis Goodwin. Overview of the TAC drug-drug interaction extraction from drug labels track. In *Proc. Text Analysis Conference (TAC)*, 2018. tac.nist.gov/publications/2018/papers.html 48

Tim Dettmers, Pasquale Minervini, Pontus Stenetorp, and Sebastian Riedel. Convolutional 2D knowledge graph embeddings. In *Proc. 32nd AAAI Conference on Artificial Intelligence, the 30th Innovative Applications of Artificial Intelligence (IAAI), and the 8th AAAI Symposium on Educational Advances in Artificial Intelligence (EAAI)*, pages 1811–1818, New Orleans, LA, February 2–7, 2018. www.aaai.org/ocs/index.php/AAAI/AAAI18/paper/view/17366 138, 146

Jacob Devlin, Ming-Wei Chang, Kenton Lee, and Kristina Toutanova. BERT: Pre-training of deep bidirectional transformers for language understanding. *ArXiv Preprint*, 2018. arxiv.org/abs/1810.04805 110, 115, 131, 150

Jacob Devlin, Ming-Wei Chang, Kenton Lee, and Kristina Toutanova. BERT: Pre-training of deep bidirectional transformers for language understanding. In *Proc. Conference of the North American Chapter of the Association for Computational Linguistics: Human Language Technologies, Volume 1 (Long and Short Papers)*, pages 4171–4186, 2019. www.aclweb.org/anthology/N19-1423 DOI: 10.18653/v1/N19-1423 110, 115, 131, 150

Cícero Nogueira dos Santos, Bing Xiang, and Bowen Zhou. Classifying relations by ranking with convolutional neural networks. In *Proc. 53rd Annual Meeting of the Association for Computational Linguistics and the 7th International Joint Conference on Natural Language Processing*, pages 626–634, 2015. DOI: 10.3115/v1/p15-1061 149, 153

Doug Downey, Oren Etzioni, and Stephen Soderland. A probabilistic model of redundancy in information extraction. In *Proc. 19th International Joint Conference on Artificial Intelligence*, pages 1034–1041, Edinburgh, Scotland, July 30–August 5, 2005. DOI: 10.21236/ada454763 93, 97

Doug Downey, Oren Etzioni, and Stephen Soderland. Analysis of a probabilistic model of redundancy in unsupervised information extraction. *Artificial Intelligence*, 174(11):726–748, 2010. DOI: 10.1016/j.artint.2010.04.024 97

Pamela Downing. On the creation and use of English noun compounds. *Language*, 53(4):810–842, 1977. DOI: 10.2307/412913 18, 23, 26

Jinhua Du, Jingguang Han, Andy Way, and Dadong Wan. Multi-level structured self-attentions for distantly supervised relation extraction. In *Proc. Conference on Empirical Methods in Natural Language Processing*, pages 2216–2225, Association for Computational Linguistics, Brussels, Belgium, 2018. www.aclweb.org/anthology/D18-1245 DOI: 10.18653/v1/d18-1245 141

Kawin Ethayarajh, David Duvenaud, and Graeme Hirst. Towards understanding linear word analogies. In *Proc. 57th Annual Meeting of the Association for Computational Linguistics*, pages 3253–3262, Florence, Italy, 2019. DOI: 10.18653/v1/p19-1315 114, 127

Oren Etzioni, Michael Cafarella, Doug Downey, Ana-Maria Popescu, Tal Shaked, Stephen Soderland, Daniel S. Weld, and Alexander Yates. Unsupervised named-entity extraction from the Web: An experimental study. *Artificial Intelligence*, 165(1):91–134, 2005. DOI: 10.1016/j.artint.2005.03.001 105

Anthony Fader, Stephen Soderland, and Oren Etzioni. Identifying relations for open information extraction. In *Proc. Conference on Empirical Methods in Natural Language Processing*, pages 1535–1545, Edinburgh, UK, July 26–29, 2011. 14, 92, 97, 105

Miao Fan, Deli Zhao, Qiang Zhou, Zhiyuan Liu, Thomas Fang Zheng, and Edward Y. Chang. Distant supervision for relation extraction with matrix completion. In *Proc. 52nd Annual Meeting of the Association for Computational Linguistics (Volume 1: Long Papers)*, pages 839–849, Baltimore, MD, 2014. www.aclweb.org/anthology/P14-1079 DOI: 10.3115/v1/p14-1079 137

Miao Fan, Qiang Zhou, Thomas Fang Zheng, and Ralph Grishman. Distributed representation learning for knowledge graphs with entity descriptions. *Pattern Recognition Letters*, 93(2017):31–37, 2016. DOI: 10.1016/j.patrec.2016.09.005 159

Michael Färber, Frederic Bartscherer, Carsten Menne, and Achim Rettinger. Linked data quality of dbpedia, freebase, opencyc, wikidata, and yago. *Semantic Web*, 9(1):77–129, 2018. DOI: 10.3233/sw-170275 49, 50

Christiane Fellbaum, Ed. *WordNet – An Electronic Lexical Database*. MIT Press, 1998. DOI: 10.2307/417141 14, 24

Jun Feng, Minlie Huang, Li Zhao, Yang Yang, and Xiaoyan Zhu. Reinforcement learning for relation classification from noisy data. In *32nd AAAI Conference on Artificial Intelligence*, 2018. 142

Gregory Finley, Stephanie Farmer, and Serguei Pakhomov. What analogies reveal about word vectors and their compositionality. In *Proc. 6th Joint Conference on Lexical and Computational Semantics (*SEM)*, pages 1–11, Association for Computational Linguistics, 2017. www.aclweb.org/anthology/S17-1001 DOI: 10.18653/v1/s17-1001 129

Gottlob Frege. *Begriffschrift*. Louis Nebert, Halle, 1879. 12

Ruiji Fu, Jiang Guo, Bing Qin, Wanxiang Che, Haifeng Wang, and Ting Liu. Learning semantic hierarchies via word embeddings. In *Proc. 52nd Annual Meeting of the Association for Computational Linguistics (Volume 1: Long Papers)*, pages 1199–1209, Baltimore, MD, 2014. www.aclweb.org/anthology/P14-1113 DOI: 10.3115/v1/p14-1113 151

George W. Furnas, Scott Deerwester, Susan T. Dumais, Thomas K. Landauer, Richard A. Harshman, Lynn A. Streeter, and Karen E. Lochbaum. Information retrieval using a singular value decomposition model of latent semantic structure. In *Proc. 11th Annual International ACM SIGIR Conference on Research and Development in Information Retrieval*, pages 465–480, 1988. DOI: 10.1145/62437.62487 112

Tianyu Gao, Xu Han, Hao Zhu, Zhiyuan Liu, Peng Li, Maosong Sun, and Jie Zhou. FewRel 2.0: Towards more challenging few-shot relation classification. In *Proc. Conference on Empirical Methods in Natural Language Processing and International Joint Conference on Natural Language Processing (EMNLP-IJCNLP)*, pages 6250–6255, 2019. www.aclweb.org/anthology/D19-1649 DOI: 10.18653/v1/d19-1649 135

Alberto García-Durán and Mathias Niepert. Learning graph representations with embedding propagation. In *Proc. 31st International Conference on Neural Information Processing Systems*, pages 5125–5136, 2017. 148

Jean Claude Gardin. *SYNTOL*. Graduate School of Library Service, Rutgers, the State University (Rutgers Series on Systems for the Intellectual Organization of Information, Susan Artandi Ed.), New Brunswick, NJ, 1965. 12

Matt Gardner and Tom Mitchell. Efficient and expressive knowledge base completion using subgraph feature extraction. In *Proc. Conference on Empirical Methods in Natural Language Processing*, pages 1488–1498, Association for Computational Linguistics, 2015. aclweb.org/anthology/D15-1173 DOI: 10.18653/v1/d15-1173 104, 134, 145

Matt Gardner, Partha Pratim Talukdar, Bryan Kisiel, and Tom Mitchell. Improving learning and inference in a large knowledge-base using latent syntactic cues. In *Proc. Conference on Empirical Methods in Natural Language Processing*, pages 833–838, Association for Computational Linguistics, 2013. www.aclweb.org/anthology/D13-1080 155

Matt Gardner, Partha Talukdar, Jayant Krishnamurthy, and Tom Mitchell. Incorporating vector space similarity in random walk inference over knowledge bases. In *Proc. Conference on Empirical Methods in Natural Language Processing (EMNLP)*, pages 397–406, Association for Computational Linguistics, Doha, Qatar, 2014. www.aclweb.org/anthology/D14-1044 DOI: 10.3115/v1/d14-1044 104, 120, 155

Dirk Geeraerts. *Theories of Lexical Semantics*. Oxford University Press, 2010. DOI: 10.1093/acprof:oso/9780198700302.001.0001 15

Maayan Geffet and Ido Dagan. The distributional inclusion hypotheses and lexical entailment. In *Proc. 43rd Annual Meeting on Association for Computational Linguistics, (ACL)*, pages 107–114, 2005. DOI: 10.3115/1219840.1219854 86

Peter Gerstl and Simone Pribbenow. Midwinters, end games, and body parts: A classification of part-whole relations. *International Journal of Human-Computer Studies*, 43:865–889, 1995. DOI: 10.1006/ijhc.1995.1079 24

Roxana Girju, Adriana Badulescu, and Dan Moldovan. Learning semantic constraints for the automatic discovery of part-whole relations. In *Proc. Human Language Technology Conference of the North American Chapter of the Association for Computational Linguistics*, Edmonton, Alberta, Canada, May 27–June 1, 2003, pages 80–87, 2003. DOI: 10.3115/1073445.1073456 68

Roxana Girju, Ana-Maria Giuglea, Marian Olteanu, Ovidiu Fortu, Orest Bolohan, and Dan Moldovan. Support vector machines applied to the classification of semantic relations in nominalized noun phrases. In *Proc. HLT-NAACL Workshop on Computational*

Lexical Semantics, pages 68–75, Association for Computational Linguistics, 2004. DOI: 10.3115/1596431.1596441 53, 67

Roxana Girju, Dan Moldovan, Marta Tatu, and Daniel Antohe. On the semantics of noun compounds. *Computer Speech and Language*, 19:479–496, 2005. DOI: 10.1016/j.csl.2005.02.006 19, 21, 22

Roxana Girju, Preslav Nakov, Vivi Nastase, Stan Szpakowicz, Peter Turney, and Deniz Yuret. Classification of semantic relations between nominals. *Language Resources and Evaluation*, 43(2):105–121, 2009. DOI: 10.1007/s10579-009-9083-2 34, 49

Ian Goodfellow, Jean Pouget-Abadie, Mehdi Mirza, Bing Xu, David Warde-Farley, Sherjil Ozair, Aaron Courville, and Yoshua Bengio. Generative adversarial nets. In *Advances in Neural Information Processing Systems*, pages 2672–2680, 2014. DOI: 10.1145/3422622 139

Ian Goodfellow, Yoshua Bengio, and Aaron Courville. *Deep Learning*. MIT Press, 2016. www.deeplearningbook.org DOI: 10.1007/978-3-642-36657-4_1 109

Matthew R. Gormley, Mo Yu, and Mark Dredze. Improved relation extraction with feature-rich compositional embedding models. In *Proc. Conference on Empirical Methods in Natural Language Processing*, pages 1774–1784, Association for Computational Linguistics, Lisbon, Portugal, 2015. www.aclweb.org/anthology/D15-1205 DOI: 10.18653/v1/d15-1205 125

Rebecca Green, Carol A. Bean, and Sung Hyon Myaeng (Eds.). *The Semantics of Relationships: An Interdisciplinary Perspective*. Kluwer Academic Publishers, 2002. DOI: 10.1007/978-94-017-0073-3 30

Mark A. Greenwood and Mark Stevenson. Improving semi-supervised acquisition of relation extraction patterns. In *Proc. ACL Workshop on Information Extraction Beyond the Document*, Sydney, Australia, 2006. DOI: 10.3115/1641408.1641412 82

Jakob Grimm. *Deutsche Grammatik, Theil 2*. Dieterich, Göttingen, 1826. 17

Ralph Grishman and Beth Sundheim. Message understanding conference-6: A brief history. In *Proc. 16th Conference on Computational Linguistics COLING*, 1:466–471, 1996. DOI: 10.3115/992628.992709 32

Aditya Grover and Jure Leskovec. node2vec: Scalable feature learning for networks. In *Proc. 22nd ACM SIGKDD International Conference on Knowledge Discovery and Data Mining*, pages 855–864, 2016. DOI: 10.1145/2939672.2939754 122

Pankaj Gupta, Hinrich Schütze, and Bernt Andrassy. Table filling multi-task recurrent neural network for joint entity and relation extraction. In *Proc. COLING, 26th International Conference on Computational Linguistics: Technical Papers*, pages 2537–2547, 2016. 152

Harsha Gurulingappa, Abdul Mateen Rajput, Angus Roberts, Juliane Fluck, Martin Hofmann-Apitius, and Luca Toldo. Development of a benchmark corpus to support the automatic extraction of drug-related adverse effects from medical case reports. *Journal of Biomedical Informatics*, 45(5):885–892, 2012. DOI: 10.1016/j.jbi.2012.04.008 48

Michael Gutmann and Aapo Hyvarinen. Noise-contrastive estimation of unnormalized statistical models, with applications to natural image statistics. *The Journal of Machine Learning Research*, 13(1):307–361, 2012. 144

Kelvin Guu, John Miller, and Percy Liang. Traversing knowledge graphs in vector space. In *Proc. Conference on Empirical Methods in Natural Language Processing*, pages 318–327, Association for Computational Linguistics, 2015. aclweb.org/anthology/D15-1038 DOI: 10.18653/v1/d15-1038 146

Ben Hachey, Claire Grover, and Richard Tobin. Datasets for generic relation extraction. *Journal of Natural Language Engineering*, 18(1):21–59, 2011. DOI: 10.1017/s1351324911000106 45

Kyungsook Han, Byungkyu Park, Hyongguen Kim, Jinsun Hong, and Jong Park. HPID: The human protein interaction database. *Bioinformatics*, 20(15):2466–2470, 2004. DOI: 10.1093/bioinformatics/bth253 42

Xianpei Han and Le Sun. Global distant supervision for relation extraction. In *Proc. 30th AAAI Conference on Artificial Intelligence (AAAI-16)*, pages 2950–2956, 2016. 102

Xu Han, Hao Zhu, Pengfei Yu, Ziyun Wang, Yuan Yao, Zhiyuan Liu, and Maosong Sun. FewRel: A large-scale supervised few-shot relation classification dataset with state-of-the-art evaluation. In *Proc. Conference on Empirical Methods in Natural Language Processing (EMNLP)*, pages 4803–4809, 2018. www.aclweb.org/anthology/D18-1514 DOI: 10.18653/v1/d18-1514 135

Roy Harris. *Reading Saussure: A Critical Commentary on the Cours le Linquistique Generale*. Open Court, La Salle, IL, 1987. DOI: 10.2307/3732096 12

David Haussler. Convolution kernels on discrete structures. *Technical Report UCSC-CRL-99-10*, Computer Science Department, University of California at Santa Cruz, 1999. 61

Luheng He, Kenton Lee, Mike Lewis, and Luke Zettlemoyer. Deep semantic role labeling: What works and what's next. In *Proc. 55th Annual Meeting of the Association for Computational Linguistics (Volume 1: Long Papers)*, pages 473–483, 2017. www.aclweb.org/anthology/P17-1044 DOI: 10.18653/v1/p17-1044 71

Shizhu He, Kang Liu, Guoliang Ji, and Jun Zhao. Learning to represent knowledge graphs with Gaussian embedding. In *Proc. 24th ACM International on Conference on Information and Knowledge Management, (CIKM)*, pages 623–632, New York, 2015. DOI: 10.1145/2806416.2806502 144

Marti A. Hearst. Automatic acquisition of hyponyms from large text corpora. In *Proc. 14th International Conference on Computational Linguistics (COLING)*, Nantes, France, 1992. DOI: 10.3115/992133.992154 14, 76, 79, 80, 87, 89, 152

Iris Hendrickx, Su Nam Kim, Zornitsa Kozareva, Preslav Nakov, Diarmuid Ó Séaghdha, Sebastian Padó, Marco Pennacchiotti, Lorenza Romano, and Stan Szpakowicz. SemEval-2010 task 8: Multi-way classification of semantic relations between pairs of nominals. In *Proc. 5th International Workshop on Semantic Evaluation*, pages 33–38, Association for Computational Linguistics, Uppsala, Sweden, 2010. www.aclweb.org/anthology/S10-1006 34, 49

Johannes M. Heuckmann, Michael Hölzel, Martin L. Sos, Stefanie Heynck, Hyatt Balke-Want, Mirjam Koker, Martin Peifer, Jonathan Weiss, Christine M. Lovly, Christian Grütter, Daniel Rauh, William Pao, and Roman K. Thomas. ALK mutations conferring differential resistance to structurally diverse ALK inhibitors. *Clinical Cancer Research*, 17(23):7394–7401, 2011. www.ncbi.nlm.nih.gov/pmc/articles/PMC3382103/ DOI: 10.1158/1078-0432.ccr-11-1648 160

Jerry R. Hobbs, Douglas E. Appelt, John Bear, David J. Israel, Megumi Kameyama, Mark E. Stickel, and Mabry Tyson. FASTUS: A cascaded finite-state transducer for extracting information from natural-language text. In Emmanuel Roche and Yves Schabes, Eds., *Finite-State Language Processing*, pages 383–406, The MIT Press, 1997. arxiv.org/abs/cmp-lg/9705013 58

Sepp Hochreiter and Jürgen Schmidhuber. Long short-term memory. *Neural Computation*, 9(8):1735–1780, 1997. DOI: 10.1162/neco.1997.9.8.1735 126

Raphael Hoffmann, Congle Zhang, and Daniel Weld. Learning 5000 relational extractors. In *Proc. 48th Annual Meeting of the Association for Computational Linguistics*, pages 286–295, Uppsala, Sweden, July 11–16, 2010. 105

Raphael Hoffmann, Congle Zhang, Xiao Ling, Luke Zettlemoyer, and Daniel S. Weld. Knowledge-based weak supervision for information extraction of overlapping relations. In *Proc. 49th Annual Meeting of the Association for Computational Linguistics: Human Language Technologies—Volume 1, (HLT)*, pages 541–550, Association for Computational Linguistics, Stroudsburg, PA, 2011. dl.acm.org/citation.cfm?id=2002472.2002541 101, 136

Florentina Hristea and George Miller. WordNet nouns: Classes and instances. *Computational Linguistics*, 32(1):1–3, 2006. DOI: 10.1162/coli.2006.32.1.1 23

Chih-Wei Hsu and Chih-Jen Lin. A comparison of methods for multiclass support vector machines. *IEEE Transactions on Neural Networks*, 13(2):415–425, 2002. DOI: 10.1109/72.991427 58

Lawrence Hunter and Bretonnel K. Cohen. Biomedical language processing perspective: What's beyond PubMed? *Molecular Cell*, 21:589–594, 2006. DOI: 10.1016/j.molcel.2006.02.012 3

Ignacio Iacobacci, Mohammad Taher Pilehvar, and Roberto Navigli. SensEmbed: Learning sense embeddings for word and relational similarity. In *Proc. 53rd Annual Meeting of the Association for Computational Linguistics and the 7th International Joint Conference on Natural Language Processing (Volume 1: Long Papers)*, pages 95–105, Beijing, China, 2015. www.aclweb.org/anthology/P15-1010 115
DOI: 10.3115/v1/p15-1010

Nancy Ide and Jean Véronis. Introduction to the special issue on word-sense disambiguation: The state of the art. *Computational Linguistics*, 24(1):2–40, 1998. dl.acm.org/citation.cfm?id=972719.972721 53

Nancy Ide, Jean Veronis, Susan Warwick-Armstrong, and Nicoletta Calzolari. Principles for encoding machine-readable dictionaries. In *5th Euralex International Congress*, pages 239–246, University of Tampere, Finland, 1992. 77

Sharmistha Jat, Siddhesh Khandelwal, and Partha P. Talukdar. Improving distantly supervised relation extraction using word and entity based attention. *ArXiv Preprint*, 2018. arxiv.org/abs/1804.06987 134

Otto Jespersen. *A Modern English Grammar on Historical Principles Part VI: Morphology*. Ejaar Munksgaard, Copenhagen, 1942. DOI: 10.4324/9780203715970 17, 26

Guoliang Ji, Shizhu He, Liheng Xu, Kang Liu, and Jun Zhao. Knowledge graph embedding via dynamic mapping matrix. In *Proc. 53rd Annual Meeting of the Association for Computational Linguistics and the 7th International Joint Conference on Natural Language Processing (Volume 1: Long Papers)*, pages 687–696, 2015. DOI: 10.3115/v1/p15-1067 144

Guoliang Ji, Kang Liu, Shizhu He, and Jun Zhao. Knowledge graph completion with adaptive sparse transfer matrix. In *Proc. 30th AAAI Conference on Artificial Intelligence*, 2016. 144

Guoliang Ji, Kang Liu, Shizhu He, and Jun Zhao. Distant supervision for relation extraction with sentence-level attention and entity descriptions. In *Proc. 31st AAAI Conference on Artificial Intelligence (AAAI)*, pages 3060–3066, 2017. 141

Heng Ji and Ralph Grishman. Knowledge base population: Successful approaches and challenges. In *Proc. 49th Annual Meeting of the Association for Computational Linguistics: Human Language Technologies*, pages 1148–1158, 2011. www.aclweb.org/anthology/P11-1115 7

Shaoxiong Ji, Shirui Pan, Erik Cambria, Pekka Marttinen, and Philip S. Yu. A survey on knowledge graphs: Representation, acquisition and applications. *ArXiv Preprint*, 2020. arxiv.org/abs/2002.00388 119, 138, 144

Robin Jia, Cliff Wong, and Hoifung Poon. Document-level N-ary relation extraction with multiscale representation learning. In *Proc. Conference of the North American Chapter of the Association for Computational Linguistics: Human Language Technologies, Volume 1 (Long and Short Papers)*, pages 3693–3704, Minneapolis, MN, 2019. www.aclweb.org/anthology/N19-1370 DOI: 10.18653/v1/n19-1370 161

Jing Jiang and ChengXiang Zhai. Instance weighting for domain adaptation in NLP. In *Proc. 45th Annual Meeting of the Association for Computational Linguistics, (ACL)*, pages 264–271, Prague, Czech Republic, 2007. www.aclweb.org/anthology/P07-1034 54

Xiaotian Jiang, Quan Wang, and Bin Wang. Adaptive convolution for multi-relational learning. In *Proc. Conference of the North American Chapter of the Association for Computational Linguistics: Human Language Technologies, Volume 1 (Long and Short Papers)*, pages 978–987, Minneapolis, MN, 2019. DOI: 10.18653/v1/n19-1103 146

Thorsten Joachims, Nello Cristianini, and John Shawe-Taylor. Composite kernels for hypertext categorisation. In *Proc. 18th International Conference on Machine Learning (ICML)*, Williamstown, MA, 2001. 62

Ian T. Jolliffe. *Principal Component Analysis*. Springer Series in Statistics, Springer-Verlag, New York, 2002. DOI: 10.1007/b98835 112

Shivram Dattatray Joshi. *Patañjali's Vyākaraṇa-Mahābhaṣya: Samarthāhnika (P 2.1.1). Edited with Translation and Explanatory Notes*. University of Poona Press, Poona, 1968. 12

Daniel Jurafsky and James H. Martin. *Speech and Language Processing: An Introduction to Natural Language Processing, Computational Linguistics, and Speech Recognition*, 2nd ed., Prentice Hall, 2009. 30, 69

Rohit J. Kate and Raymond Mooney. Joint entity and relation extraction using card-pyramid parsing. In *Proc. 14th Conference on Computational Natural Language Learning*, pages 203–212, Association for Computational Linguistics, Uppsala, Sweden, 2010. www.aclweb.org/anthology/W10-2924 69

Charles Kemp, Joshua B. Tenenbaum, Thomas L. Griffiths, Takeshi Yamada, and Naonori Ueda. Learning systems of concepts with an infinite relational model. In *Proc. 21st National Conference on Artificial Intelligence—Volume 1, (AAAI)*, pages 381–388, AAAI Press, 2006. 94

Christopher S. G. Khoo and Jin-Cheon Na. Semantic relations in information science. *Annual Review of Information Science and Technology*, 40(1):157–228, 2006. DOI: 10.1002/aris.1440400112 26, 30

Jin-Dong Kim, Tomoko Ohta, Sampo Pyysalo, Yoshinobu Kano, and Jun'ichi Tsujii. Overview of BioNLP'09 shared task on event extraction. In *Proc. BioNLP09, Workshop at NAACL-HTL*, Association for Computations Linguistics, Boulder, CO, 2009. DOI: 10.3115/1572340.1572342 28

Su Nam Kim and Timothy Baldwin. Automatic interpretation of compound nouns using Word-Net similarity. In *Proc. 2nd International Joint Conference on Natural Language Processing*, pages 945–956, Jeju, Korea, 2005. DOI: 10.1007/11562214_82 39, 40

Judith L. Klavans, Martin S. Chodorow, and Nina Wacholder. Building a knowledge base from parsed definitions. In George Heidorn, Karen Jensen, and Steve Richardson, Eds., *Natural Language Processing: The PLNLP Approach*, Kluwer, New York, 1992. DOI: 10.1007/978-1-4615-3170-8_10 77

Stanley Kok and Pedro Domingos. Statistical predicate invention. In *Proc. 24th International Conference on Machine Learning*, pages 433–440, 2007. DOI: 10.1145/1273496.1273551 94

Lili Kotlerman, Ido Dagan, Idan Szpektor, and Maayan Zhitomirsky-Geffet. Directional distributional similarity for lexical inference. *Natural Language Engineering*, 16(4):359–389, 2010. DOI: 10.1017/s1351324910000124 86

Bhushan Kotnis and Vivi Nastase. Learning knowledge graph embeddings with type regularizer. In *Proc. Knowledge Capture Conference, (K-CAP)*, pages 19:1–19:4, ACM, 2017. 120 DOI: 10.1145/3148011.3154466

Bhushan Kotnis and Vivi Nastase. Analysis of the impact of negative sampling on link prediction in knowledge graphs. In *Workshop on Knowledge Base Construction, Reasoning and Mining (KBCOM)*, 2018. arxiv.org/abs/1708.06816 144

Zornitsa Kozareva and Eduard Hovy. A semi-supervised method to learn and construct taxonomies using the Web. In *Proc. Conference on Empirical Methods in Natural Language Processing*, pages 1110–1118, Cambridge, MA, October 9–11, 2010. 89, 90, 91

Zornitsa Kozareva, Ellen Riloff, and Eduard Hovy. Semantic class learning from the Web with hyponym pattern linkage graphs. In *Proc. 46th Annual Meeting of the Association for Computational Linguistics ACL: HLT*, pages 1048–1056, 2008. 89

Martin Krallinger, Florian Leitner, Carlos Rodriguez-Penagos, and Alfonso Valencia. Overview of the protein-protein interaction annotation extraction task of BioCreative II. *Genome Biology*, 9(Supplement 2), 2008. DOI: 10.1186/gb-2008-9-s2-s4 46

Frank R. Kschischang, Brendan J. Frey, and Hans-Andrea Loeliger. Factor graphs and the sum-product algorithm. *IEEE Transactions on Information Theory*, 47(2):498–519, 2001. DOI: 10.1109/18.910572 102

Henry Kučera and Winthrop Nelson Francis. *Computational Analysis of Present-Day American English*. Brown University Press, Providence, RI, 1967. 17

L. T. F. Gamut. *Logic, Language, and Meaning, Volume 1: Introduction to Logic.* University of Chicago Press, Chicago, IL, 1991. DOI: 10.7208/chicago/9780226791678.001.0001 12

John Lafferty, Andrew McCallum, and Fernando Pereira. Conditional random fields: Probabilistic models for segmenting and labeling sequence data. In *Proc. 18th International Conference on Machine Learning*, pages 282–289, Williams College, MA, June 27–30, 2001. 64, 99

Zhenzhong Lan, Mingda Chen, Sebastian Goodman, Kevin Gimpel, Piyush Sharma, and Radu Soricut. ALBERT: A lite BERT for self-supervised learning of language representations. In *International Conference on Learning Representations, (ICLR)*, 2020. 115

Ni Lao, Tom Mitchell, and William W. Cohen. Random walk inference and learning in a large scale knowledge base. In *Proc. Conference on Empirical Methods in Natural Language Processing*, pages 529–539, Association for Computational Linguistics, 2011. www.aclweb.org/anthology/D11-1049 145, 155

Ni Lao, Amarnag Subramanya, Fernando Pereira, and William W. Cohen. Reading the Web with learned syntactic-semantic inference rules. In *Proc. Joint Conference on Empirical Methods in Natural Language Processing and Computational Natural Language Learning*, pages 1017–1026, Association for Computational Linguistics, 2012. www.aclweb.org/anthology/D12-1093 155

Maria Lapata. The disambiguation of nominalizations. *Computational Linguistics*, 28(3):357–388, 2002. DOI: 10.1162/089120102760276018 5

Mirella Lapata and Frank Keller. The Web as a baseline: Evaluating the performance of unsupervised Web-based models for a range of NLP tasks. In *Proc. Human Language Technology Conference and Conference on Empirical Methods in Natural Language Processing*, pages 121–128, Boston, MA, 2004. 19

Mark Lauer. Designing statistical language learners: Experiments on noun compounds. Ph.D. thesis, Department of Computing, Macquarie University, 1995. 19, 23

Matt Le, Stephen Roller, Laetitia Papaxanthos, Douwe Kiela, and Maximilian Nickel. Inferring concept hierarchies from text corpora via hyperbolic embeddings. *ArXiv Preprint*, 2019. arXiv.org/abs/1902.00913 DOI: 10.18653/v1/p19-1313 151, 152

Yann LeCun and Yoshua Bengio. Convolutional networks for images, speech, and time series. *The Handbook of Brain Theory and Neural Networks*, 3361(10):255–258, 1995. 149

Douglas B. Lenat and R. V. Guha. *Building Large Knowledge-Based Systems: Representation and Inference in the CYC Project.* Addison-Wesley, Reading, MA, 1990. 13, 24

Alessandro Lenci and Giulia Benotto. Identifying hypernyms in distributional semantic spaces. In *SEM: The First Joint Conference on Lexical and Computational Semantics—Volume 1: Proc. Main Conference and the Shared Task, and Volume 2: Proc. 6th International Workshop on Semantic Evaluation (SemEval)*, pages 75–79, Association for Computational Linguistics, Montréal, Canada, 2012. www.aclweb.org/anthology/S12-1012 86

Rosemary Leonard. *The Interpretation of English Noun Sequences on the Computer*. North Holland, Amsterdam, 1984. 19

Judith N. Levi. *The Syntax and Semantics of Complex Nominals*. Academic Press, New York, 1978. DOI: 10.2307/412592 5, 17, 18, 21, 22, 23

Omer Levy and Yoav Goldberg. Neural word embedding as implicit matrix factorization. In *Advances in Neural Information Processing Systems*, pages 2177–2185, 2014a. 119

Omer Levy and Yoav Goldberg. Linguistic regularities in sparse and explicit word representations. In *Proc. 18th Conference on Computational Natural Language Learning*, pages 171–180, Association for Computational Linguistics, 2014b. www.aclweb.org/anthology/W14-1618 DOI: 10.3115/v1/w14-1618 129

Omer Levy, Minjoon Seo, Eunsol Choi, and Luke Zettlemoyer. Zero-shot relation extraction via reading comprehension. In *Proc. 21st Conference on Computational Natural Language Learning (CoNLL)*, pages 333–342, Association for Computational Linguistics, 2017. www.aclweb.org/anthology/K17-1034 DOI: 10.18653/v1/k17-1034 159

Charles N. Li. Semantics and the structure of compounds in Chinese. Ph.D. thesis, University of California, Berkeley, 1971. 17

Jiao Li, Yueping Sun, Robin J. Johnson, Daniela Sciaky, Chih-Hsuan Wei, Robert Leaman, Allan Peter Davis, Carolyn J. Mattingly, Thomas C. Wiegers, and Zhiyong Lu. BioCreative V CDR task corpus: A resource for chemical disease relation extraction. *Database*, 2016. DOI: 10.1093/database/baw068 46

Pengshuai Li, Xinsong Zhang, Weijia Jia, and Hai Zhao. GAN driven semi-distant supervision for relation extraction. In *Proc. Conference of the North American Chapter of the Association for Computational Linguistics: Human Language Technologies, Volume 1 (Long and Short Papers)*, pages 3026–3035, Minneapolis, MN, 2019a. www.aclweb.org/anthology/N19-1307 DOI: 10.18653/v1/N19-1307 140

Qi Li and Heng Ji. Incremental joint extraction of entity mentions and relations. In *Proc. 52nd Annual Meeting of the Association for Computational Linguistics (Volume 1: Long Papers)*, pages 402–412, Baltimore, MD, 2014. www.aclweb.org/anthology/P14-1038 DOI: 10.3115/v1/p14-1038 69, 152, 153

Xiaoya Li, Fan Yin, Zijun Sun, Xiayu Li, Arianna Yuan, Duo Chai, Mingxin Zhou, and Jiwei Li. Entity-relation extraction as multi-turn question answering. In *Proc. 57th Annual Meeting of the Association for Computational Linguistics*, pages 1340–1350, 2019b. www.aclweb.org/anthology/P19-1129 DOI: 10.18653/v1/p19-1129 159

Percy Liang, Michael I. Jordan, and Dan Klein. Learning dependency-based compositional semantics. In *Proc. 49th Annual Meeting of the Association for Computational Linguistics*, Portland, OR, June 19–24, 2011. DOI: 10.1162/coli_a_00127 28

Yan Liang, Xin Liu, Jianwen Zhang, and Yangqiu Song. Relation discovery with out-of-relation knowledge base as supervision. In *Proc. Conference of the North American Chapter of the Association for Computational Linguistics: Human Language Technologies, Volume 1 (Long and Short Papers)*, pages 3280–3290, Minneapolis, MN, 2019. www.aclweb.org/anthology/N19-1332 DOI: 10.18653/v1/n19-1332 162

Marc Light, Eric Brill, Eugene Charniak, Mary Harper, Ellen Riloff, and Ellen Voorhees, Eds. *ANLP-NAACL Workshop: Reading Comprehension Tests as Evaluation for Computer-Based Language Understanding Systems*, 2000. www.aclweb.org/anthology/W00-0600 159

Dekang Lin and Patrick Pantel. Discovery of inference rules for question-answering. *Natural Language Engineering*, 7(4):343–360, 2001. DOI: 10.1017/s1351324901002765 92

Thomas Lin, Mausam, and Oren Etzioni. Identifying functional relations in Web text. In *Proc. Conference on Empirical Methods in Natural Language Processing*, pages 1266–1276, Cambridge, MA, October 9–11, 2010. 97

Thomas Lin, Oren Etzioni, et al. Entity linking at web scale. In *Proc. Joint Workshop on Automatic Knowledge Base Construction and Web-Scale Knowledge Extraction*, pages 84–88, Association for Computational Linguistics, 2012. 157

Yankai Lin, Zhiyuan Liu, Maosong Sun, Yang Liu, and Xuan Zhu. Learning entity and relation embeddings for knowledge graph completion. In *Proc. 29th AAAI Conference on Artificial Intelligence, (AAAI)*, pages 2181–2187, AAAI Press, 2015. dl.acm.org/citation.cfm?id=2886521.2886624 144

Yankai Lin, Shiqi Shen, Zhiyuan Liu, Huanbo Luan, and Maosong Sun. Neural relation extraction with selective attention over instances. In *Proc. 54th Annual Meeting of the Association for Computational Linguistics (Volume 1: Long Papers)*, pages 2124–2133, Berlin, Germany, 2016. www.aclweb.org/anthology/P16-1200 DOI: 10.18653/v1/p16-1200 140

Qi Liu, Maximilian Nickel, and Douwe Kiela. Hyperbolic graph neural networks. In *Advances in Neural Information Processing Systems*, pages 8230–8241, 2019a. 148

Tianyi Liu, Xinsong Zhang, Wanhao Zhou, and Weijia Jia. Neural relation extraction via inner-sentence noise reduction and transfer learning. In *Proc. Conference on Empirical Methods in Natural Language Processing*, pages 2195–2204, Association for Computational Linguistics, Brussels, Belgium, 2018. www.aclweb.org/anthology/D18-1243 DOI: 10.18653/v1/d18-1243 141

Yang Liu, Furu Wei, Sujian Li, Heng Ji, Ming Zhou, and Houfeng Wang. A dependency-based neural network for relation classification. In *Proc. 53rd Annual Meeting of the Association for Computational Linguistics and the 7th International Joint Conference on Natural Language Processing (Volume 2: Short Papers)*, pages 285–290, 2015. www.aclweb.org/anthology/P15-2047 DOI: 10.3115/v1/p15-2047 127, 129, 130, 149

Yang Liu, Yifeng Zeng, Yingke Chen, Jing Tang, and Yinghui Pan. Self-improving generative adversarial reinforcement learning. In *Proc. 18th International Conference on Autonomous Agents and MultiAgent Systems*, pages 52–60, 2019b. 143

Yinhan Liu, Myle Ott, Naman Goyal, Jingfei Du, Mandar Joshi, Danqi Chen, Omer Levy, Mike Lewis, Luke Zettlemoyer, and Veselin Stoyanov. RoBERTa: A robustly optimized BERT pretraining approach. *ArXiv Preprint*, 2019c. arxiv.org/abs/1907.11692 116

Colin Lockard, Prashant Shiralkar, and Xin Luna Dong. OpenCeres: When open information extraction meets the semi-structured web. In *Proc. Conference of the North American Chapter of the Association for Computational Linguistics: Human Language Technologies, Volume 1 (Long and Short Papers)*, pages 3047–3056, Minneapolis, MN, 2019. www.aclweb.org/anthology/N19-1309 DOI: 10.18653/v1/N19-1309 157

Huma Lodhi, Craig Saunders, John Shawe-Taylor, Nello Cristianini, and Christopher J. C. H. Watkins. Text classification using string kernels. *Journal of Machine Learning Research*, 2:419–444, 2002. www.jmlr.org/papers/v2/lodhi02a.html 62

Bo Long, Zhongfei (Mark) Zhang, Xiaoyun Wu, and Philip S. Yu. Spectral clustering for multi-type relational data. In *Proc. 23rd International Conference on Machine Learning (ICML)*, pages 585–592, 2006. DOI: 10.1145/1143844.1143918 121

Wei Lu, Hwee Tou Ng, Wee Sun Lee, and Luke S. Zettlemoyer. A generative model for parsing natural language to meaning representations. In *Proc. Conference on Empirical Methods in Natural Language Processing, (EMNLP)*, pages 783–792, 2008. dl.acm.org/citation.cfm?id=1613715.1613815 DOI: 10.3115/1613715.1613815 28

Yi Luan, Luheng He, Mari Ostendorf, and Hannaneh Hajishirzi. Multi-task identification of entities, relations, and coreferencefor scientific knowledge graph construction. In *Proc. Conference on Empirical Methods in Natural Language Processing (EMNLP)*, pages 3219–3232, 2018. DOI: 10.18653/v1/d18-1360 48

Yi Luan, Dave Wadden, Luheng He, Amy Shah, Mari Ostendorf, and Hannaneh Hajishirzi. A general framework for information extraction using dynamic span graphs. In *Proc. Conference of the North-American Chapter of the Association for Computational Linguistics: Human Language Technologies, Volume 1 (Long and Short Papers)*, pages 3036–3046, 2019. www.aclweb.org/anthology/N19-1308 DOI: 10.18653/v1/n19-1308 153, 154

Christopher Manning and Hinrich Schütze. *Foundations of Statistical Natural Language Processing*. MIT Press, Cambridge, 1999. 58

Diego Marcheggiani and Ivan Titov. Discrete-state variational autoencoders for joint discovery and factorization of relations. *Transactions of the Association for Computational Linguistics*, 4:231–244, 2016. www.aclweb.org/anthology/Q16-1017 DOI: 10.1162/tacl_a_00095 162

Mitchell Marcus, Beatrice Santorini, and Mary Marcinkiewicz. Building a large annotated corpus of English: The Penn Treebank. *Computational Linguistics*, 19(2):313–330, 1994. DOI: 10.21236/ada273556 39

Eric Margolis and Stephen Laurence, Eds. *Concepts: Core Readings*. A Bradford Book, 1999. 11

Cynthia Matuszek, John Cabral, Michael Witbrock, and John DeOliveira. An introduction to the syntax and content of Cyc. In *Proc. AAAI Spring Symposium on Formalizing and Compiling Background Knowledge and Its Applications to Knowledge Representation and Question Answering*, pages 44–49, 2006. 24

Mausam, Michael Schmitz, Robert Bart, Stephen Soderland, and Oren Etzioni. Open language learning for information extraction. In *Proc. Conference on Empirical Methods in Natural Language Processing*, Jeju Island, Korea, July 12–14, 2012, pages 523–534, 2012. 92, 105

Andrew McCallum and Wei Li. Early results for named entity recognition with conditional random fields, feature induction and Web-enhanced lexicons. In *Proc. 7th Conference on Natural Language Learning at HLT-NAACL—Volume 4, (CONLL)*, pages 188–191, 2003. dx.doi.org/10.3115/1119176.1119206 DOI: 10.3115/1119176.1119206 64

Bryan McCann, Nitish Shirish Keskar, Caiming Xiong, and Richard Socher. The natural language decathlon: Multitask learning as question answering. *ArXiv Preprint*, 2018. arxiv.org/abs/1806.08730 159

John McCarthy. Programs with common sense. In *Proc. Teddington Conference on the Mechanization of Thought Processes*, 1958. 13

Warren S. McCulloch and Walter H. Pitts. A logical calculus of the ideas immanent in nervous activity. *Bulletin of Mathematical Biophysics*, 5:115–133, 1943. DOI: 10.1007/bf02478259 107

Ryan McDonald, Fernando Pereira, Seth Kulik, Scott Winters, Yang Jin, and Pete White. Simple algorithms for complex relation extraction with applications to biomedical IE. In *Proc. 43rd Annual Meeting of the Association for Computational Linguistics (ACL)*, Ann Arbor, MI, 2005. DOI: 10.3115/1219840.1219901 71

Tomáš Mikolov, Martin Karafiát, Lukáš Burget, Jan Černocký, and Sanjeev Khudanpur. Recurrent neural network based language model. In *11th Annual Conference of the International Speech Communication Association*, 2010. 125

Tomas Mikolov, Kai Chen, Greg Corrado, and Jeffrey Dean. Efficient estimation of word representations in vector space. *ArXiv Preprint*, 2013a. arxiv.org/abs/1301.3781 145

Tomas Mikolov, Ilya Sutskever, Kai Chen, Greg S. Corrado, and Jeff Dean. Distributed representations of words and phrases and their compositionality. In C. J.C. Burges, L. Bottou, M. Welling, Z. Ghahramani, and K. Q. Weinberger, Eds., *Advances in Neural Information Processing Systems 26*, pages 3111–3119, 2013b. 113

Tomas Mikolov, Wen-tau Yih, and Geoffrey Zweig. Linguistic regularities in continuous space word representations. In *Proc. Conference of the North American Chapter of the Association for Computational Linguistics: Human Language Technologies*, pages 746–751, Atlanta, GA, 2013c. 107, 113, 115, 129

Marvin Minsky. A framework for representing knowledge. In Patrick Winston, Ed., *The Psychology of Computer Vision*, pages 211–277, McGraw Hill, 1975. dspace.mit.edu/bitstream/handle/1721.1/6089/AIM-306.pdf DOI: 10.7551/mitpress/4626.003.0005 27

Mike Mintz, Steven Bills, Rion Snow, and Dan Jurafsky. Distant supervision for relation extraction without labeled data. In *Proc. Joint Conference of the 47th Annual Meeting of the ACL and the 4th International Joint Conference on Natural Language Processing of the AFNLP: Volume 2, (ACL)*, pages 1003–1011, 2009. dl.acm.org/citation.cfm?id=1690219.1690287 DOI: 10.3115/1690219.1690287 99, 100, 102, 135

Jeff Mitchell and Mirella Lapata. Composition in distributional models of semantics. *Cognitive Science*, 34(8):1388–1429, 2010. DOI: 10.1111/j.1551-6709.2010.01106.x 125

Tom Mitchell. *Machine Learning*. McGraw Hill, 1997. 58

Tom Mitchell, W. Cohen, E. Hruschka, P. Talukdar, B. Yang, J. Betteridge, A. Carlson, B. Dalvi, M. Gardner, B. Kisiel, J. Krishnamurthy, N. Lao, K. Mazaitis, T. Mohamed, N. Nakashole, E. Platanios, A. Ritter, M. Samadi, B. Settles, R. Wang, D. Wijaya, A. Gupta, X. Chen, A. Saparov, M. Greaves, and J. Welling. Never-ending learning. *Communications of the ACM*, 61(5):103–115, 2018. cacm.acm.org/magazines/2018/5/227193-never-ending-learning/fulltext DOI: 10.1145/3191513 104

Makoto Miwa and Mohit Bansal. End-to-end relation extraction using LSTMs on sequences and tree structures. In *Proc. 54th Annual Meeting of the Association for Computational Linguistics (Volume 1: Long Papers)*, pages 1105–1116, Berlin, Germany, 2016. www.aclweb.org/anthology/P16-1105 DOI: 10.18653/v1/p16-1105 132, 152, 153

Makoto Miwa and Yutaka Sasaki. Modeling joint entity and relation extraction with table representation. In *Proc. Conference on Empirical Methods in Natural Language Processing (EMNLP)*, pages 1858–1869, Association for Computational Linguistics, Doha, Qatar, 2014. www.aclweb.org/anthology/D14-1200 DOI: 10.3115/v1/d14-1200 69, 70, 152

Thahir Mohamed, Estevam Hruschka Jr., and Tom Mitchell. Discovering relations between noun categories. In *Proc. Conference on Empirical Methods in Natural Language Processing*, Edinburgh, UK, July 26–29, 2011, pages 1447–1455, 2011. 104

Dan Moldovan, Adriana Badulescu, Marta Tatu, Daniel Antohe, and Roxana Girju. Models for the semantic classification of noun phrases. In *Proc. HLT-NAACL Workshop on Computational Lexical Semantics*, pages 60–67, Association for Computational Linguistic, Boston, MA, 2004. DOI: 10.3115/1596431.1596440 68

Alessandro Moschitti. Efficient convolution kernels for dependency and constituent syntactic trees. *Proc. 17th European Conference on Machine Learning (ECML)*, 2006. dit.unitn.it/moschitt/articles/ECML2006.pdf DOI: 10.1007/11871842_32 61, 62

Lynne M. Murphy. *Semantic Relations and the Lexicon*. Cambridge University Press, Cambridge, UK, 2003. DOI: 10.1017/cbo9780511486494 26, 30

Preslav Nakov. Noun compound interpretation using paraphrasing verbs: Feasibility study. In *LNAI Volume 5253: Proc. 13th International Conference on Artificial Intelligence: Methodology, Systems and Applications (AIMSA)*, pages 103–117, Springer, 2008a. DOI: 10.1007/978-3-540-85776-1_10 23

Preslav Nakov. Improved statistical machine translation using monolingual paraphrases. In *Proc. 16th European Conference on Artificial Intelligence*, pages 338–342, Valencia, Spain, August 23–27, 2008b. 3

Preslav Nakov and Marti Hearst. UCB: System description for SemEval Task #4. In *Proc. 4th International Workshop on Semantic Evaluations (SemEval)*, pages 366–369, Prague, Czech Republic, 2007. DOI: 10.3115/1621474.1621554 55

Preslav Nakov and Marti Hearst. Solving relational similarity problems using the Web as a corpus. In *Proc. 46th Annual Meeting of the Association for Computational Linguistics: Human Language Technologies*, pages 452–460, Columbus, OH, June 15–20, 2008. 34

Preslav Nakov and Zornitsa Kozareva. Combining relational and attributional similarity for semantic relation classification. In *Proc. International Conference Recent Advances in Natural Language Processing*, pages 323–330, RANLP Organising Committee, Hissar, Bulgaria, 2011. aclweb.org/anthology/R11-1045 34

Vivi Nastase and Michael Strube. Transforming Wikipedia into a large-scale multilingual concept network. *Artificial Intelligence*, 194:62–85, 2013. DOI: 10.1016/j.artint.2012.06.008 44

Vivi Nastase and Stan Szpakowicz. Exploring noun-modifier semantic relations. In *Proc. 5th International Workshop on Computational Semantics (IWCS)*, pages 285–301, Tilburg, The Netherlands, 2003. 19, 20, 21, 22, 29, 38, 39, 53, 67, 72

Vivi Nastase, Jelber Sayyad-Shirabad, Marina Sokolova, and Stan Szpakowicz. Learning noun-modifier semantic relations with corpus-based and WordNet-based features. In *Proc. 21st National Conference on Artificial Intelligence*, pages 781–787, Boston, MA, 2006. 53, 67

Roberto Navigli. Word sense disambiguation: A survey. *ACM Computing Surveys*, 41(2):1–69, 2009. DOI: 10.1145/1459352.1459355 53

Claire Nédellec. Learning language in logic-genic interaction extraction challenge. In *Proc. ICML Workshop on Learning Language in Logic (LLL)*, Bonn, Germany, 2005. 45

Arvind Neelakantan, Jeevan Shankar, Alexandre Passos, and Andrew McCallum. Efficient non-parametric estimation of multiple embeddings per word in vector space. In *Proc. Conference on Empirical Methods in Natural Language Processing (EMNLP)*, pages 1059–1069, Association for Computational Linguistics, Doha, Qatar, 2014. www.aclweb.org/anthology/D14-1113 DOI: 10.3115/v1/d14-1113 115

Arvind Neelakantan, Benjamin Roth, and Andrew McCallum. Compositional vector space models for knowledge base completion. In *Proc. 53rd Annual Meeting of the Association for Computational Linguistics and the 7th International Joint Conference on Natural Language Processing (Volume 1: Long Papers)*, pages 156–166, Association for Computational Linguistics, 2015. aclweb.org/anthology/P15-1016 DOI: 10.3115/v1/p15-1016 146

Thien Huu Nguyen and Ralph Grishman. Relation extraction: Perspective from convolutional neural networks. In *Proc. 1st Workshop on Vector Space Modeling for Natural Language Processing*, pages 39–48, Association for Computational Linguistics, Denver, CO, 2015. www.aclweb.org/anthology/W15-1506 DOI: 10.3115/v1/w15-1506 149

Truc-Vien T. Nguyen, Alessandro Moschitti, and Giuseppe Riccardi. Convolution kernels on constituent, dependency and sequential structures for selation extraction. In *Proc. Conference on Empirical Methods in Natural Language Processing*, Singapore, August 6–7, 2009. DOI: 10.3115/1699648.1699684 61, 62

Maximilian Nickel and Douwe Kiela. Learning continuous hierarchies in the Lorentz model of hyperbolic geometry. *ArXiv Preprint*, 2018. arXiv.org/abs/1806.03417 115, 148, 152

Maximilian Nickel, Volker Tresp, and Hans-Peter Kriegel. A three-way model for collective learning on multi-relational data. In *Proc. ICML*, 2011. 110, 117, 138, 144, 145

Maximilian Nickel, Kevin Murphy, Volker Tresp, and Evgeniy Gabrilovich. A review of relational machine learning for knowledge graphs. *Proc. IEEE*, 104(1):11–33, 2016a. DOI: 10.1109/jproc.2015.2483592 118, 119, 144

Maximilian Nickel, Lorenzo Rosasco, and Tomaso Poggio. Holographic embeddings of knowledge graphs. In *Proc. 30th AAAI Conference on Artificial Intelligence, (AAAI)*, pages 1955–1961. AAAI Press, 2016b. dl.acm.org/citation.cfm?id=3016100.3016172 119, 145

Maximillian Nickel and Douwe Kiela. Poincaré embeddings for learning hierarchical representations. In *Advances in Neural Information Processing Systems (NIPS)*, pages 6338–6347, 2017. 115, 116, 145

Mathias Niepert. Discriminative Gaifman models. In *Proc. 30th International Conference on Neural Information Processing Systems, (NIPS)*, pages 3413–3421, Curran Associates Inc., 2016. 148

Madhav Nimishakavi, Uday Singh Saini, and Partha P. Talukdar. Relation schema induction using tensor factorization with side information. *ArXiv Preprint*, 2016. arxiv.org/abs/1605.04227 DOI: 10.18653/v1/d16-1040 157, 158

Adolf Noreen. *Vårt Språk*, vol. 5. C. W. K. Gleerups Förlag, Lund, 1904. 17

J. Terry Nutter. A lexical relation hierarchy. *Technical Report TR-89-06*, (eprints.cs.vt.edu/archive/00000143/01/TR-89-06.pdf), Virginia Polytechnic Institute and State University, Department of Computer Science, 1989. 24

Diarmuid Ó Séaghdha. Learning compound noun semantics. Ph.D. thesis, University of Cambridge, 2008. 19

Diarmuid Ó Séaghdha and Ann Copestake. Co-occurrence contexts for noun compound interpretation. In *Proc. ACL Workshop on a Broader Perspective on Multiword Expressions*, pages 57–64, Association for Computational Linguistics, 2007. DOI: 10.3115/1613704.1613712 17, 18, 39, 41

Diarmuid Ó Séaghdha and Ann Copestake. Semantic classification with distributional kernels. In *Proc. 22nd International Conference on Computational Linguistics*, pages 649–656, Manchester, UK, 2008. DOI: 10.3115/1599081.1599163 34, 51, 60

Diarmuid Ó Séaghdha and Ann Copestake. Using lexical and relational similarity to classify semantic relations. In *Proc. 12th Conference of the European Chapter of the Association for Computational Linguistics (EACL)*, Athens, Greece, 2009. DOI: 10.3115/1609067.1609136 62

Alberto Paccanaro and Geoffrey E. Hinton. Learning hierarchical structures with linear relational embedding. In T. G. Dietterich, S. Becker, and Z. Ghahramani, Eds., *Advances in Neural Information Processing Systems 14*, pages 857–864, Curran Associates, Inc., 2002. papers.nips.cc/paper/2068-learning-hierarchical-structures-with-linear-relational-embedding.pdf 120

Marius Paşca, Dekang Lin, Jeffrey Bigham, Andrei Lifchits, and Alpa Jain. Names and similarities on the Web: Fact extraction in the fast lane. In *Proc. 21st International Conference on Computational Linguistics and 44th Annual Meeting of the Association for Computational Linguistics*, Sydney, Australia, July 17–21, 2006, pages 809–816, 2006a. DOI: 10.3115/1220175.1220277 84

Marius Paşca, Dekang Lin, Jeffrey Bigham, Andrei Lifchits, and Alpa Jain. Organizing and searching the World-Wide Web of facts—step one: the one-million fact extraction challenge. In *Proc. 21st National Conference on Artificial Intelligence*, Boston, MA, July 16–20, 2006, pages 1400–1405, 2006b. 84

Martha Palmer, Daniel Gildea, and Nianwen Xue. *Semantic Role Labeling*. Synthesis Lectures on Human Language Technologies. Morgan & Claypool, 2010. www.morganclaypool.com/doi/abs/10.2200/S00239ED1V01Y200912HLT006 DOI: 10.2200/S00239ED1V01Y200912HLT006 71

Patrick Pantel and Dekang Lin. Discovering word senses from text. In *Proc. 8th ACM SIGKDD Conference on Knowledge Discovery and Data Mining*, Edmonton, Alberta, Canada, July 23–26, 2002, pages 613–619, 2002. DOI: 10.1145/775047.775138 51, 88

Patrick Pantel and Marco Pennacchiotti. Espresso: Leveraging generic patterns for automatically harvesting semantic relations. In *Proc. 21st International Conference on Computational Linguistics and 44th Annual Meeting of the Association for Computational Linguistics*, Sydney, Australia, July 17–21, 2006, pages 113–120, 2006. DOI: 10.3115/1220175.1220190 83

Patrick Pantel and Deepak Ravichandran. Automatically labeling semantic classes. In *Proc. Human Language Technology Conference of the North American Chapter of the Association for Computational Linguistics*, Boston, MA, May 2–7, 2004, pages 321–328, 2004. 88

Yannis Papanikolaou, Ian Roberts, and Andrea Pierleoni. Deep bidirectional transformers for relation extraction without supervision. In *Proc. 2nd Workshop on Deep Learning Approaches for Low-Resource NLP (DeepLo)*, pages 67–75, 2019. www.aclweb.org/anthology/D19-6108 DOI: 10.18653/v1/d19-6108 162

Robert Parker, David Graff, Junbo Kong, Ke Chen, and Kazuaki Maeda. English Gigaword, 5th ed., 2011. catalog.ldc.upenn.edu/LDC2011T07 DOI: 10.35111/wk4f-qt80 56, 87

Siddharth Patwardhan and Ellen Riloff. Effective information extraction with semantic affinity patterns and relevant regions. In *Proc. Joint Conference on Empirical Methods in Natural Language Processing and Computational Language Learning*, Prague, Czech Republic, June 28–30, 2007, pages 717–727, 2007. 14

Charles Sanders Peirce. Existential graphs. [Unpublished manuscript reprinted in Justus Buchler (Ed.), *The Philosophy of Peirce: Selected Writings*, Harcourt, Brace & Co., 1940], 1909. 13

Thomas Pellissier Tanon, Denny Vrandečić, Sebastian Schaffert, Thomas Steiner, and Lydia Pintscher. From freebase to Wikidata: The great migration. In *Proc. 25th International Conference on World Wide Web, (WWW)*, pages 1419–1428, 2016. DOI: 10.1145/2872427.2874809 42

Nanyun Peng, Hoifung Poon, Chris Quirk, Kristina Toutanova, and Wen-tau Yih. Cross-sentence N-ary relation extraction with graph LSTMs. *Transactions of the Association for Computational Linguistics*, 5:101–115, 2017. www.aclweb.org/anthology/Q17-1008 DOI: 10.1162/tacl_a_00049 132, 133, 161

Jeffrey Pennington, Richard Socher, and Christopher Manning. Glove: Global vectors for word representation. In *Proc. Conference on Empirical Methods in Natural Language Processing (EMNLP)*, pages 1532–1543, Association for Computational Linguistics, Doha, Qatar, 2014. www.aclweb.org/anthology/D14-1162 DOI: 10.3115/v1/d14-1162 115

Bryan Perozzi, Rami Al-Rfou, and Steven Skiena. DeepWalk: Online learning of social representations. In *Proc. 20th ACM SIGKDD International Conference on Knowledge Discovery and Data Mining, (KDD)*, pages 701–710, 2014. DOI: 10.1145/2623330.2623732 122, 145

Matthew Peters, Mark Neumann, Mohit Iyyer, Matt Gardner, Christopher Clark, Kenton Lee, and Luke Zettlemoyer. Deep contextualized word representations. In *Proc. Conference of the North American Chapter of the Association for Computational Linguistics: Human Language Technologies, Volume 1 (Long Papers)*, pages 2227–2237, New Orleans, LA, 2018. www.aclweb.org/anthology/N18-1202 DOI: 10.18653/v1/n18-1202 115

Daniele Pighin and Alessandro Moschitti. On reverse feature engineering of syntactic tree kernels. In *Proc. 14th Conference on Computational Natural Language Learning (CONLL)*, Boulder, CO, 2010. 63

Mohammad Taher Pilehvar and Nigel Collier. De-conflated semantic representations. In *Proc. Conference on Empirical Methods in Natural Language Processing*, pages 1680–1690, Association for Computational Linguistics, Austin, TX, 2016. www.aclweb.org/anthology/D16-1174 DOI: 10.18653/v1/d16-1174 115

Jim Pitman. *Combinatorial Stochastic Processes*. Springer-Verlag, Berlin, 2006. works.bepress. com/jim_pitman/1 94

Barbara Plank and Alessandro Moschitti. Embedding semantic similarity in tree kernels for domain adaptation of relation extraction. In *Proc. 51st Annual Meeting of the Association for Computational Linguistics (Volume 1: Long Papers)*, pages 1498–1507, Sofia, Bulgaria, 2013. www.aclweb.org/anthology/P13-1147 63

Hoifung Poon, Janara Christensen, Pedro Domingos, Oren Etzioni, Raphael Hoffmann, Chloe Kiddon, Thomas Lin, Xiao Ling, Mausam, Alan Ritter, Stefan Schoenmackers, Stephen Soderland, Dan Weld, Fei Wu, and Congle Zhang. Machine reading at the University of Washington. In *Proc. NAACL/HLT 1st International Workshop on Formalisms and Methodology for Learning by Reading*, pages 87–95, 2010. 96, 104

James Pustejovsky. *The Generative Lexicon*. MIT Press, Cambridge, MA, 1995. 67

James Pustejovsky, José M. Castaño, Jason Zhang, M. Kotecki, and B. Cochran. Robust relational parsing over biomedical literature: Extracting *inhibit* relations. In *Proc. 7th Pacific Symposium on Biocomputing (PSB)*, Lihue, Hawaii, 2002. DOI: 10.1142/9789812799623_0034 80

Sampo Pyysalo, Antti Airola, Juho Heimonen, Jari Björne, Filip Ginter, and Tapio Salakoski. Comparative analysis of five protein-protein interaction corpora. *BMC Bioinformatics*, 9(Supplement 3), 2008. DOI: 10.1186/1471-2105-9-s3-s6 45

Longhua Qian and Guodong Zhou. Clustering-based stratified seed sampling for semi-supervised relation classification. In *Proc. Conference on Empirical Methods in Natural Language Processing*, pages 346–355, Association for Computational Linguistics, Cambridge, MA, 2010. www.aclweb.org/anthology/D10-1034 86

Longhua Qian, Guodong Zhou, Fang Kong, Qiaoming Zhu, and Peide Qian. Exploiting constituent dependencies for tree kernel-based semantic relation extraction. In *Proc. 22nd International Conference on Computational Linguistics (Coling)*, pages 697–704, Coling Organizing Committee, Manchester, UK, 2008. www.aclweb.org/anthology/C08-1088 DOI: 10.3115/1599081.1599169 63

Longhua Qian, Guodong Zhou, Fang Kong, and Qiaoming Zhu. Semi-supervised learning for semantic relation classification using stratified sampling strategy. In *EMNLP*, 2009. DOI: 10.3115/1699648.1699690 86

Pengda Qin, Weiran Xu, and William Yang Wang. DSGAN: Generative adversarial training for distant supervision relation extraction. In *Proc. 56th Annual Meeting of the Association for Computational Linguistics (Volume 1: Long Papers)*, pages 496–505, Melbourne, Australia, 2018a. www.aclweb.org/anthology/P18-1046 DOI: 10.18653/v1/p18-1046 139

Pengda Qin, Weiran Xu, and William Yang Wang. Robust distant supervision relation extraction via deep reinforcement learning. In *Proc. 56th Annual Meeting of the Association for Computational Linguistics (Volume 1: Long Papers)*, pages 2137–2147, Melbourne, Australia, 2018b. www.aclweb.org/anthology/P18-1199 DOI: 10.18653/v1/p18-1199 142

Ciyang Qing, Ulle Endriss, Raquel Fernández, and Justin Kruger. Empirical analysis of aggregation methods for collective annotation. In *Proc. COLING, the 25th International Conference on Computational Linguistics: Technical Papers*, pages 1533–1542, Dublin City University and Association for Computational Linguistics, 2014. www.aclweb.org/anthology/C14-1145 49

Ross Quillian. A revised design for an understanding machine. *Mechanical Translation*, 7:17–29, 1962. 14

Chris Quirk and Hoifung Poon. Distant supervision for relation extraction beyond the sentence boundary. In *Proc. 15th Conference of the European Chapter of the Association for Computational Linguistics: Volume 1, Long Papers*, pages 1171–1182, Valencia, Spain, 2017. www.aclweb.org/anthology/E17-1110 DOI: 10.18653/v1/e17-1110 103, 160

Randolph Quirk, Sidney Greenbaum, Geoffrey Leech, and Jan Svartvik. *A Comprehensive Grammar of the English Language*. Longman, London and New York, 1985. 4

Colin Raffel, Noam Shazeer, Adam Roberts, Katherine Lee, Sharan Narang, Michael Matena, Yanqi Zhou, Wei Li, and Peter J. Liu. Exploring the limits of transfer learning with a unified text-to-text transformer. *ArXiv Preprint*, 2019. arxiv.org/abs/1910.10683 116

Lance Ramshaw and Mitch Marcus. Text chunking using transformation-based learning. In *Proc. 3rd Workshop on Very Large Corpora*, ACL, 1995. DOI: 10.1007/978-94-017-2390-9_10 64

Lev Ratinov and Dan Roth. Design challenges and misconceptions in named entity recognition. In *Proc. 13th Conference on Computational Natural Language Learning, (CoNLL)*, pages 147–155, 2009. dl.acm.org/citation.cfm?id=1596374.1596399 DOI: 10.3115/1596374.1596399 64

Alexander Ratner, Stephen H. Bach, Henry Ehrenberg, Jason Fries, Sen Wu, and Christopher Ré. Snorkel: Rapid training data creation with weak supervision. In *Proc. VLDB Endowment International Conference on Very Large Data Bases*, 11(3):269–282, NIH Public Access, 2017. DOI: 10.14778/3157794.3157797 97

Deepak Ravichandran and Eduard Hovy. Learning surface text patterns for a question answering system. In *Proc. 40th Annual Meeting of the Association for Computational Linguistics*, pages 41–47, Philadelphia, PA, July 7–12, 2002. DOI: 10.3115/1073083.1073092 14, 82

Soumya Ray and Mark Craven. Representing sentence structure in hidden Markov models for information extraction. In *Proc. 17th International Joint Conference on Artificial Intelligence—Volume 2, (IJCAI)*, pages 1273–1279, Morgan Kaufmann Publishers Inc., San Francisco, CA, 2001. dl.acm.org/citation.cfm?id=1642194.1642264 65, 66

Xiang Ren, Zeqiu Wu, Wenqi He, Meng Qu, Clare R. Voss, Heng Ji, Tarek F. Abdelzaher, and Jiawei Han. Cotype: Joint extraction of typed entities and relations with knowledge bases. In *Proc. 26th International Conference on World Wide Web*, pages 1015–1024, International World Wide Web Conferences Steering Committee, 2017. DOI: 10.1145/3038912.3052708 69, 120

Sebastian Riedel, Limin Yao, and Andrew McCallum. Modeling relations and their mentions without labeled text. In *Proc. European Conference on Machine Learning and Knowledge Discovery in Databases: Part III, (ECML PKDD)*, pages 148–163, Springer-Verlag, Berlin, Heidelberg, 2010. dl.acm.org/citation.cfm?id=1889788.1889799 DOI: 10.1007/978-3-642-15939-8_10 100, 102, 135

Sebastian Riedel, Limin Yao, Andrew McCallum, and M. Benjamin Marlin. Relation extraction with matrix factorization and universal schemas. In *Proc. Conference of the North American Chapter of the Association for Computational Linguistics: Human Language Technologies*, pages 74–84, 2013. aclweb.org/anthology/N13-1008 123, 156, 157

Ellen Riloff and Rosie Jones. Learning dictionaries for information extraction by multi-level bootstrapping. In *Proc. 16th National Conference on Artificial Intelligence*, pages 474–479, Orlando, FL, July 18–22, 1999. 80, 84

Alan Ritter, Luke Zettlemoyer, Mausam, and Oren Etzioni. Modeling missing data in distant supervision for information extraction. *Transactions of the Association for Computational Linguistics*, 1:367–378, 2013. DOI: 10.1162/tacl_a_00234 101

Angus Roberts, Robert Gaizauskas, Mark Hepple, and Yikun Guo. Mining clinical relationships from patient narratives. *BMC Bioinformatics*, 9(Supplement 11), 2008. DOI: 10.1186/1471-2105-9-s11-s3 71

Stephen Roller, Douwe Kiela, and Maximilian Nickel. Hearst patterns revisited: Automatic hypernym detection from large text corpora. In *Proc. 56th Annual Meeting of the Association for Computational Linguistics (Volume 2: Short Papers)*, pages 358–363, Melbourne, Australia, 2018. www.aclweb.org/anthology/P18-2057 DOI: 10.18653/v1/p18-2057 87, 88

Barbara Rosario and Marti Hearst. Classifying the semantic relations in noun compounds via a domain-specific lexical hierarchy. In *Proc. Conference on Empirical Methods in Natural Language Processing*, pages 82–90, Pittsburgh, PA, June 3–4, 2001. 28, 47, 53

Barbara Rosario and Marti Hearst. Multi-way relation classification: Application to protein-protein interactions. In *Proc. Human Language Technology Conference and Conference on Empirical Methods in Natural Language Processing*, pages 732–739, Vancouver, British Columbia, Canada, 2005. DOI: 10.3115/1220575.1220667 46, 66

Barbara Rosario and Marti A. Hearst. Classifying semantic relations in bioscience texts. In *Proc. 42nd Annual Meeting of the Association for Computational Linguistics*, pages 430–437, Barcelona, Spain, July 21–26, 2004. DOI: 10.3115/1218955.1219010 28, 46, 66, 72

Barbara Rosario, Marti Hearst, and Charles Fillmore. The descent of hierarchy, and selection in relational semantics. In *Proc. 40th Annual Meeting of the Association for Computational Linguistics*, pages 417–424, Philadelphia, PA, July 7–12, 2002. DOI: 10.3115/1073083.1073125 67

Frank. Rosenblatt. The perceptron: A probabilistic model for information storage and organization in the brain. *Psychological Review*, 65(6):386–408, 1958. DOI: 10.1037/h0042519 107

Benjamin Rosenfeld and Ronen Feldman. Using corpus statistics on entities to improve semi-supervised relation extraction from the Web. In *Proc. 45th Annual Meeting of the Association for Computational Linguistics*, pages 600–607, Prague, Czech Republic, June 23–30, 2007. 84

Gaetano Rossiello, Alfio Gliozzo, Robert Farrell, Nicolas Fauceglia, and Michael Glass. Learning relational representations by analogy using hierarchical siamese networks. In *Proc. Conference of the North American Chapter of the Association for Computational Linguistics: Human Language Technologies, Volume 1 (Long and Short Papers)*, pages 3235–3245, Minneapolis, MN, 2019. www.aclweb.org/anthology/N19-1327 DOI: 10.18653/v1/n19-1327 150

Dan Roth and Wen-Tau Yih. Global inference for entity and relation identification via a linear programming formulation. In *Introduction to Statistical Relational Learning*, MIT Press, 2007. DOI: 10.7551/mitpress/7432.003.0022 69, 152

Chengsen Ru, Jintao Tang, Sasha Li, Songxian Xie, and Ting Wang. Using semantic similarity to reduce wrong labels in distant supervision for relation extraction. *Information Processing and Management*, 54(4):593–608, 2018. DOI: 10.1016/j.ipm.2018.04.002 136

David E. Rumelhart, Geoffrey E. Hinton, and Ronald J. Williams. Learning representations by back-propagating errors. *Nature*, 323(6088):533–536, 1986. DOI: 10.1038/323533a0 107, 120

Stuart Russell and Peter Norvig. *Artificial Intelligence: A Modern Approach*, 4th ed., Pearson, 2020. DOI: 10.1093/oso/9780190905033.003.0012 13, 30

Enrico Santus, Frances Yung, Alessandro Lenci, and Chu-Ren Huang. EVALution 1.0: An evolving semantic dataset for training and evaluation of distributional semantic models. In *Proc. 4th Workshop on Linked Data in Linguistics: Resources and Applications*, pages 64–69, Association for Computational Linguistics, Beijing, China, 2015. www.aclweb.org/anthology/W15-4208 DOI: 10.18653/v1/w15-4208 38, 87

Enrico Santus, Anna Gladkova, Stefan Evert, and Alessandro Lenci. The CogALex-V shared task on the corpus-based identification of semantic relations. In *Proc. 5th Workshop on Cognitive Aspects of the Lexicon (CogALex-V)*, pages 69–79, The COLING Organizing Committee, Osaka, Japan, 2016. 38

Franco Scarselli, Marco Gori, Ah Chung Tsoi, Markus Hagenbuchner, and Gabriele Monfardini. The graph neural network model. *IEEE Transactions on Neural Networks and Learning Systems*, 20(1):61–80, 2009. dx.doi.org/10.1109/TNN.2008.2005605 DOI: 10.1109/tnn.2008.2005605 131, 147

Michael Schlichtkrull, Thomas N. Kipf, Peter Bloem, Rianne Van Den Berg, Ivan Titov, and Max Welling. Modeling relational data with graph convolutional networks. In *European Semantic Web Conference*, pages 593–607, Springer, 2018. DOI: 10.1007/978-3-319-93417-4_38 148

Jürgen Schmidhuber. Artificial curiosity based on discovering novel algorithmic predictability through coevolution. In *Proc. Congress on Evolutionary Computation-CEC99 (Cat. No. 99TH8406)*, 3:1612–1618, IEEE, 1999. DOI: 10.1109/cec.1999.785467 139

Rico Sennrich, Barry Haddow, and Alexandra Birch. Neural machine translation of rare words with subword units. In *Proc. 54th Annual Meeting of the Association for Computational Linguistics (Volume 1: Long Papers)*, pages 1715–1725, 2016. www.aclweb.org/anthology/P16-1162 DOI: 10.18653/v1/p16-1162 115

Minjoon Seo, Aniruddha Kembhavi, Ali Farhadi, and Hannaneh Hajishirzi. Bidirectional attention flow for machine comprehension. *ArXiv Preprint*, 2017. arxiv.org/abs/1611.01603 159

John Shawe-Taylor and Nello Cristianini. *Kernel Methods for Pattern Analysis*. Cambridge University Press, Cambridge, UK, 2004. DOI: 10.1017/cbo9780511809682 60

Peng Shi and Jimmy Lin. Simple BERT models for relation extraction and semantic role labeling. *ArXiv Preprint*, 2019. arxiv.org/abs/1904.05255 151

Vered Shwartz and Ido Dagan. Paraphrase to explicate: Revealing implicit noun-compound relations. In *Proc. 56th Annual Meeting of the Association for Computational Linguistics (Volume 1: Long Papers)*, pages 1200–1211, Melbourne, Australia, 2018. www.aclweb.org/anthology/P18-1111 DOI: 10.18653/v1/p18-1111 150

Vered Shwartz, Yoav Goldberg, and Ido Dagan. Improving hypernymy detection with an integrated path-based and distributional method. *ArXiv Preprint*, 2016. arxiv.org/abs/1603.06076 DOI: 10.18653/v1/p16-1226 151

Vered Shwartz, Enrico Santus, and Dominik Schlechtweg. Hypernyms under siege: Linguistically-motivated artillery for hypernymy detection. In *Proc. 15th Conference of the European Chapter of the Association for Computational Linguistics: Volume 1, Long Papers*, pages 65–75, 2017. www.aclweb.org/anthology/E17-1007 DOI: 10.18653/v1/e17-1007 86, 87

Ajit Paul Singh and Geoffrey J. Gordon. Relational learning via collective matrix factorization. In *Proc. 14th ACM SIGKDD International Conference on Knowledge Discovery and Data Mining*, 2008. DOI: 10.1145/1401890.1401969 121

Gaurav Singh and Parminder Bhatia. Relation extraction using explicit context conditioning. In *Proc. Conference of the North-American Chapter of the Association for Computational Linguistics: Human Language Technologies, Volume 1 (Long and Short Papers)*, pages 1442–1447, 2019. www.aclweb.org/anthology/N19-1147 DOI: 10.18653/v1/n19-1147 161

Push Singh, Thomas Lin, Erik T. Mueller, Grace Lim, Travell Perkins, and Wan Li Zhu. Open mind common sense: Knowledge acquisition from the general public. In *Proc. 1st International Conference on Ontologies, Databases, and Applications of Semantic for Large Scale Information Systems*, 2002. DOI: 10.1007/3-540-36124-3_77 14

Sameer Singh, Sebastian Riedel, Brian Martin, Jiaping Zheng, and Andrew McCallum. Joint inference of entities, relations, and coreference. In *Proc. Workshop on Automated Knowledge Base Construction (AKBC)*, pages 1–6, 2013. DOI: 10.1145/2509558.2509559 69

Rion Snow, Daniel Jurafsky, and Andrew Y. Ng. Learning syntactic patterns for automatic hypernym discovery. In *Proc. 19th Conference on Neural Information Processing Systems (NIPS)*, pages 1297–1304, 2005. 99

Livio Baldini Soares, Nicholas FitzGerald, Jeffrey Ling, and Tom Kwiatkowski. Matching the blanks: Distributional similarity for relation learning. In *Proc. 57th Annual Meeting of the Association for Computational Linguistics*, pages 2895–2905, 2019. DOI: 10.18653/v1/p19-1279 130, 131

Richard Socher, Eric H. Huang, Jeffrey Pennington, Andrew Y. Ng, and Christopher D. Manning. Dynamic pooling and unfolding recursive autoencoders for paraphrase detection. In *Proc. 24th International Conference on Neural Information Processing Systems, (NIPS)*, pages 801–809, Curran Associates Inc., 2011a. dl.acm.org/citation.cfm?id=2986459.2986549 134

Richard Socher, Cliff Chiung-Yu Lin, Andrew Y. Ng, and Christopher D. Manning. Parsing natural scenes and natural language with recursive neural networks. In *Proc. 28th International Conference on International Conference on Machine Learning, (ICML)*, pages 129–136, Omnipress, 2011b. dl.acm.org/citation.cfm?id=3104482.3104499 126

Richard Socher, Brody Huval, Christopher D. Manning, and Andrew Y. Ng. Semantic compositionality through recursive matrix-vector spaces. In *Proc. Joint Conference on Empirical Methods in Natural Language Processing and Computational Natural Language Learning, (EMNLP-CoNLL)*, pages 1201–1211, Association for Computational Linguistics, Stroudsburg, PA, 2012. dl.acm.org/citation.cfm?id=2390948.2391084 34, 129

Richard Socher, Danqi Chen, Christopher D. Manning, and Andrew Y. Ng. Reasoning with neural tensor networks for knowledge base completion. In C. J. C. Burges, L. Bottou, M. Welling, Z. Ghahramani, and K. Q. Weinberger, Eds., *Advances in Neural Information Processing Systems 26*, pages 926–934, Curran Associates, Inc., 2013. papers.nips.cc/paper/5028-reasoning-with-neural-tensor-networks-for-knowledge-base-completion.pdf 145

John F. Sowa. *Conceptual Structures: Information Processing in Mind and Machine*. Addison-Wesley, 1984. 28

Karen Spärck Jones. Synonymy and semantic classification. Ph.D. thesis, University of Cambridge, 1964. 14

Nitish Srivastava, Geoffrey Hinton, Alex Krizhevsky, Ilya Sutskever, and Ruslan Salakhutdinov. Dropout: A simple way to prevent neural networks from overfitting. *Journal of Machine Learning Research*, 15(56):1929–1958, 2014. jmlr.org/papers/v15/srivastava14a.html 110

Mark Stevenson. Fact distribution in information extraction. *Language Resources and Evaluation*, 40(2):183–201, 2006. DOI: 10.1007/s10579-006-9014-4 71

Mark Stevenson and Mark A. Greenwood. A semantic approach to IE pattern induction. In *Proc. 43rd Annual Meeting of the Association for Computational Linguistics (ACL)*, Ann Arbor, MI, 2005. DOI: 10.3115/1219840.1219887 82

M. Steyvers and T. Griffiths. Probabilistic topic models. In *Latent Semantic Analysis: A Road to Meaning*. Lawrence Erlbaum, 2006. DOI: 10.4324/9780203936399.ch21 113

Paul Studtmann. Aristotle's categories. In Edward N. Zalta, Ed., *The Stanford Encyclopedia of Philosophy*. The Metaphysics Research Lab, Center for the Study of Language and Information, Stanford University, 2008. plato.stanford.edu/plato.stanford.edu/archives/fall2008/entries/aristotle-categories/ DOI: 10.1093/oxfordhb/9780195187489.013.0004 11

Sen Su, Ningning Jia, Xiang Cheng, Shuguang Zhu, and Ruiping Li. Exploring encoder-decoder model for distant supervised relation extraction. In *Proc. 27th International Joint*

Conference on Artificial Intelligence (IJCAI), pages 4389–4395, 2018. DOI: 10.24963/ijcai.2018/610 137

Stanley Y. W. Su. A semantic theory based upon interactive meaning. *Computer Sciences Technical Report #68*, University of Wisconsin, 1969. 19

Ang Sun, Ralph Grishman, and Satoshi Sekine. Semi-supervised relation extraction with large-scale word clustering. In *Proc. 49th Annual Meeting of the Association for Computational Linguistics: Human Language Technologies*, pages 521–529, Portland, OR, 2011. www.aclweb.org/anthology/P11-1053 51

Shaohua Sun, Ni Lao, Rahul Gupta, and Dave Orr. 50,000 lessons on how to read: A relation extraction corpus, 2013. research.googleblog.com/2013/04/50000-lessons-on-how-to-read-relation.html 134

Mihai Surdeanu, Julie Tibshirani, Ramesh Nallapati, and Christopher D. Manning. Multi-instance multi-label learning for relation extraction. In *Proc. Joint Conference on Empirical Methods in Natural Language Processing and Computational Natural Language Learning, (EMNLP-CoNLL)*, pages 455–465, Association for Computational Linguistics, Stroudsburg, PA, 2012. dl.acm.org/citation.cfm?id=2390948.2391003 101, 103, 136

Ilya Sutskever and Geoffrey E. Hinton. Using matrices to model symbolic relationship. In D. Koller, D. Schuurmans, Y. Bengio, and L. Bottou, Eds., *Advances in Neural Information Processing Systems 21*, pages 1593–1600, Curran Associates, Inc., 2009. papers.nips.cc/paper/3482-using-matrices-to-model-symbolic-relationship.pdf 121

Jun Suzuki, Tsutomu Hirao, Yutaka Sasaki, and Eisaku Maeda. Hierarchical directed acyclic graph kernel: Methods for structured natural language data. In *Proc. 41st Annual Meeting of the Association for Computational Linguistics (ACL)*, Sapporo, Japan, 2003. DOI: 10.3115/1075096.1075101 61

Kumutha Swampillai and Mark Stevenson. Extracting relations within and across sentences. In Galia Angelova, Kalina Bontcheva, Ruslan Mitkov, and Nicolas Nicolov, Eds., *Proc. Recent Advances in Natural Language Processing (RANLP)*, pages 25–32, 2011. www.aclweb.org/anthology/R11-1004/ 54, 71, 72

Don R. Swanson. Two medical literatures that are logically but not bibliographically connected. *Journal of the American Society for Information Science*, 38(4):228–233, 1987. DOI: 10.1002/(sici)1097-4571(198707)38:4<228::aid-asi2>3.0.co;2-g 3, 75

Ryo Takahashi, Ran Tian, and Kentaro Inui. Interpretable and compositional relation learning by joint training with an autoencoder. In *Proc. 56th Annual Meeting of the Association for Computational Linguistics (Volume 1: Long Papers)*, pages 2148–2159, Melbourne, Australia, 2018. www.aclweb.org/anthology/P18-1200 DOI: 10.18653/v1/p18-1200 146

Shingo Takamatsu, Issei Sato, and Hiroshi Nakagawa. Reducing wrong labels in distant supervision for relation extraction. In *Proc. 50th Annual Meeting of the Association for Computational Linguistics (Volume 1: Long Papers)*, pages 721–729, Jeju Island, Korea, 2012. www.aclweb.org/anthology/P12-1076 100

Lucien Tesnière. *Éléments de Syntaxe Structurale*. C. Klincksieck, Paris, 1959. 1

Sebastian Thrun and Lorien Pratt. *Learning to Learn*. Springer Science and Business Media, 2012. DOI: 10.1007/978-1-4615-5529-2_1 72, 76

Kristina Toutanova, Danqi Chen, Patrick Pantel, Hoifung Poon, Pallavi Choudhury, and Michael Gamon. Representing text for joint embedding of text and knowledge bases. In *Proc. Conference on Empirical Methods in Natural Language Processing*, pages 1499–1509, Association for Computational Linguistics, Lisbon, Portugal, 2015. www.aclweb.org/anthology/D15-1174 DOI: 10.18653/v1/d15-1174 123, 155

Kristina Toutanova, Victoria Lin, Wen-Tau Yih, Hoifung Poon, and Chris Quirk. Compositional learning of embeddings for relation paths in knowledge base and text. In *Proc. 54th Annual Meeting of the Association for Computational Linguistics (Volume 1: Long Papers)*, pages 1434–1444, 2016. www.aclweb.org/anthology/P16-1136 DOI: 10.18653/v1/p16-1136 156

Stephen Tratz and Eduard Hovy. A taxonomy, dataset, and classifier for automatic noun compound interpretation. In *Proc. 48th Annual Meeting of the Association for Computational Linguistics*, pages 678–687, Uppsala, Sweden, 2010. 19, 21, 22, 39

Théo Trouillon, Christopher R. Dance, Johannes Welbl, Sebastian Riedel, Éric Gaussier, and Guillaume Bouchard. Knowledge graph completion via complex tensor factorization. *ArXiv Preprint*, 2017. arxiv.org/abs/1702.06879 134, 138, 145

Peter Turney. Expressing implicit semantic relations without supervision. In *Proc. 21st International Conference on Computational Linguistics and 44th Annual Meeting of the Association for Computational Linguistics*, pages 313–320, Sydney, Australia, July 17–21, 2006a. www.aclweb.org/anthology/P/P06/P06-1040 DOI: 10.3115/1220175.1220215 56

Peter Turney. Similarity of semantic relations. *Computational Linguistics*, 32(3):379–416, 2006b. DOI: 10.1162/coli.2006.32.3.379 50, 56

Peter Turney and Michael Littman. Corpus-based learning of analogies and semantic relations. *Machine Learning*, 60(1–3):251–278, 2005. DOI: 10.1007/s10994-005-0913-1 55, 95

Lucy Vanderwende. Algorithm for the automatic interpretation of noun sequences. In *Proc. 15th International Conference on Computational Linguistics*, pages 782–788, Kyoto, Japan, August 5–9, 1994. DOI: 10.3115/991250.991272 19, 21, 22

Shikhar Vashishth, Rishabh Joshi, Sai Suman Prayaga, Chiranjib Bhattacharyya, and Partha Talukdar. RESIDE: Improving distantly-supervised neural relation extraction using side information. In *Proc. Conference on Empirical Methods in Natural Language Processing*, pages 1257–1266, Association for Computational Linguistics, Brussels, Belgium, 2018. www.aclweb.org/anthology/D18-1157 DOI: 10.18653/v1/d18-1157 138

Patrick Verga, David Belanger, Emma Strubell, Benjamin Roth, and Andrew McCallum. Multilingual relation extraction using compositional universal schema. In *Proc. Conference of the North American Chapter of the Association for Computational Linguistics: Human Language Technologies*, pages 886–896, 2016. aclweb.org/anthology/N16-1103 DOI: 10.18653/v1/n16-1103 157

Patrick Verga, Arvind Neelakantan, and Andrew McCallum. Generalizing to unseen entities and entity pairs with rowless universal schema. In *Proc. 15th Conference of the European Chapter of the Association for Computational Linguistics: Volume 1, Long Papers*, pages 613–622, Valencia, Spain, 2017. www.aclweb.org/anthology/E17-1058 DOI: 10.18653/v1/e17-1058 157

Patrick Verga, Emma Strubell, and Andrew McCallum. Simultaneously self-attending to all mentions for full-abstract biological relation extraction. In *Proc. Conference of the North American Chapter of the Association for Computational Linguistics: Human Language Technologies, Volume 1 (Long Papers)*, pages 872–884, 2018. www.aclweb.org/anthology/N18-1080 DOI: 10.18653/v1/n18-1080 161

David Wadden, Ulme Wennberg, Yi Luan, and Hannaneh Hajishirzi. Entity, relation, and event extraction with contextualized span representations. In *Proc. Conference on Empirical Methods in Natural Language Processing and the 9th International Joint Conference on Natural Language Processing (EMNLP-IJCNLP)*, pages 5784–5789, 2019. www.aclweb.org/anthology/D19-1585 DOI: 10.18653/v1/d19-1585 154

Chang Wang, James Fan, Aditya Kalyanpur, and David Gondek. Relation extraction with relation topics. In *Proc. Conference on Empirical Methods in Natural Language Processing (EMNLP)*, Edinburgh, UK, 2011. 56

Guanying Wang, Wen Zhang, Ruoxu Wang, Yalin Zhou, Xi Chen, Wei Zhang, Hai Zhu, and Huajun Chen. Label-free distant supervision for relation extraction via knowledge graph embedding. In *Proc. Conference on Empirical Methods in Natural Language Processing*, pages 2246–2255, Association for Computational Linguistics, Brussels, Belgium, 2018. www.aclweb.org/anthology/D18-1248 DOI: 10.18653/v1/d18-1248 137

Hai Wang and Hoifung Poon. Deep probabilistic logic: A unifying framework for indirect supervision. In *Proc. Conference on Empirical Methods in Natural Language Processing*, pages 1891–1902, Association for Computational Linguistics, Brussels, Belgium, 2018. www.aclweb.org/anthology/D18-1215 DOI: 10.18653/v1/d18-1215 161

Haoyu Wang, Vivek Kulkarni, and William Yang Wang. Dolores: Deep contextualized knowledge graph embeddings. In *Automated Knowledge Base Construction*, 2020. openreview.net/forum?id=ajrveGQBl0 122

Hong Wang, Wenhan Xiong, Mo Yu, Xiaoxiao Guo, Shiyu Chang, and William Yang Wang. Sentence embedding alignment for lifelong relation extraction. In *Proc. Conference of the North American Chapter of the Association for Computational Linguistics: Human Language Technologies, Volume 1 (Long and Short Papers)*, pages 796–806, Minneapolis, MN, 2019. www.aclweb.org/anthology/N19-1086 DOI: 10.18653/v1/n19-1086 163

Quan Wang, Zhendong Mao, Bin Wang, and Li Guo. Knowledge graph embedding: A survey of approaches and applications. *IEEE Transactions on Knowledge and Data Engineering*, 29(12):2724–2743, 2017. DOI: 10.1109/tkde.2017.2754499 119, 138, 144

Zhen Wang, Jianwen Zhang, Jianlin Feng, and Zheng Chen. Knowledge graph embedding by translating on hyperplanes. In *28th AAAI Conference on Artificial Intelligence*, 2014. DOI: 10.1016/j.knosys.2020.106564 144

Beatrice Warren. Semantic patterns of noun-noun compounds. Ph.D. thesis, Actr Universitatis Gothoburgensis, Göteborg, 1978. 17, 21, 22, 29

Melanie Weber and Maximilian Nickel. Curvature and representation learning: Identifying embedding spaces for relational data. *NeurIPS Relational Representation Learning*, 2018. 122

Julie Weeds, Daoud Clarke, Jeremy Reffin, David Weir, and Bill Keller. Learning to distinguish hypernyms and co-hyponyms. In *Proc. COLING, the 25th International Conference on Computational Linguistics: Technical Papers*, pages 2249–2259, Dublin City University and Association for Computational Linguistics, 2014. www.aclweb.org/anthology/C14-1212 38, 87

Chih-Hsuan Wei, Yifan Peng, Robert Leaman, Allan Peter Davis, Carolyn J. Mattingly, Jiao Li, Thomas C. Wiegers, and Zhiyong Lu. Assessing the state of the art in biomedical relation extraction: Overview of the BioCreative V chemical-disease relation (CDR) task. *Database*, 2016. DOI: 10.1093/database/baw032 46

Gerhard Weikum, Gjergji Kasneci, Maya Ramanath, and Fabian Suchanek. Database and information-retrieval methods for knowledge discovery. *Communications of the ACM*, 52(4):56–64, 2009. DOI: 10.1145/1498765.1498784 44

Joseph Weizenbaum. ELIZA—A computer program for the study of natural language communication between man and machine. *Communications of the ACM*, 9(1):36–45, 1966. DOI: 10.1145/365153.365168 13

Jason Weston, Antoine Bordes, Oksana Yakhnenko, and Nicolas Usunier. Connecting language and knowledge bases with embedding models for relation extraction. In *Proc. Conference on Empirical Methods in Natural Language Processing*, pages 1366–1371, Association for Computational Linguistics, 2013. www.aclweb.org/anthology/D13-1136 157

Anna Wierzbicka. Apples are not a kind of fruit: The semantics of human categorization. *American Ethnologist*, 11:313–328, 1984. DOI: 10.1525/ae.1984.11.2.02a00060 23, 42

Terry Winograd. Understanding natural language. *Cognitive Psychology*, 3(1):1–191, 1972. DOI: 10.1016/0010-0285(72)90002-3 13

Morton E. Winston, Roger Chaffin, and Douglas Herrmann. A taxonomy of part-whole relations. *Cognitive Science*, 11(4):417–444, 1987. dx.doi.org/10.1207/s15516709cog1104_2 DOI: 10.1207/s15516709cog1104_2 23, 24, 82

Ian H. Witten, Eibe Frank, Mark A. Hall, and Christopher J. Pal. *Data Mining: Practical Machine Learning Tools and Techniques*, 4th ed., Morgan Kaufmann, 2016. DOI: 10.1016/C2015-0-02071-8 58

Fei Wu and Daniel S. Weld. Autonomously semantifying wikipedia. In *Proc. ACM 16th Conference on Information and Knowledge Management (CIKM)*, pages 41–50, Lisbon, Portugal, November 6–9, 2007. DOI: 10.1145/1321440.1321449 99, 105

Fei Wu and Daniel S. Weld. Open information extraction using Wikipedia. In *Proc. 48th Annual Meeting of the Association for Computational Linguistics*, pages 118–127, Uppsala, Sweden, July 11–16, 2010. 91, 105

Han Xiao, Minlie Huang, and Xiaoyan Zhu. TransG: A generative model for knowledge graph embedding. In *Proc. 54th Annual Meeting of the Association for Computational Linguistics (Volume 1: Long Papers)*, 1:2316–2325, 2016. DOI: 10.18653/v1/p16-1219 138, 144

Ruobing Xie, Zhiyuan Liu, Jia Jia, Huanbo Luan, and Maosong Sun. Representation learning of knowledge graphs with entity descriptions. In *Proc. AAAI*, pages 2659–2665, 2016. 159

Kun Xu, Yansong Feng, Songfang Huang, and Dongyan Zhao. Semantic relation classification via convolutional neural networks with simple negative sampling. *ArXiv Preprint*, 2015. arxiv.org/abs/1506.07650 DOI: 10.18653/v1/d15-1062 153

Yan Xu, Ran Jia, Lili Mou, Ge Li, Yunchuan Chen, Yangyang Lu, and Zhi Jin. Improved relation classification by deep recurrent neural networks with data augmentation. In *Proc. COLING, the 26th International Conference on Computational Linguistics: Technical Papers*, pages 1461–1470, The COLING Organizing Committee, Osaka, Japan, 2016. www.aclweb.org/anthology/C16-1138 127, 128, 149

Bishan Yang, Wen-tau Yih, Xiaodong He, Jianfeng Gao, and Li Deng. Embedding entities and relations for learning and inference in knowledge bases. In *Proc. International Conference on Representation Learning*, 2015. 138, 144, 145

Kaijia Yang, Liang He, Xin-yu Dai, Shujian Huang, and Jiajun Chen. Exploiting noisy data in distant supervision relation classification. In *Proc. Conference of the North American Chapter of the Association for Computational Linguistics: Human Language Technologies, Volume 1 (Long and Short Papers)*, pages 3216–3225, Minneapolis, MN, 2019. www.aclweb.org/anthology/N19-1325 DOI: 10.18653/v1/n19-1325 142

Roman Yangarber. Counter-training in discovery of semantic patterns. In *Proc. 41st Annual Meeting of the Association for Computational Linguistics*, pages 343–350, Sapporo, Japan, July 7–12, 2003. DOI: 10.3115/1075096.1075140 84

Limin Yao, Aria Haghighi, Sebastian Riedel, and Andrew McCallum. Structured relation discovery using generative models. In *Proc. Conference on Empirical Methods in Natural Language Processing*, pages 1456–1466, Association for Computational Linguistics, 2011. www.aclweb.org/anthology/D11-1135 92, 93

Yuan Yao, Deming Ye, Peng Li, Xu Han, Yankai Lin, Zhenghao Liu, Zhiyuan Liu, Lixin Huang, Jie Zhou, and Maosong Sun. DocRED: A large-scale document-level relation extraction dataset. In *Proc. ACL*, pages 764–777, 2019. DOI: 10.18653/v1/p19-1074 134

Alexander Yates and Oren Etzioni. Unsupervised resolution of objects and relations on the Web. In *Proc. Human Language Technologies: The Conference of the North American Chapter of the Association for Computational Linguistics*, pages 121–130, Rochester, NY, April 22–27, 2007. 93

Alexander Yates and Oren Etzioni. Unsupervised methods for determining object and relation synonyms on the Web. *Journal of Artificial Intelligence Research*, 34:255–296, 2009. DOI: 10.1613/jair.2772 92

Zhi-Xiu Ye and Zhen-Hua Ling. Distant supervision relation extraction with intra-bag and inter-bag attentions. In *Proc. Conference of the North American Chapter of the Association for Computational Linguistics: Human Language Technologies, Volume 1 (Long and Short Papers)*, pages 2810–2819, Minneapolis, MN, 2019. www.aclweb.org/anthology/N19-1288 DOI: 10.18653/v1/n19-1288 140

Xiaofeng Yu and Wai Lam. Jointly identifying entities and extracting relations in encyclopedia text via a graphical model approach. In *Coling: Posters*, pages 1399–1407, Coling Organizing Committee, Beijing, China, 2010. www.aclweb.org/anthology/C10-2160 69

Dmitry Zelenko, Chinatsu Aone, and Anthony Richardella.   Kernel methods for relation extraction.   *Journal of Machine Learning Research*, 3:1083–1106, 2003. DOI:
10.3115/1118693.1118703 61

Daojian Zeng, Kang Liu, Siwei Lai, Guangyou Zhou, Jun Zhao, et al. Relation classification
via convolutional deep neural network. In *COLING*, pages 2335–2344, 2014. 149, 150

Daojian Zeng, Kang Liu, Yubo Chen, and Jun Zhao. Distant supervision for relation extraction via piecewise convolutional neural networks. In *Proc. Conference on Empirical Methods in
Natural Language Processing*, pages 1753–1762, Association for Computational Linguistics,
2015. aclweb.org/anthology/D15-1203 DOI: 10.18653/v1/d15-1203 136

Xiangrong Zeng, Daojian Zeng, Shizhu He, Kang Liu, and Jun Zhao. Extracting relational facts
by an end-to-end neural model with copy mechanism. In *Proc. 56th Annual Meeting of the
Association for Computational Linguistics (Volume 1: Long Papers)*, pages 506–514, Melbourne,
Australia, 2018. www.aclweb.org/anthology/P18-1047 DOI: 10.18653/v1/p18-1047 154

Dongxu Zhang, Subhabrata Mukherjee, Colin Lockard, Luna Dong, and Andrew McCallum.
OpenKI: Integrating open information extraction and knowledge bases with relation infer-
ence. In *Proc. Conference of the North American Chapter of the Association for Computational
Linguistics: Human Language Technologies, Volume 1 (Long and Short Papers)*, pages 762–772,
Minneapolis, MN, 2019a. www.aclweb.org/anthology/N19-1083 DOI: 10.18653/v1/N19-
1083 157

Min Zhang, Jie Zhang, Jian Su, and GuoDong Zhou. A composite kernel to extract relations between entities with both flat and structured features. In *Proc. 21st International
Conference on Computational Linguistics and 44th Annual Meeting of the Association for Computational Linguistics*, pages 825–832, 2006. www.aclweb.org/anthology/P06-1104 DOI:
10.3115/1220175.1220279 63

Ningyu Zhang, Shumin Deng, Zhanlin Sun, Guanying Wang, Xi Chen, Wei Zhang, and Huajun Chen. Long-tail relation extraction via knowledge graph embeddings and graph convolution networks. In *Proc. Conference of the North American Chapter of the Association for
Computational Linguistics: Human Language Technologies, Volume 1 (Long and Short Papers)*,
pages 3016–3025, Minneapolis, MN, 2019b. DOI: 10.18653/v1/n19-1306 148, 159

Yuhao Zhang, Victor Zhong, Danqi Chen, Gabor Angeli, and Christopher D. Manning.
Position-aware attention and supervised data improve slot filling. In *Proc. Conference on Empirical Methods in Natural Language Processing (EMNLP)*, pages 35–45, 2017. nlp.stanford.
edu/pubs/zhang2017tacred.pdf DOI: 10.18653/v1/d17-1004 134

Yuhao Zhang, Peng Qi, and Christopher D. Manning. Graph convolution over pruned dependency trees improves relation extraction. In *Proc. Conference on Empirical Methods in Natural*

Language Processing, pages 2205–2215, Association for Computational Linguistics, Brussels, Belgium, 2018. DOI: 10.18653/v1/d18-1244 132

Zhu Zhang. Weakly-supervised relation classification for information extraction. In *Proc. 13th ACM International Conference on Information and Knowledge Management, (CIKM)*, pages 581–588, 2004. DOI: 10.1145/1031171.1031279 85

Shubin Zhao and Ralph Grishman. Extracting relations with integrated information using kernel methods. In *Proc. 43rd Annual Meeting of the Association for Computational Linguistics (ACL)*, pages 419–426, Ann Arbor, MI, 2005. www.aclweb.org/anthology/P05-1052 DOI: 10.3115/1219840.1219892 63

Suncong Zheng, Jiaming Xu, Peng Zhou, Hongyun Bao, Zhenyu Qi, and Bo Xu. A neural network framework for relation extraction: Learning entity semantic and relation pattern. *Knowledge-Based Systems*, 114:12–23, 2016. www.sciencedirect.com/science/article/pii/S0950705116303501 DOI: 10.1016/j.knosys.2016.09.019 149

Suncong Zheng, Feng Wang, Hongyun Bao, Yuexing Hao, Peng Zhou, and Bo Xu. Joint extraction of entities and relations based on a novel tagging scheme. In *Proc. 55th Annual Meeting of the Association for Computational Linguistics (Volume 1: Long Papers)*, pages 1227–1236, Vancouver, Canada, 2017. www.aclweb.org/anthology/P17-1113 152, 153

GuoDong Zhou, Min Zhang, DongHong Ji, and QiaoMing Zhu. Tree kernel-based relation extraction with context-sensitive structured parse tree information. In *Proc. Joint Conference on Empirical Methods in Natural Language Processing and Computational Natural Language Learning (EMNLP-CoNLL)*, pages 728–736, Association for Computational Linguistics, Prague, Czech Republic, 2007. www.aclweb.org/anthology/D07-1076 63

Guodong Zhou, Longhua Qian, and Qiaoming Zhu. Label propagation via bootstrapped support vectors for semantic relation extraction between named entities. *Computer Speech and Language*, 23(4):464–478, 2009. DOI: 10.1016/j.csl.2009.03.001 85, 102

Jie Zhou, Ganqu Cui, Zhengyan Zhang, Cheng Yang, Zhiyuan Liu, and Maosong Sun. Graph neural networks: A review of methods and applications. *ArXiv Preprint*, 2018. arxiv.org/abs/1812.08434 132, 147

Yan Zhou, Murat Kantarcioglu, Bhavani Thuraisingham, and Bowei Xi. Adversarial support vector machine learning. In *Proc. 18th ACM SIGKDD International Conference on Knowledge Discovery and Data Mining, (KDD)*, pages 1059–1067, 2012. DOI: 10.1145/2339530.2339697 139

Karl E. Zimmer. Some general observations about nominal compounds. *Stanford Working Papers on Linguistic Universals*, 5:C1–C21, 1971. 18

Pierre Zweigenbaum, Dina Demner-Fushman, Hong Yu, and Kevin B. Cohen. Frontiers of biomedical text mining: Current progress. *Briefings in Bioinformatics*, 8(5):358–375, 2007. DOI: 10.1093/bib/bbm045 45

Authors' Biographies

VIVI NASTASE

Vivi Nastase[1] holds a Ph.D. from the University of Ottawa. A research associate at the University of Stuttgart, she works mainly on lexical semantics, semantic relations, knowledge acquisition, and language evolution.

STAN SZPAKOWICZ

Stan Szpakowicz[2] holds a Ph.D. from Warsaw University, and a D.Sc. from the Institute of Informatics, Polish Academy of Sciences. Now an emeritus professor of Computer Science at the University of Ottawa, he has dabbled in NLP since 1969. His interests in the past several years include semantic relations and lexical resources.

PRESLAV NAKOV

Preslav Nakov[3] holds a Ph.D. from the University of California, Berkeley. He leads the Tanbih mega-project, developed in collaboration with MIT, which aims to limit the impact of fake news, propaganda, and media bias.

DIARMUID Ó SÉAGDHA

Diarmuid Ó Séagdha[4] holds a Ph.D. from the University of Cambridge. He works for Apple, and is a Visiting Industrial Fellow at the UC's NLIP Research Group. His interests revolve around the application of machine learning techniques to semantic processing tasks.

[1] Institute for Natural Language Processing, University of Stuttgart, Germany
vivi.nastase@ims.uni-stuttgart.de
[2] School of Electrical Engineering and Computer Science, University of Ottawa, Canada
szpak@eecs.uottawa.ca
[3] Qatar Computing Research Institute, Hamad bin Khalifa University, Qatar
pnakov@hbku.edu.qa
[4] Apple
do242@cam.ac.uk

Index